D1566373

MORE PRAISE FOR *GROW FAST GROW RIGHT*

"Once again, Andrew Sherman proves that he's got his finger on the pulse of entrepreneurship. It's all about growth, and if anyone knows the hard-and-fast key strategies of business expansion, it's this veteran observer of business trends. Grow Fast Grow Right *provides a vital blueprint that will aid entrepreneurs and managers alike in their efforts to stay focused."*

DON J. DEBOLT, PRESIDENT, INTERNATIONAL FRANCHISE ASSOCIATION

"Andrew Sherman's work is always thorough, and this is no exception. If you're trying to grow your company, Grow Fast Grow Right *is a must. It's a complete reference to the ins and outs of raising capital and managing growth."*

RIPLEY HOTCH, EDITOR IN CHIEF, *SUCCESS* MAGAZINE

"If I were limited to five experts with which to build a dream team to help me grow my company, Andrew J. Sherman would be on that list. With this book, EVERY business owner can put Andrew on their dream team."

JIM BLASINGAME, HOST OF *THE SMALL BUSINESS ADVOCATE* AND AUTHOR OF *SMALL BUSINESS IS LIKE A BUNCH OF BANANAS*

*"*Grow Fast Grow Right *is a must-read for all executives seeking to maximize profits and expand their company in a demanding 21st century. Sherman should be applauded for turning a complex topic into a manageable guide."*

GREG LEBEDEV, CHIEF OPERATING OFFICER, U.S. CHAMBER OF COMMERCE

"Very comprehensive, but easy to read . . . Sherman has captured the key elements of corporate growth: building a platform, the human side, the capital requirements, internal and external growth strategies, and managing the challenges of growth."

RUSS ROBB, PRESIDENT, ASSOCIATION FOR CORPORATE GROWTH

*"The next best thing to having direct access to Andrew's sage advice is his most important work to date—*Grow Fast Grow Right. *If you are truly serious about effectively managing your firm's resources and growth, this book is an indispensable guide."*

KAREN KERRIGAN, PRESIDENT AND CEO, SMALL BUSINESS & ENTREPRENEURSHIP COUNCIL, AND FOUNDER, WOMEN ENTREPRENEURS, INC. (WE INC.)

"One of the greatest challenges to building a successful business is knowing when and how to grow. Grow Fast Grow Right *is a must-read for any business executive serious about running their enterprise."*

JOE WATSON, CEO, WITHOUT EXCUSES

"Sherman is a teacher, adviser, publisher, and visionary who lays out a candid and comprehensive approach toward growing your business. Sherman offers the commonsense approach that entrepreneurs need to hear."

JIM GARRETTSON, PRESIDENT, POTOMAC OFFICERS CLUB AND EXECUTIVEBIZ

"Andrew gets to the heart of what makes some rapid-growth businesses succeed and others fail. He first makes the critical distinction between a weak foundation for growth and the ability to achieve sustained growth. He then identifies those traits in companies that ultimately succeed. Andrew's work is a blueprint of how to grow a business at a rational and, most important, sustainable rate."

BRIAN ANDERSON, SENIOR VICE PRESIDENT AND DIRECTOR OF SPECIAL PROJECTS, *INC.* AND *FAST COMPANY* MAGAZINES

ANDREW J. SHERMAN

GROW *fast*
GROW *right*

12 STRATEGIES TO ACHIEVE BREAKTHROUGH BUSINESS GROWTH

KAPLAN PUBLISHING

This publication is designed to provide accurate and authoritative information in regard to the subject matter covered. It is sold with the understanding that the publisher is not engaged in rendering legal, accounting, or other professional service. If legal advice or other expert assistance is required, the services of a competent professional should be sought.

Editorial Director: Jennifer Farthing
Senior Managing Editor, Production: Jack Kiburz
Typesetter: the dotted i
Cover Designer: Design Literate

Published by Kaplan Publishing,
a division of Kaplan, Inc.

Printed in the United States of America

07 08 09   10 9 8 7 6 5 4 3 2 1

Library of Congress Cataloging-in-Publication Data

Sherman Andrew J.
  Grow fast grow right : 12 strategies to achieve breakthrough business growth / Andrew J. Sherman
    p. cm.
  Includes index.
  ISBN-13: 978-1-4195-9324-6
  ISBN-10: 1-4195-9324-2
  1. Small business—United States—Management. 2. Small business—United States—Planning. 3. Small business—United States—Growth. I. Title.
  HD62.7.S5266 2007
  658.4'06–dc22

                                                            2006029695

Kaplan Publishing books are available at special quantity discounts to use for sales promotions, employee premiums, or educational purposes. Please call our Special Sales Department to order or for more information at 800-621-9621, ext. 4444, e-mail kaplanpubsales@kaplan.com, or write to Kaplan Publishing, 30 South Wacker Drive, Suite 2500, Chicago, IL 60606-7481.

DEDICATION

For Judy, Matthew, and Jennifer
A family that grows together stays together

After 25 years of teaching, writing, and working with clients of all sizes and from all industries on the legal and strategic aspects of business growth, it would take me several hundred pages to acknowledge everyone who has helped me along this exciting path.

First, I want to thank my partners and the excellent lawyers and staff at Dickstein Shapiro LLP for their support, particularly Fred Lowther for his mentoring and guidance, Jim Kelly for his friendship, and Mike Nannes for his tremendous leadership. A special thanks to Al Schieffer for 12 years of loyalty, hard work, and still going strong. I also want to applaud the tireless efforts of Jason Gerbsman, our general manager at Grow Fast Grow Right (GFGR), who makes sure that all the trains are running on time. Our GFGR Dream Team is the best resource and board of advisors that any company leader could ever wish for. I especially want to thank Dream Team members John Hrastar, Mary MacPherson, and Dave Gardy for all of their support. I very much appreciate the friendship of Jack Maier at Legacy Partners, Ed Mathias at Carlyle, Mark Stevens at MSCO, Bill Poster at GFGR, and the many others who have been wonderful mentors and friends. A special thanks to my assistant, Jo Lynch, for her loyalty, dedication, and organizational skills.

At Kaplan, I owe a large debt of gratitude to the leadership of Jennifer Farthing and her editorial and production team, including Jack Kiburz, Brigit Dermott, and Krystal Villanosa, for all of their support and hard work on the editing and organization of the manuscript. I look forward to great things ahead.

Finally, my wife, Judy, and children, Matthew and Jennifer, again deserve a lot of recognition for their patience with me, chapter after chapter taking time away from them. I am very proud of their accomplishments, and they seem to be growing up as fast as many of my rapid-growth clients.

C o n t e n t s

After 25 years of working as a legal and strategic advisor to growing companies of all sizes and in a variety of industries, 16 years of teaching business growth strategy courses in the MBA programs at University of Maryland and Georgetown University, and the publication of 14 books on business growth topics, I launched Grow Fast Grow Right® *(www.growfastgrowright* *.com)* in 2004 as an educational and training company for executives and leaders of growing companies. The content and focus of our programs is designed to help leaders strike that delicate balance between growing quickly and growing properly.

Our programs are organized around the three key strategic business growth pillars that support a foundation for growth that optimizes shareholder value, human capital, financial capital, and intellectual capital. Within each pillar are four specific value drivers that facilitate smart and strategic business growth.

This book is organized around the Grow Fast Grow Right proprietary content, its 3 pillars, and 12 value drivers. Following two chapters that discuss laying the groundwork for growth, each of the 12 value drivers has a chapter devoted to the concepts, best practices, and war stories that make up the Grow Fast Grow Right curriculum. The Appendix is devoted to resources and business groups that support the needs and challenges of growing companies.

Our Grow Fast Grow Right content helps leaders of growing companies answer some fundamental questions, such as *how* and *when* to grow. Armed with the answers to these questions, leaders can then develop and implement concrete action items and specific growth strategies. The Grow Fast Grow Right proprietary content also addresses more specific issues, such as the following: What strategies should be used to facilitate growth? How do you know whether these strategies are appropriate for your business? Are there problems with your business structure that need resolving before you can implement the growth strategy selected? How can you build on your strengths and compensate for your weaknesses?

How might the growth strategy selected present new risks or make you vulnerable? To whom? Is this the right *time* to grow? That is, have you put a proper foundation for growth in place? Is capital available to fuel growth? Are market conditions ripe for growth opportunities?

The various challenges and problems associated with building a company will take a toll on the entrepreneurs and decision makers who are trusted with meeting business growth objectives. Growth causes a wide variety of changes, all of which present different management, legal, and financial challenges. Growth means that new employees will be hired who will be looking to the top management of the company for leadership. Growth means that the company's management will become increasingly decentralized, which may create greater levels of internal politics, protectionism, and dissension over the goals and projects that the company should pursue. Growth means that the company's market share will expand, necessitating new strategies for dealing with larger competitors. Growth also means that additional capital will be required, creating new responsibilities to shareholders, investors, and institutional lenders. Thus, growth brings with it a variety of changes in the company's structure, needs, and objectives.

The plans and strategies developed by management in order to cope with the changes caused by rapid growth cannot be made in a vacuum. The legal implications, costs, benefits, and risks of each proposed decision, transaction, plan, or strategy must be understood. An understanding of the legal issues raised by the inevitable changes that are caused by business growth is a necessary prerequisite to effectively managing the organization and to ensuring the long-term success and continued profitability of the company.

Business growth is truly a double-edged sword. When it's controlled and well managed, it has the potential of providing tremendous rewards to the managers and shareholders of the company. When growth is uncontrolled and poorly planned, it often leads to financial distress and failure. For many companies, rapid growth is the only way to survive in highly competitive industries. These companies are faced with a choice of either acting quickly to capture additional market share or sitting on the sidelines and watching others play the game.

Do these competitive conditions justify unplanned and unbridled growth, where sound management, legal, and accounting principles are disregarded? Certainly not. But these conditions do mean that the need of the organization to grow must be tempered by the need to understand that meaningful, long-term, profitable growth is the by-product of effective management and planning. A strategy that focuses on sensible and logical growth dictates that managers create a balance between the need for organizational flexibility that can quickly seize market opportunities, adapt to changes in the marketplace, and develop creative solutions for problems that arise *versus* the need for controlled and well-managed expansion plans. Failure to create this balance will result in a vulnerability to attack by competitors, creditors, hostile employees, and creative takeover specialists.

A commitment to growing the company properly will invariably trigger the need for management to undertake greater risks. These risks must be managed from a legal and financial perspective, as must the changes that the organization will experience as a result of the growth. Accelerated growth will mean that these risks and changes will occur with greater frequency and with more serious implications. The legal requirements and restrictions that affect most business objectives and transactions will typically retard the rate at which a company can grow.

Over the years, I have found that very few things are more professionally rewarding than advising growing companies on the strategies that will be most effective to build shareholder value and meet growth objectives. I truly hope that *Grow Fast, Grow Right* becomes a resource and a tool that helps your company leverage its strengths and achieve its full potential, and I hope that you enjoy the journey as you follow the business growth path.

Andrew J. Sherman
Bethesda, Maryland
July 2006

1

UNDERSTANDING THE GROW FAST GROW RIGHT BASIC PRINCIPLES

At Grow Fast Grow Right®, we believe that there are key areas of the company that drive its growth and performance. A business exists to generate profitable revenue streams, create opportunities for its employees, support its channel relationships, and maximize shareholder value. We call these key areas value drivers. The leadership of the company needs to stay focused on these value drivers and to make its decisions and guide the company's growth according to them.

As discussed in the Preface, we organize these value drivers into the three pillars that support a secure foundation and strategy for growth: Human Capital, Financial Capital, and Intellectual Capital. *If the 12 value drivers within these three pillars are strategically optimized, then a company will both grow fast and grow right.* Each chapter in this book provides strategies, best practices, and war stories about each value driver to help you formulate a growth plan and strategy that meets your company's objectives. Some value drivers may be more relevant to your company than others, and a few may not apply at all. Some value drivers may represent opportunities for growth, and others may represent areas of weaknesses. Some may be building blocks that are necessary to build a foundation that will support growth goals and objectives, and other value drivers may represent cracks in that foundation. Still others may serve as cornerstones on which more weight can be placed. Take another look at the chart of the Grow Fast Grow Right foundation in Figure 1.1 in order to understand the role and importance of each building block.

VALUE DRIVER ACID TESTS

In our Grow Fast Grow Right® training programs and seminars, we encourage CEOs and team leaders to put their companies and the 12 value drivers through a series of acid tests in order to assess the current state of their companies. Two such tests are discussed here.

1. *"Eyes of the Buyer" Acid Test.* Treat your company as if it were for sale every day, even if your exit is ten or more years away. What would

FIGURE 1.1 *The Grow Fast Grow Right Foundation*

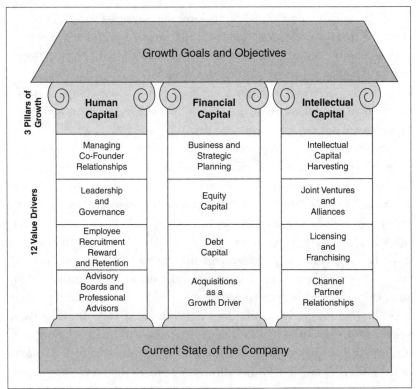

a buyer find compelling about your company? How could you build on these strengths? What would they find troubling? How would you correct these weaknesses? **Strategic exercise:** Draft a Letter of Intent as if a deal with a buyer had been made. What price would be paid? Why? How would you work to improve that value? What conditions to closing would a buyer impose? Why?

2. *"Understanding Your Obituary" Acid Test.* If your comapny went out of business tomorrow, would anyone care? Why might it die? Who would cry at its funeral? How long before your employees land elsewhere? How long before your customers find an alternative solution? **Strategic exercise:** Draft a three- to six-word epitaph for your company's gravestone. How should it be remembered? What fatal error did you make? The reality of seeing it on a gravestone can help you focus on your survival for many years to come.

From our seminars throughout North America with CEOs and leaders of growing companies, some of the epitaphs that we have seen include:

"Day Late and a Dollar Short"
"Won the Battle But Lost the War"
"Grew Too Fat and Lazy"
"Strayed Too Far from Our Core"
"Didn't Make It across the Chasm"
"No Good Opportunity Went Unmissed"
And my favorite: "We Died Trying," which is a reminder not to confuse activity with results when building a growing company.

UNDERSTANDING THE DNA
OF GROWTH COMPANIES

What factors drive a company to fast-track business growth? What is the genealogy that motivates an entrepreneurial growth company to get bigger, faster, diversify, enter new markets, and develop new products?

The Edison syndrome. Some companies develop a culture of creativity and innovation that drives them toward new product development and technological breakthroughs. The pride of inventiveness and skillful management combine to provide the fuel for growth. Cisco Systems, Apple, 3M, and Johnson Industries are examples of modern success stories that are driven by innovation—both internally and via acquisition of developing companies and technologies.

Fear. Some companies are driven by fear of competition: the fear of missing an opportunity or the fear of not being the market leader. Andy Grove, the founder of Intel, wrote "only the paranoid survive," and certainly fear of failure or the insecurity of a company's leadership can, if harnessed properly, be a strong motivator for growth.

Boredom. One entrepreneur I met recently told me that he and his team decided to triple the size of their building supplies conglomerate through recapitalizing, establishing new offices, and acquiring existing businesses primarily because they got bored. When all the trains are running on time, the entrepreneurial challenge can be significantly diminished. Many companies remain stagnant (and often begin to slowly deteriorate) because ownership and management have become "fat, dumb, and happy" with the EBITA and cash flow. They transform from gazelles to elephants, unless their leaderships develop new challenges. When companies stop evolving, they may also eventually lose key employees, key customers, and other key strategic relationships. Never, ever take business growth for granted. Getting bored easily and always striving for new challenges can be strong characteristics for a growth company.

Publish or perish. Some industries, particularly those that are technology driven, mimic the publish-or-perish culture of the academic tenure track. They must continue to be productive and innovative or the markets and their customers will punish and abandon them. Misjudging a market or mistiming the release of a new product can be very costly.

First mover advantage/the land grab. Many emerging industries are driven by the first mover advantage; that is, the company that gets its product or service out the fastest and begins building brand equity with its targeted group of customers. This gold rush–style market dynamic becomes a market and business growth motivator because strategies must be put in place to be *first* to market, *first* to build brand, and so on. The theory here is that the company that grabs the most market share the fastest wins the battle and the war. This business growth motivator came under attack after the market crash in 2000 when a "best beats first" mentality crept into the marketplace. Being the first to market in the dot-com era didn't guaranty that a company would be around 12 months later. For example, first mover search engine Netscape is now a smaller piece of a much larger but struggling AOL/Time Warner pie, while Google, which improved but certainly did not invent the search engine, enjoys a robust 45 percent of the market share, leaving early pioneers such as Lycos and Alta Vista in the dust.

Ego. The stereotypical public image of an entrepreneur at the helm of a growth company is that he has an ego the size of the state of Texas. It is often but not always true that entrepreneurs have very large egos, and this self-confidence and self-pride become the motivators for continued business growth. *A successful company cannot be built on ego alone.* If the founder views the company basically as a monument to himself, then it will surely fail at some point. Similarly, if individual greed is at the heart of the compensation and ownership structure, then the company will often fail or lose momentum. The better entrepreneurs, including Sam Walton or Bill Gates, take great pride in helping thousands of employees and shareholders build wealth, knowing that their rewards will be even greater if everyone around them prospers. Ego and greed must be kept in balance with the needs of the company as a whole. The entrepreneur or management team that is focused on the enrichment of its employees, the satisfaction of its customers, and a steady increase in its shareholder value will build wealth by helping instead of hurting others along the way.

The "chip on my shoulder" phenomenon. Many entrepreneurs at the helm of rapid growth companies have some external motivating factors that drive them to succeed day in and day out. They may have been the kid who never got picked in schoolyard basketball, was from a broken home, or grew up under difficult economic or social conditions. This "chip-on-the-shoulder" syndrome becomes part of the corporate culture, and employees who shared similar backgrounds are attracted to a culture where "geeks rule" or "David beats Goliath" or "the nice guy gets the girl." Americans often cheer for and reward the underdog, and many companies have grown and flourished because resources were made available to them so that they could overcome past and present hurdles.

THE IMPORTANCE OF MOMENTUM

Momentum is a critical component of all seven of the key motivators for growth discussed above. The leadership must ensure that the resources and the systems are in place to facilitate forward progress toward stated objectives. Every day, week, month, quarter, and year, management must establish benchmarks and milestones and must measure progress against these goals. A loss of momentum for an extended period of time can be detrimental and will hinder a company's ability to raise additional rounds of capital or get access to other resources needed for continued business growth. Companies rarely lose momentum if they measure performance against these benchmarks and focus on maintaining high employee motivation and strong customer relationships. The "Big Mo," as it is often known to entrepreneurs and venture capitalists, is critical to continued success.

COMMON TRAITS AND BEST PRACTICES OF SUCCESSFUL RAPID-GROWTH COMPANIES

Growth companies share common traits and best practices that contribute to their success. These include:

FIGURE 1.2 *The Business Growth Strategic Decision Path*

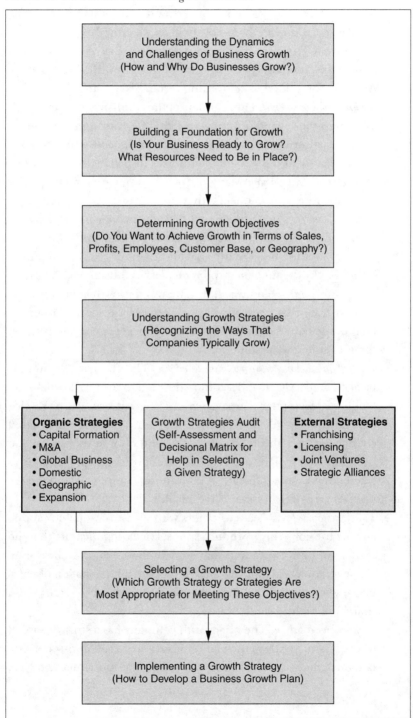

- *Beyond seed capital.* The company has received early rounds of capital, and the challenge shifts from "How do we get start-up capital?" to "We've been seeded but now how do we grow?"
- *Proven team.* The team has demonstrated an ability to work together and to execute, and peers and employees view them as leaders. Are they committed to reinvesting resources into the company?
- *Scalable business model.* The founders of the company have developed a business model and infrastructure that fits with *current* customer demand patterns but that also can *evolve profitability* as demand patterns increase and the market embraces its products and services.
- *Recognizable innovation.* Many of today's rapid-growth companies are truly innovative pioneers; they are focused on creating products and services that are ten times faster, cheaper, or more convenient for the user than the competition. Rapid-growth companies often aim for ten times as the goal because they realize and understand that by the time the product or service hits the marketplace, it will only be three times better. The rapid-growth company must demonstrate that its products and services are several orders of magnitude better and more valuable for targeted customers to get them to switch to its solution.
- *Intellectual vision and an ability to evolve.* The company's founders have created a vision and a culture devoted to the intellectual challenge of developing a great idea into a great product or service that customers will line up for. The founders have anticipated change—stayed ahead of the curve—and also have ensured that the company's plans are flexible enough to change directions when circumstances dictate. A continuing commitment to the development of new initiatives is critical.
- *Loyal customer base.* Real customers who gladly have paid real dollars for the company's products and services demonstrate that the team's solutions work and that somebody wants what they offer. These customers are initially attracted to the differentiation of product or service, and the company's ability to deliver creates mind share and builds brand loyalty.
- *Competitive analysis.* The fast-growth company has a strong sense of where it is currently in the marketplace and has demonstrated sustainable competitive advantage by being first to the marketplace,

by building brand, or by developing a portfolio of intellectual property that creates barriers to entry. It finds an initial niche to exploit and then begins building around that opening in the market.

- *Financial performance.* The company has developed a stream of durable revenues and profits that are built on a foundation of defensible accounting and revenue recognition practices.

- A *healthy attitude toward future and risk.* Rapid-growth companies understand how to put risk into proper perspective. They understand that entrepreneurial companies need to be prepared to fail in order to succeed. They view some degree of failure as inevitable, and this culture of resiliency helps them quickly rebound without getting overly discouraged. These companies know how to learn from their mistakes (and when and where possible to avoid making them twice); the acceptance and encouragement of risk are part of their culture that drives ongoing innovation.

- *Commitment to empowerment.* The leadership of the company is committed to empowering team members at all levels with the resources and the decision-making authority to do their jobs effectively and without excessive red tape or internal politics. The leaders of the company continuously set goals and milestones, communicate these goals to employees at all levels, and regularly measure the company's performance against these benchmarks. The company develops compensation and reward systems around the accomplishment of (and the ability to exceed) these benchmarks.

- *Always monitoring competitive trends.* The more successful rapid-growth companies are never caught with their heads in the sand. They devote capital and resources to developing market information systems and to gathering and analyzing market intelligence. They carefully monitor key market trends, indicators, and moves made by their competitors.

- *The art of spin control.* Rapid-growth companies learn quickly how to manage the rumor mill. Along the growth path, these companies are especially vulnerable to attacks from jealous competitors, disgruntled employees, and Wall Street analysts. The smarter companies stay ahead of this information and control the flow of data effectively. When bad news does hit, they deal with the problem in a direct and straightforward manner that will often prevent employees and customers from running for the hills.

THE STRATEGIC AUDIT AS A PREREQUISITE FOR DEFINING OBJECTIVES

The strategic audit is a tool for assessing the current state of your company—the foundation for your three pillars of growth—and the means to determine the best growth strategy. It will evaluate the strength of the current management and advisory team; define the key sections of the *business growth strategic plan,* which needs to be drafted; examine the current systems, distribution channels, and financial resources that are available to determine whether the plans for growth can be supported; and look at industry trends and macroeconomic factors that will either support and expedite your growth plans or serve as a barrier to implementation. It is also an important way to *benchmark* your company's performance to date and plans for growth against other direct or indirect competitors that are similarly situated.

The strategic audit may reveal that your initial set of growth objectives were misdirected, overly conservative, too aggressive, or just plain inconsistent with current market trends. It will serve as a reality test and an opportunity to refine objectives before resources are expended to implement the wrong set of objectives. The business growth strategic plan can be shaped accordingly, or resources that are missing can be put in place to achieve the original plan.

CATEGORIES OF GROWTH

The strategic audit should also help your company define which specific categories or aspects of your business you intend to grow. For example, your business plan may revolve around a desire to grow profits while holding the number of employees steady, or it may be that you need to grow the number of distribution channels while holding the number of new products and services steady (or vice versa). The process of choosing *which* aspects of the business are slated for growth and *what* strategy will be most effective for meeting these objectives is a critical part of the overall growth planning process. Many categories of business operations could be targeted for growth, as demonstrated by Figure 1.3.

It is often the case that growth strategies are developed to solve a specific problem or to help jump over a hurdle in the business growth evolution. The need to stay competitive, the need to foster creativity and innovation, the need to encourage career advancement among top management, the need to build your brand, the challenge of overseas expansion, the need to strengthen the balance sheet, and the need to better leverage your portfolio of intellectual property may be problems your company is facing. The *right* growth strategy can solve these, *if* it is formulated and implemented properly.

Not *all* growth is accomplished through the establishment of external strategic relationships. Some types of business growth are more internally focused, or organic. These strategies include raising capital to build additional locations, hiring more sales staff, or developing additional products. Another type of organic growth is accomplished through mergers and acquisitions, where the growing company chooses to *buy* third parties in

FIGURE 1.3 *Understanding Categories of Growth*

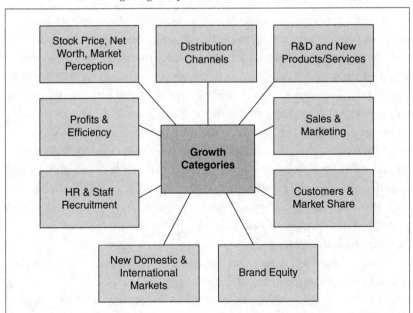

lieu of establishing strategic relationships with them. Many acquirers use strategic relationships as a due diligence precursor to an actual acquisition.

AVOIDING SOME OF THE CLASSIC
BUSINESS GROWTH PROBLEMS

Growth spurts can hit a company at any time, especially in a fast-moving economy and fast-paced business environment. The impetus for growth could be the development of new technology, the demise of a competitor (or even a weakness), the hiring of new personnel, the infusion of fresh capital, newly discovered opportunities or marketing breakthroughs, or a favorable shift in economic conditions. These developments can happen over an extended period of time or virtually overnight. When they happen quickly, some of the more common challenges include decreased cash flow, mismanagement, lack of customer service responsiveness, overhead costs out of control, communications logjams, high employee turnover, inexperienced senior management, and a slippage in quality control. The key to managing this process is for management to anticipate the downside of a given growth strategy or set of market conditions and use that knowledge to provide impetus for growth plans.

These problems can take a company quickly off its growth path or lead to a violent crash if not properly navigated. Steps that can help keep the company on course include getting high-quality advice from consultants and professional advisors and recruiting senior executives to help support the founders as they manage the growth and provide training to employees so they understand the implications of business growth. Other steps to help the growing company stay on course as it works toward its growth objectives include developing strong financial controls and accounting/reporting systems (to manage and monitor the *costs* of growth), the raising of additional capital (to ensure enough "ammunition" for the battle), and finding the discipline to stay focused on the end game (*to* make sure the growth phenomenon does not fuel the founders' egos and lead to lavish spending or perks).

Rapidly growing smaller companies need to place new emphasis on relationship management, building valuable networks, and leveraging intangible assets to assist in the leveling of the playing field to compete against larger companies. The ability to leverage your knowledge, to establish key strategic relationships (and maintain them as "happy marriages"), to be flexible in establishing *new* relationships as necessary, and to bring products and services to the market *faster* (using these strategic relationships), gives small and medium companies an edge over the larger elephants they compete against. Think gazelle, which navigates its way to survival by being nimble, fast, and smart to compensate for the size and strength of larger animals. In this new economy, fast beats slow, knowledge triumphs over traditional assets, and information is king.

2

DEVELOPING A BUSINESS GROWTH PLAN

To Grow Fast *and* Grow Right, you need to develop a game plan. You need to take the time to map out where you are, what you have achieved, where you are going, and how you plan to head in that direction. Effective business and strategic planning is *critical* to a company's long-term success and its ability to raise capital and grow successfully. As a result, bankers, accountants, consultants, and academics have written volumes about business growth plans. Yet, it seems that the more information there is, the more confused people get. There's no one right answer. A business growth plan should tell a story, make an argument, and conservatively predict the future. All companies have different stories to tell, different arguments to make, and different futures to predict.

Business growth planning is the process of setting goals, explaining the objectives, and then mapping out a strategy to achieve these goals and objectives. A well-written plan maps out the best growth path, as well as the rationale for the selection of the strategy over other alternatives. In essence, a business growth plan is the articulation and explanation of *why* your chosen strategy makes sense, *what* resources you will need to implement the growth strategy, *who* the team will be that will have the vision and leadership to execute the growth strategy, and *what* path you will follow to get there. It will also answer the following questions:

- Who are you?
- What do you do?
- What is your business model? (How do you make money? Who is your customer? What problem do you solve? How do you solve the problem better, faster, or cheaper than other available solutions?)
- How do your customers pay you?
- How loyal are they?
- How should you grow?
- Why is this strategy better than others that may be available?
- What do you need to implement the growth strategy selected?
- How crowded is the market?
- What vehicles (and at what costs) will you use to sell the customer *your* product or service? Why is this the best vehicle?
- What market research have you done to be sure that anyone *wants* to buy this product or service at this price—or at all?
- Does your company truly modify the way business is being done in your industry or is this more of a fad or a trend?

Nobody has a crystal ball that can predict what will work and what won't—neither the savviest investor nor the most veteran entrepreneur. The better the analysis, the better the chances that most of the goals set forth in the business growth plan will be achieved.

Building your small company into something much larger is a marathon, not a sprint. If you think of growing your business as a NASCAR season—a series of long races that build toward a long-term goal where you accumulate experience, victories, and defeats—then the following five smart ways to build your business are:

1. **Double-check the functionality of your racecar before putting it on the fast track.** Do you have the right foundation in place to grow your business? What are the strategic prerequisites? To grow your small business successfully, your company should have a strong foundation from which your growth strategy will be built, launched, and monitored. As you build a platform for growth, make sure that the relevant components listed below are firmly in place:
   - **A clearly defined mission statement,** vision and core values that management has adopted and your employees have embraced.

Your employees must be committed to sharing and living by these core values to achieve corporate goals. If your mission statement sits on a plaque behind your desk, it's not embedded in the corporate culture, and that means your company is not yet in a position to grow effectively or efficiently.

- **A proven business model or format** that will serve as a basis or as the blueprint for the growth strategy selected. The business model must have been tested, refined, and operated successfully and should be consistently profitable. The success of the business model should not be too dependent on the physical presence or specific expertise of the founders of the system.

- **Proven methods of operation and proprietary processes** that can be explained in a comprehensive operations manual and that cannot be easily duplicated by competitors. The processes must maintain their value to any market-channel partners over an extended period of time, and be enforced through clearly drafted and objective quality-control standards.

- **Comprehensive training programs for employees and any market-channel partners.** The programs should integrate the latest education and training technologies and take place both at your headquarters and on-site at the channel partner's proposed location at the outset of the relationship and on an ongoing basis.

- **A commitment to, and genuine understanding of, your customers.** A company positioned for growth has taken the time to understand the short-term as well as long-term needs and wants of its customers, and modified its organization and products to meet these needs and wants.

- **A demonstrated market demand for the products and services** developed by your company that will be distributed through channels created by the growth strategy selected. Your company's products and services should meet certain minimum quality standards and not be subject to rapid shifts in consumer preferences (e.g., fads). They should also be proprietary in nature. Market research and analysis should be sensitive to trends in the economy and your industry, the plans of direct and indirect competitors, and shifts in consumer preferences.

2. **Chart your course.** Have you drafted a business plan that will navigate your course and that will identify the human and financial resources needed to get there? Does the plan include a sensitivity analysis to anticipate the inevitable surprises that the market will throw at you? In other words, what are the what-ifs? If you have drafted a plan recently, then you may need to dust if off. Did you meet the goals and objectives set for the company the last time you engaged in the planning process? Why or why not?

3. **Make sure the car is filled with gas.** Financial capital is the fuel that serves the growth engine. How will you finance your growth plans? Will you take on debt or seek equity capital? How do the needs of these sources of capital differ? Are you looking for capital which is more financially reward-driven or more strategic in nature?

4. **Make sure you have an experienced driver that others trust.** Fans rally around the driver, not the car. Who is leading the company and how did he or she get there? Do people trust the driver and his or her vision for winning the race? Are they willing to work for longer hours and at less pay to help the company achieve its growth objectives? In *Good to Great*, Jim Collins discusses the importance of having the right people on the right bus in the right seats. While I would never advocate entering a bus into a NASCAR race, the parallel to growing a small business is very clear. Our rapidly developing service- and technology-driven economy has made managing human resources more important than ever. The age of the knowledge worker and the role of human capital in building a company can be a significant challenge to small and growing business owners who compete every day with large competitors to recruit and retain qualified personnel. In an economy in which unemployment has reached an all-time low, skilled technical labor is at a premium, and the dynamics of the employer/employee relationship are changing quickly. The owner of a growing company needs to stay abreast of new trends and developments in the law. These include technology-enabled telecommuting and the option of working from home, new legal rights for temporary workers, and the divided loyalties of the multi-employer "free agent."

5. **Select your pit crew carefully.** Think of your channel partners as your pit crew. Channel partners are the relationships that you will build to assist you in bringing your product or service to the targeted end-customer. Who are they? How should they be selected? How effective have they been once they are in place? It will be difficult to grow if your current channel partner systems and relationships are *not* working. If this is the case, then whose fault is it? Did you choose too hastily, or did you fail to support your partners?

Do You Really Need a Business Plan?

Some members of the business and academic communities challenge whether an entrepreneur really needs a business plan. They claim that preparing one is a waste of time because the marketplace moves so rapidly. This is like asking a pilot to fly without navigation equipment, or a ship's captain to set sail without a nautical map—it's a bad idea. There are many reasons to prepare a business plan, including:

- **To explain**—to yourself and others—why a viable opportunity exists
- **To provide a road map** for the future direction of the business
- **To hold the founders accountable** for performance goals, and to demonstrate that you have put together a capable and balanced management team that is able to execute the strategy and implement the business plan
- **To provide a schedule** and a time frame for meeting key milestones
- **To identify what resources will be needed** to accomplish objectives and *when* they will be needed
- **To mitigate the risks of future business failure** by identifying potential bottlenecks and problems that will affect the growth of the company and offering possible solutions
- **To provide internal financial controls** and direction

PREPARING THE PLAN

A well-written business growth plan doesn't *oversell* the good, *undersell* the bad, or *ignore* the ugly! Essentially, it is a plan to manage the risks and challenges involved in implementing a new growth strategy. Business growth plans should acknowledge that growth and success are moving targets by anticipating as many future events or circumstances that will affect the company's objectives.

Here's an outline of the elements that should be included in a business growth plan.

I. **Executive summary**
   A. Brief history of your company
   B. Overview of your products and services
   C. Background of your management team (summary)
   D. Mission statement (Why are you in this business?)
   E. Summary of your company's financial performance to date (when applicable)
   F. Key features of your market

II. **The company: an overview**
   A. Organizational and management structure
   B. Operational and management policies
   C. Description of products and services (both current and anticipated)
   D. Overview of trends in the industry and marketplace in which you compete (or plan to compete)
   E. Key strengths and weaknesses of your company

III. **Growth strategy analysis**
   A. Articulate growth strategy selected
   B. How and why did you adopt this growth strategy?
   C. What hurdles and risks might you encounter in the implementation of this strategy?
   D. What resources will you need to implement this strategy?

IV. **Market analysis**
   A. Extended description of the markets in which you compete (size, trends, growth, etc.)

    B. Analysis of key competitors and likely future competitors (and how will your business model and growth strategy change or evolve to face the new competitors?)

    C. Description and analysis of key customers and clients (current and anticipated)

    D. Market research supporting current and anticipated product lines

    E. Analysis of barriers to entry and your sustainable competitive advantage

V. Marketing and advertising strategy

    A. Strategies for reaching current and anticipated customers/ clients

    B. Pricing policies and strategies

    C. Advertising and public relations plans and strategies

    D. Discussion of potential market partners and strategic alliances

VI. Financial plan and strategies

    A. Summary of financial performance for last three to five years

    B. Current financial condition (includes recent income statements and balance sheets as attachments)

    C. Projected financial condition (forecasts for three to five years)

    D. Extended discussion of anticipated allocation of proceeds and parallel budgets

VII. Suggested exhibits and attachments

    A. Résumés of key members of your management team

    B. Organizational chart

    C. Timetables for completion of goals and objectives

    D. Copies of key documents and contracts

    E. Copies of recent media coverage

    F. Pictures of key products or advertising materials for services offered

    G. List of customer and professional references

Business plans are used by both start-up as well as existing companies. For example, a company that has been operating for 15 or more years, but is planning to enter the next stage in its development, will need to draft a business plan in order to raise the necessary capital. In any situation, the business plan should be prepared with the assistance of a financial consultant, the investment banker, and the internal management team, as well as with the input and editorial advice of attorneys and accountants.

Be aware of some of the more common misperceptions when drafting your business plan.

#1   Myth: *BUSINESS PLANS ARE ONLY FOR START-UP COMPANIES.*

REALITY: Companies at all stages of development need to prepare business plans either to plan or finance a specific project *or* for general expansion, financing, mergers or acquisitions, *or* the overall improvement of the company's financial and managerial performance.

#2   Myth: *BUSINESS PLANS SHOULD BE AS DETAILED AND SLICK AS POSSIBLE. THE MORE MONEY AND TIME THAT IS SPENT PREPARING THE PLAN, THE BETTER CHANCE THAT THE PROJECT WILL BE FINANCED.*

REALITY: Sophisticated investors will not have the time to review hundreds of pages of text. The plan must be concise, well-written, and should focus on the lender's or investor's principal areas of concern. Avoid overly technical descriptions of the company's processes or operations. Investors will commit funds based on the quality and clarity of the document's content, not its thickness or its style. Although business plans ought to be presented professionally, a very expensive binder or presentation will often demonstrate inefficient resource management.

#3   Myth: *BUSINESS PLANS SHOULD EMPHASIZE IDEAS AND CONCEPTS, NOT PEOPLE.*

REALITY: Many entrepreneurs fear that if the success of a company depends too heavily on any specific person, an investor will shy away. Although this is partially true, any experienced venture capitalist will tell you that they would prefer to invest in a company that has great people and only a good concept, rather than a great concept and a weak management team. Ultimately, lenders and investors will commit funds based on the strength of the management team.

#4 Myth: *ONLY THE FOUNDING ENTREPRENEUR SHOULD PREPARE THE BUSI-
NESS PLAN.*

REALITY: Most entrepreneurs are highly skilled in a particular profession or area of management. As a result, they may not
necessarily possess the ability to prepare a business plan in
a form that prospective lenders or investors are accus-
tomed to. Ideally, the plan should be developed by a team
of managers within the company and then reviewed by
qualified experts, such as accountants, attorneys, and the
board of directors. However, the business plan should never
be prepared solely by outside advisors without the input of
internal management. A venture capitalist will be quick to
recognize a "cooked" plan, or one that reflects the views
and efforts of professional advisors rather than the company's management team who are responsible for running
the company on a day-to-day basis.

#5 Myth: *BUSINESS PLANS SHOULD BE DISTRIBUTED AS WIDELY AS POSSIBLE.*

REALITY: The business plan will inevitably contain information that
is proprietary and confidential to the company. Therefore,
distribution should be controlled, and careful records should
be kept as to whom has been provided with copies of the
plan. The cover sheet should contain a conspicuously positioned management disclaimer reminding the reader that
these are only the *plans* of the company, the success of
which cannot be assured, as well as a notice of proprietary
information. All applicable federal and state securities laws
must be carefully considered if the business plan is intended
as a financing proposal. However, the plan should not be
used in lieu of a formal private placement memorandum
(discussed later in this chapter.) Finally, certain institutional investors will only consider investing in certain kinds
of companies or industries. Research these criteria before
sending a business plan in order to save both the time and
resources of all concerned parties.

#6 Myth: *A BUSINESS PLAN SHOULD FOLLOW A SPECIFIED FORMAT, REGARD-LESS OF THE INDUSTRY IN WHICH THE COMPANY OPERATES.*

REALITY: While it may be true that all companies face certain common challenges in the areas of marketing, management, administration, and finance, companies at different stages of growth face different problems, and those operating in different industries will require different sets of topics that must be included in the business plan. For example, plans for a start-up manufacturing company may be far more concerned with financing of the plant, equipment, patents, inventory, and production schedules than an already established service-oriented company that may be more focused on personnel, marketing costs, and the protection of trade secrets and goodwill.

#7 Myth: *IN PREPARING THE BUSINESS PLAN, OPTIMISM SHOULD PREVAIL OVER REALISM.*

REALITY: The business plan should demonstrate the enthusiasm of the founders of the company as well as generate excitement in the reader; however, it should be credible and accurate. Investors will want to know all the company's strengths *and* weaknesses. In fact, a realistic discussion of the company's problems, along with a reasonable plan for dealing with these various risks and challenges, will have a positive impact on the prospective investor. As a general rule, investors will feel more comfortable investing in someone who has learned from previous business failures rather than a person who has never managed a company. Finally, any budgets, sales projections, company valuations, or related forecasts should be well-substantiated with accompanying footnotes, for both legal and business reasons. Unrealistic or unsubstantiated financial projections and budgets will reveal inexperience or lack of attention to detail to an interested investor. It may even lead to litigation by disgruntled investors if there are wide disparities between what was represented and what actually happened.

#8   Myth: *WHEN PREPARING A BUSINESS PLAN, THE EXECUTIVE SUMMARY SHOULD BE WRITTEN FIRST.*

REALITY: Institutional investors are exposed to hundreds of business plans in any given month and as a result they only devote a few minutes to the initial review of each business plan. Only those plans that capture their interest will be given a more thorough review. The Executive Summary (generally one to three pages in length) will be the first, and possibly the last, impression that the company makes on the investor. Thus, if the reader's attention is not captured in these first few minutes, he or she is not likely to complete the review of the plan. The Executive Summary should contain all the information that will be critical in the investment decision, such as:

- Nature of the company and its founders
- Amount of money sought
- Allocation of the proceeds
- Summary of key financial projections
- Overview of marketing considerations

Entrepreneurs often make the mistake of writing the Executive Summary *first*, before the main components of the business plan have been drafted. It is much more effective to prepare the main body of the plan, and then draft the Executive Summary last in order to ensure consistency. The Executive Summary is then truly a preview of the details of the plan.

#9   Myth: *BUSINESS PLANS ARE ONLY WRITTEN WHEN A COMPANY NEEDS TO RAISE CAPITAL.*

REALITY: Although most business plans are written in connection with the search for capital, a well-written business plan will also serve a variety of beneficial functions to the company and its management team. The completed business plan serves as

- a management tool that serves as a road map for growth;
- a realistic self-appraisal of the company's progress to date, as well as projected goals and objectives;

- a foundation for the development of a more detailed strategic and growth management plan (especially after the proposed financing has been successfully completed).

THE IMPORTANCE OF STRATEGIC PLANNING FOR BUSINESS GROWTH

In a company's early stages, the emphasis is on survival. Among the key concerns are how do we properly launch and grow the company by attracting and sustaining customers, and what resources will we need to support the strategy selected? But what happens later? Once an emerging growth company reaches its initial set of fundamental goals, the focus shifts away from mere business planning to strategic planning for growth. Strategic planning is an ongoing process that seeks to *build* and *improve* the following key areas:

- Quality and sophistication of the technology used by the emerging company to support its customers
- Quality and sophistication of the training and support systems
- Value and recognition of the emerging company's brand from the perspective of customer awareness
- Development of operating systems, practices, and procedures based upon internal company "best practices" as well as overall industry "best practices"
- Exploration of new domestic and international markets
- Organization of supplier councils, co-branding alliances, and other key strategic relationships
- Development of strategies for alternative sites and related new market penetration strategies
- Development of advanced branding and intellectual property protection strategies

The strategic planning process should manifest itself in periodic meetings among the emerging growth company's leadership, periodic strategic planning retreats, and a written strategic plan that should be updated

Key Strategic Planning Issues

- What are the common characteristics of our targeted customers?
- What are the common characteristics of our most successful employees?
- What can we do to attract more people like this in the recruitment and selection process?
- What are the five greatest strengths of our company?
- What are five greatest strengths of our system?
- What is being done to build on these strengths?
- What are our five biggest problems?
- What are we doing to resolve these problems?

annually. The strategic planning meetings and retreats could focus on a specific theme, such as:

- Brand building and leveraging
- Rebuilding trust and value with customers
- Litigation prevention and compliance
- International opportunities in the global village
- Leadership and productivity issues
- Financial management and performance issues
- Improved recruitment of women and minorities
- Technology and communications systems improvement
- Alternative site and nontraditional location analysis
- Co-branding and brand-extension licensing
- Building systems for improving internal communication

Any or all of these topics are appropriate for one meeting or for discussion on a continuing basis. An outside facilitator, such as an industry expert, or the emerging growth company's senior management team, could lead the strategic planning meeting.

The end result of an effective strategic planning meeting is to develop a list of specific action items. You may be able to implement some action items right away, and others may take time.

The strategic planning process is a commitment to strive for the *continuous improvement* of your business growth objective. The process is designed to ensure that maximum value is being delivered, day in and day out, to the growing company's executive team, employees, shareholders, vendors and suppliers, and, of course, its customers. It is about not being afraid to ask: Where are we? Where do we want to be? What do we need to do to get there? What is currently standing in our way of achieving these objectives? It is about making sure that the company takes the time to develop a mission statement and define a collective vision and then develop a series of plans to achieve these goals. Executives must stay *focused* on these objectives and provide leadership to both the balance of the growing company's leadership team and the customers by explaining *how* these objectives will be achieved. The focus must be on brand equity, customer value and loyalty, and shareholder profitability. The guidelines and protocols for internal communications must encourage honesty and openness, without fear of retaliation or politics.

BUILDING A BUSINESS GROWTH PLAN

Once the general business and strategic-planning process has been completed, a foundation exists upon which a specific *business growth plan* can be built. The business growth plan looks at specific growth opportunities and analyzes the alternatives for implementation. For example, if a new product or technology is developed at the company, then the plan should address the following issues:

1. Should this new project be folded into an existing business division or operating unit? Why? Which one offers the best fit?
2. If not, should this new project be structured as a newly created subsidiary? If yes, what are the corporate and tax implications? What approvals may be necessary to transfer assets and resources into this new subsidiary?
3. If a new subsidiary is created, will it be wholly owned by the parent corporation? Partially owned by the employees? A corporate spin-off? Will third-party investors or strategic partners be invited to invest in the subsidiary? Which ones? How will the deal be structured?
4. Should the subsidiary be co-owned as an operating joint venture corporation with one or more joint venture partners? Which partner makes the most sense for this new venture?

Essentially, each new corporate opportunity must first be analyzed from a structural point of view before the other elements of the business growth plan can be developed. And for highly innovative rapid-growth companies, this means that up to dozens of new corporate opportunities must endure this rigid analysis each year.

The impetus for developing a business growth plan may be that innovation within the company has created new products or opportunities, but this is not always the case. As demonstrated by Figure 2.1, other growth drivers may include market-driven opportunities (e.g., the market is growing rapidly and you must grow with it or perish), increasing customer demand for your specific products or services (e.g., customers are pulling you into a growth strategy), or the problems or failures faced by a given competitor (e.g., the hole created by their troubles presents a growth opportunity). These types of growth drivers do not typically require a corporate venturing analysis, but they nevertheless dictate the need for a business growth plan.

FIGURE 2.1 *Key Components of a Business Growth Plan*

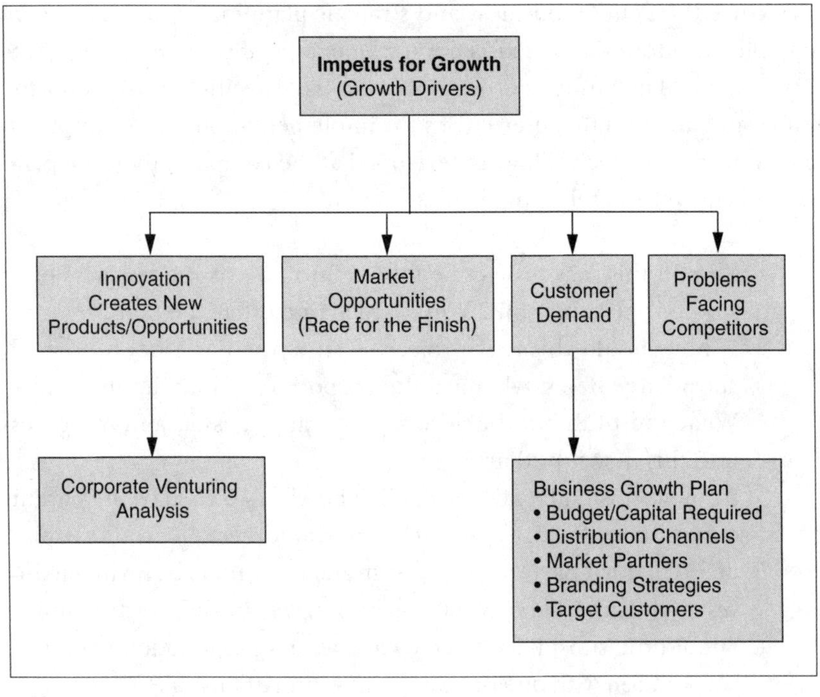

KEY COMPONENTS OF THE BUSINESS GROWTH PLAN

A well-prepared business growth plan builds on the basic business plan and strategic plan discussed earlier in this chapter, but also specifically focuses on:

- What capital will be required to develop a working budget to create the business growth plan?
- What are the distribution channels that need to be strengthened or built in order to implement the business growth plan?
- What market partners will we need to implement the business growth plan?
- What new branding strategies will need to be developed to position (or reposition) our company and its products or services to successfully implement the business growth plan?
- Which new or existing customer relationships need to be built in order for the business growth plan to be successful?

Budget. This section of the business growth plan analyzes the resources that will be required to implement the selected strategy. It must be conservative, realistic, and well-documented. The budget will often be driven by whether the company has decided to adopt an organic/internal growth strategy, an external growth strategy that relies prominently on the resources to be deployed by *others,* or some hybrid strategy.

Distribution channels. This section of the business growth plan analyzes *how* the product or service will reach the marketplace and the targeted consumer. Most rapid growth companies will have a *multi-channel* strategy to ensure maximum market penetration and to increase the chances of success.

Market partners. A key component of the business growth plan will be to identify the appropriate strategic market partners and get to them before your competitors, particularly if you expect to enjoy an exclusive or partially exclusive relationship. For more on this topic, see Chapter 14.

Branding strategies. The business growth plan must also analyze the company's current branding and marketing practices to see how they fit into the new growth strategy. What new advertising or sales campaigns will need to be developed? Would co-branding with other strategic partners be a way to expedite or enhance the pace of the growth? Does any repositioning of the brand (or the development of new brands or subbrands) need to be done in order to offer this new suite of services or family of products? For example, if the majority of customers associate the brand with a baseline level of quality at a very competitive price, would new product introduction that features much higher quality at an increased price require a brand overhaul or even a new brand, especially if the existing line of products or services remains intact?

Customer relationships. The business growth plan should address whether the growth strategy selected *relies on the company's ability to sell more products and services to existing customers, or is it more dependent on establishing new customer relationships?* If it is the former, what strategies will be put in place to get existing customers to spend more? If it is the latter, have these *new* customers been identified? How will they be resolved? Where are these targeted new customers currently getting their products/ services from (e.g., from whom are you asking these customers to take their business away from to give to you)?

THE IMPORTANCE OF SENSITIVITY ANALYSIS IN BUILDING A BUSINESS GROWTH PLAN

A well-drafted business growth plan must deal with the inevitable contingencies of growth. Ever-changing capital markets, customer demand patterns, the entry of new competitors, and general market conditions will burden a rapid-growth company's ability to identify specific tasks and translate them into a specific schedule. For example, if the success of the business growth plan relies upon your company's products being faster, cheaper, more reliable and capable of solving more complicated problems than those offered by your competitors, then how does the strategy change when your competitor introduces a product better, faster, and cheaper than yours? What if the customer is slow to adopt, or even recognize, the benefits of your new product or service? These are the challenges that high technology companies constantly face, and are the types of problems that the sensitivity analysis in the business growth plan seeks to address.

Sensitivity analysis is a tool for looking at a wide range of variables and assumptions in the business growth plan to determine the impact on the company and the viability of its growth plan if, and when, these planning assumptions change, which they invariably and inevitably will.

Sensitivity analysis might raise the following kinds of questions:

- Will our business growth plan still be viable if 20 percent of the target customers that we assume will adopt this new product do not? Thirty percent? Forty percent?
- What impact will it have on our business growth plan if two of the key *potential* competitors we have identified become actual competitors?
- What impact will it have on our business growth plan if we can't attract new employees or strategic partners that we have identified as critical to implementation?
- What if we can't raise the equity capital we need to implement the strategy? What if we have to give up more ownership and control than we had anticipated to raise the capital?
- If we planned to borrow money to implement the strategy, what impact would higher interest rates have on the economics of the strategy? If our customers will need to borrow to buy our products and services, what impact will higher rates have on these buying decisions?
- What if the market rejects the pricing structure that underlies the introduction of the new product or service? What if deeper discounts need to be offered to encourage customers to make the switch? What impact will this have on our margins?

The bottom line is that overly optimistic or weakly researched assumptions in your business growth plan can and will come back to haunt you. And even if you are conservative in your assumptions and conduct adequate research, there are still many variables that can and will change (see sidebar following) that will have an impact on your business growth plan and your company. Sensitivity analysis seeks to *anticipate* the changes in these variables so that you are not caught by surprise.

Variables Likely to Affect the Implementation of the Business Growth Plan

No matter how well you plan, things can and will change. Hundreds of variables will go into the development of your business growth plan. This means that thousands of things could go wrong (or right) that will affect your company's actual-to-plan performance. The actual growth results may vary depending on a wide variety of factors, including:

- Demand for your products and services
- Actions taken by your competitors, including new product introductions and enhancements
- Ability to scale your network and operations to support large numbers of customers, suppliers, and transactions
- Ability to develop, introduce, and market new products and enhancements to your existing products on a timely basis
- Changes in your pricing policies and business model or those of your competitors
- Integration of your recent acquisitions and any future acquisitions
- Ability to expand your sales and marketing operations, including hiring additional sales personnel
- Size and timing of sales of your products and services, including the recognition of a significant portion of your sales at the end of the quarter
- Success in maintaining and enhancing existing relationships, and developing new relationships with strategic partners, including systems integrators and other implementation partners
- Compensation policies that compensate sales personnel based on achieving annual quotas
- Ability to control costs
- Technological changes in your markets
- Deferrals of customer orders in anticipation of product enhancements or new products
- Customer budget cycles and changes in these budget cycles
- General economic factors, including a slowdown or recession

SOME FINAL THOUGHTS ON EFFECTIVE BUSINESS GROWTH PLANNING

Effective business growth planning is not an easy process and the chapters that follow will give your company some of the tools and strategies that you will need to remain viable and competitive. Having worked over the years with hundreds of companies of all sizes and in many different industries to develop business growth strategies, I have pulled together some tips, thoughts, and observations that should govern your planning process:

- **Have the right mix of talent to develop and maintain your plan.** The wrong planning team will yield the wrong planning decisions, leading the company down a path of disaster.
- **Think long-term but act short-term.** Be ready to modify the plan based on changes in market conditions, but without taking your eye off your long-term goals.
- **Effective business growth planning is a continuing *process*, not a stand-alone *task*.**
- **Don't buy into the mantra that planning is a thing of the past.** There are some who believe that market conditions are too dynamic and uncertain to make long-term growth-oriented strategic planning possible. This is SIMPLY NOT TRUE! In fact, fast-moving business conditions make the need for strategic planning that much more critical, provided that the plan does not sit on a shelf, but rather is monitored and modified as conditions may warrant.
- **Invest in systems that will gather competitive intelligence.** Information rules. If you don't have good data on the trends affecting your competitors and customers, you are dead in the water. The data gathered becomes a key component of your business growth plan and will trigger changes to the plan or strategy selected.
- **Protect your key assets.** You can develop business growth plans until you are blue in the face, but if the success of your strategy depends on your ability to keep and leverage your key intangible assets, then you must take the time to protect your intellectual property (see Chapter 11) and to reward and motivate your employees (Chapter 5).

- **Be sure to connect the dots.** A well-drafted business growth plan understands and anticipates how all the market forces and players fit together, taking into account social, environmental, political, and economic influences, and figuring out how these factors come together to affect your growth plans. The ability to view things at 30,000 feet and see the dynamics of your markets at this level is the key to effective growth planning. And because market conditions are never static and the relationships that connect the dots constantly change, you need to keep climbing the mountain to look down on the valley.
- **Build an organization that has a deeply rooted commitment to growth.** The commitment must begin with the leader or founder of the company whose mission and passion becomes contagious so that everyone in the company focuses their efforts on meeting business growth objectives. To achieve this, the company's leadership must clearly communicate and reinforce the growth plans, objectives, and strategies, reward those who contribute to the achievement of these goals and monitor the company's progress, changing its course and direction as necessary.
- **Don't be afraid to measure and monitor performance.** It is critical to develop an objective set of metrics for each key area of the business growth plan that can be continuously monitored and periodically measured against your key goals. The metrics may include sales, profitability, the number of new customer relationships added, the growth market partners, the number of new employees, customer satisfaction, the level of employee turnover, inventory cycles, the number of new offices opened, warranty returns or even the number of new rounds of capital raised at favorable valuation rates. Regardless of the specific metric(s) selected, the growing company must build systems to track and measure these performance indicators, and have the expertise in place to understand, analyze, and properly react to this data once it has been reported.
- **Develop high quality products and services.** As veteran entrepreneurs and professional advisors will always tell you, a business growth plan will be completely ineffective if the "dogs will not eat the dog food." At the end of the day, all business growth plans must revolve around a set of high quality products and services that customers want and need.

3

EFFECTIVE MANAGEMENT OF BUSINESS MARRIAGES

Human capital issues and their impact on the company's ability to Grow Fast *and* Grow Right must be addressed at their roots: the health and trust of the relationships among the co-founders. The clarity of the company's founders, owners, and leaders' shared version, and the openness of their communication channels, often dictates the essence of the company's culture and its ability to meet growth objectives. It's natural for entrepreneurs to look for other people to join them when they start and build companies. They may want to pair up with other people for reasons such as:

- Friendship and having a "sounding board" for discussing ideas and strategies
- Pairing technical expertise with capital or other resources in which one co-founder may be deficient
- Sharing and mitigation of risk
- Bonding among family members or friends to start new ventures together

But as John D. Rockefeller once said, "A friendship founded on business is better than a business founded on friendship." Co-founders owe it to each other as well as to their employees, customers, investors, and even their spouses to develop a genuine understanding of what brought them together in the first place, what strengths each brings to the venture, what goals and expectations hold them together, and what will happen to the business if a lack of trust or communication develops, or if there are disagreements over the future direction of the company.

It may very well be that friendship, love, or bloodlines serve as the initial impetus that brings people together to start a business, but it is foolish to assume that emotions or genetics alone will hold a business partnership together. Just like a good marriage, business co-founders must learn to communicate, compromise, and evolve together as key challenges arise. They must be able to agree on all of the key strategic issues, even if they disagree on items which may not be as critical to the long-term success of the business. They must develop a framework in which an accord is reached on key issues, such as:

- Control, governance, and decision-making
- Hiring and firing of personnel
- Capitalization of the company, and the need for additional capital contributions
- Business planning and strategic direction
- The degree and level of commitment to the company in relation to balancing other parts of their lives

Many industrial psychologists and business mediators strongly suggest that co-founders develop a Relationship Charter as a starting point for clarifying these objectives and expectations. The Relationship Charter is a broad statement of key principles that is a precursor to the more detailed Shareholders Agreement explained below. The purpose of the Relationship Charter is to assure that the co-founders can agree on a basic constitution of core values and rules. If they can't, it may be a red flag that they should reconsider starting a business together. Later in the development of the company, such an inability to agree on core values will most definitely be an impediment to growth. The development of the Relationship Charter should be from the heart, with an open and honest dialogue regarding concerns that one co-founder may have about another's commitment, loyalty, trustworthiness, personality, ability to fund the company, track record or experience, or liability for future problems. Each co-founder should do a little homework on the other's prior business experiences and relationships, by talking to former or current co-workers or business partners, friends, family, spouses, or significant others. Even asking each to provide a personal financial statement or recent tax returns is not unreasonable.

The Relationship Charter may include topics such as:

- Common goals (short, medium, and long term)
- Resources to be contributed to the business
- Loyalty and commitment to the business
- Expectations
- Values
- Principles of equity and fairness
- Communication and governance
- Procedures for resolving disagreements and rules for admitting additional partners or co-founders

Once the Relationship Charter has been prepared and adopted by all co-founders, the task of preparing a Shareholders Agreement will be considerably easier.

RELATIONSHIP ISSUES FOR CO-FOUNDERS

When multiple founders or owners start a company, it's not uncommon to have written agreements or understandings in place which *restrict* the ability of any given co-founder to pass his or her shares (and thereby ownership and control rights) on to a spouse or children. There is usually a mechanism for redeeming these shares, providing the surviving spouse or estate with either a lump-sum payment or installment payments in exchange for the shares. How and where the proceeds from this redemption will be directed are governed by the decedent's will or trust, making the matter an issue of estate planning rather than succession planning. If you are a founder of a business, make sure that you have discussed the following issues with your co-founders:

- Do we have a plan or agreement in place that determines (or controls) the ownership of the shares upon death? How will things be different in case of disability or retirement?
- How will these issues be dealt with in case of dispute that leads to a co-founder's departure from the company, such as a breach of a noncompete clause, embezzlement, or failure to perform key responsibilities?
- What formula or periodic valuation technique will we use to determine the fair value of these shares upon redemption?
- How and when will the proceeds be paid?
- If all of the co-founders are roughly the same age, and the agreement provides for mandatory redemption upon death, then who will eventually assume control of the business? If it is the last surviving co-founder (and then his or her estate), have you unintentionally created a "survival of the fittest" policy?
- If your agreement (or lack of an agreement) provides that the shares of each co-founder *can* be passed on to their spouse or heirs, can you get along with them on a long-term basis? Do you want to separate ownership from control?

UNDERSTANDING THE BUY-SELL AGREEMENT

The buy-sell agreement is a legal document that specifies how a company or its owners will redistribute ownership shares after one of the owners dies, becomes disabled, retires, or otherwise leaves the company. The basis for the agreement is a covenant by each owner (or the company) to redeem the stake of any owner who departs, eliminating many of the complications of having a surviving spouse (or even the entire family) at the ownership table. The primary goal is to avoid conflict and confusion by keeping ownership and control in the hands of those individuals who will be responsible for managing the operations of the business. The right of the remaining owners (or the company) to purchase the departing owner's shares must be provided for in some manner. This is typically accomplished through the purchase of a series of "key person" life insurance policies or some other reliable method, such as investment accounts specially designated for these purposes to ensure that cash will be available when the "triggering event" occurs. A triggering event may be death, disability, voluntary or involuntary termination (with or without cause), retirement, reaching a certain age, divorce, an acquisition or initial public offering, or some other change in personal, business, or family circumstances.

The buy-sell agreement will also dictate, among other things, when an owner can transfer his or her shares, and under what circumstances shares must be offered first to other shareholders/owners (or to the company)—known as "rights of first refusal." The agreement includes the procedures for doing so, payment terms or payment mechanism (lump-sum versus deferred or installment) to the departing owner, and procedures for resolving any disputes over valuation or nonpayment. In a family-owned business, the restrictions on ownership and transfer of the shares can be very strict, and in some cases may provide that *only* the lineal family members can be shareholders, either by initial issuance or upon transfer. The impact of a divorce and/or provisions in a prenuptial agreement should be considered when preparing these ownership restriction provisions.

To assure that the departing owner or survivors and heirs receive full value upon redemption, the agreement should spell out how the departing owner's shares will be valued, or directs that one or more outside appraisals be obtained when a triggering event occurs. Whatever method proves best for your type of business, your buy-sell agreement should provide for periodic mandatory valuations. But remember that, although valuation of your business is a vital component of an effective succession plan, valuation is not an exact science, especially for small, closely held businesses.

When your business was first organized, you and the other co-founders decided how the business would be structured—partnership, corporation, and so on. You may have agreed upon basic procedures for decision-making and governance, although these procedures may well have changed after a few years as conditions altered. There may also have been a discussion on how and when the business would be dissolved, or what would happen if a co-owner died or left the company. If you and your co-founders have not properly documented these discussions, then you may be headed for frustration, disappointment, and strained relationships unless you correct the situation as soon as possible. If you don't have a written agreement in place, or your agreement is incomplete, use the guidelines set forth below as a starting point, and consult with your corporate attorney to have a comprehensive agreement drafted. Even if you do have a comprehensive agreement, this is a good time to review its provisions. You may find the document needs updating due to a change in circumstances, the growth of the business, or due to developments in your industry.

In general, there are three basic types of buy-sell agreements:

- **Cross purchase agreements** are ideal for partnerships and corporations with small ownership groups (up to three people). The remaining owners directly purchase the departing partner's ownership interest in the business, rather than doing it through the company.
- **Stock redemption agreements** are simpler and easier to structure than Cross Purchase agreements. This makes them best suited for corporations with four or more shareholders. The corporation redeems (directly purchases) the shares of the departing owner, and the remaining owners see an increase in the value of their shares, not the number of their shares, as in a cross purchase.
- **Hybrids** are combination arrangements that usually give the corporation priority for redemption, but the shareholders have the option of directly redeeming a deceased owner's shares if the corporation is unwilling or unable to do so.

MANAGING DISPUTES AND PROBLEMS AMONG CO-FOUNDERS

Regardless of how the co-founders came together, like any business marriage, there will inevitably be bumps along the road. They may result from internal difficulties, such as a lack of communication, jealousy or differing objectives, or from external reasons, such as the influence of a spouse or key employee, competitive conditions, or changes in the technology or marketplace. Perhaps one of the most challenging hurdles that a growing company faces is a dispute among its co-founders. Virtually every company, as it achieves various stages of growth, will confront inevitable disagreements and problems among its co-founders. The balance of this

Advantages of a Buy-Sell Agreement

A buy-sell agreement has numerous advantages for the business itself, the owners, and the surviving family of a deceased owner.

Advantages for the business:

1. **Future continuity.** A buy-sell agreement helps assure the future continuation of the business. This security produces confidence and peace of mind not only for the firm's owners, but also the firm's employees, customers, suppliers, and creditors.

2. **No unintentional ownership.** A buy-sell agreement eliminates the problem of unintentional owners. Survivors usually are unqualified to help run the business. They can even interfere in its operation.

3. **Smooth redistribution of ownership.** Because each owner joins in making the agreement, the plan can provide a built-in guarantee that each owner and his or her estate will be treated equitably, regardless of who dies or leaves the business, or when.

Advantages for the surviving family members:

1. **Liquidation of the ownership interest.** A buy-sell agreement can provide the surviving family members with what they need most—a "ready market" for selling the estate's ownership interest. The survivors need the ownership shares converted into liquid funds to provide an income, to pay estate taxes and costs, or to meet other needs. A buy-sell agreement is by far the most efficient way to convert ownership into cash.

2. **Establishment of a fair price.** Through an "arm's-length" negotiation process of making a buy-sell agreement, the owners determine in advance the value or price of the shares to be purchased or redeemed from their estates. This is the best way to arrive at a fair price for each owner because no one knows who will leave or die first, and each owner can think of himself or herself as either the buyer or the seller. Negotiating a price after the fact takes away that balance and makes adversaries of the surviving owners and the decedent's estate.

chapter will attempt to look at the various reasons why co-founders have problems, and also look at some common and creative solutions to those problems. Some of these scenarios involve a third party or outside circumstance that none of the co-founders can control, yet they clearly have a direct impact on the ability of each co-founder to continue growing the business. As we shall see, basic agreements must be put in place in order to protect the co-founders from the outside world and each other. However, contracts are not enough; the agreements must be supplemented with sound management and business practices, sensitivity to psychological and ego issues, and a clear strategic development plan.

Common Problems

In my experiences working with a wide variety of small and growing companies, I have encountered some common problems and situations that can arise as a result of disagreements and conflicts among co-founders. Here are the top ten.

1. **The "high school best friend/college roommate" partner.** Many growing businesses in their early stages are founded by old college roommates or best friends who grew up and went to high school together. The mix of a personal friendship, together with a conflict in either business or personal relationships, can make the resolution of disputes especially complex. Unable to separate the personal issues from the business issues, the partners can easily run into tricky situations.
2. **The "obsolete" partner.** Often as a business grows, one or more of the co-founders are unable to keep pace with the level of sophistication or business acumen that the company now requires. He or she is no longer making a significant contribution to the business and, in essence, has become "obsolete." It's even harder when the obsolete partner is a close friend or family member.
3. **The "ego-clashing" partner.** Entrepreneurs, as leaders with strong values and integrity, also tend to have extra-large egos. These egos will typically clash from time to time. Sometimes, the clash is short-lived and easy to overcome, and other times a continuing clash of the egos creates a problem that cannot easily be resolved.

4. **The "we all have differing goals and objectives" partner.** One common situation is that the co-founders are all slowly moving in different strategic directions with different visions and plans for the course that the company should take and the markets it should enter. At this point, communication is strained and difficult as each partner has his or her own ideas of where the company should be heading. I've even seen some lose the "fire in their belly" once the company reaches a particular stage of growth, and when key goals and objectives have been met.

5. **The "silent money" partner.** Few people that I have met have ever gotten wealthy by being stupid or being silent, but entrepreneurs still want to believe there's such a thing as a "silent partner." My experience has been that most silent partners are rarely silent, and will go out of their way to interfere with the operations and management abilities of the operating partner(s).

6. **The "I want to retire early" partner.** People tend to reach personal comfort levels when they are ready to retire or just plain "burn out" at differing stages of a company's growth. Many growing companies, especially those owned by younger entrepreneurs, are founded at a time when all of the co-founders are either not married, or are in the early stages of their marriage. As the company grows so do the co-founders' families, and those with young children may feel the pressure to spend more time at home, but their absence will significantly cut their ability to continuously make a valuable contribution to the company's growth. Also, the new family may bring new income needs that the company may not be able to meet.

7. **The "hand caught in the cookie jar" or the "caught in the back room with a subordinate" partner.** When a co-founder is caught doing an illegal or unacceptable act on the company's premises it can be very, very difficult to handle the situation diplomatically. The issues—embezzlement, sexual harassment, employment discrimination, and other unacceptable or illegal acts—are sensitive, and the liability to the company is significant.

8. **The "I have an immediate need to cash out" partner.** Life often gets in the way of healthy co-founder relationships, especially when it comes to money. One co-founder's demand could result from

ordinary circumstances, such as the need to buy a home, or it could be related to less acceptable circumstances like needing to repay a gambling debt. This situation puts a strain on the relations among the co-founders. More importantly, it puts a strain on the company's ability to provide the cash to repurchase that co-founder's shares of the company. The company may not have readily available funds, and because nothing has happened by way of disability or death, there are rarely any insurance policies that can be drawn upon to fund this repurchase.

9. **The "we are getting acquired and the buyer only wants me" or "the investor wants you out" partner.** In a rapidly growing business, the exit strategy is often either the sale of the company to a third party or the registration of the company's stock in a public offering. I have often seen that the buyer of the company only wants one or two of the co-founders. Many times, the investment bankers who are handling an initial public offering ("IPO") would prefer that one or more of the co-founders step down from the company as a condition to the IPO being successful. I have even seen this scenario in venture capital settings where two or three co-founders were asked to either leave or modify their positions as a condition for the venture capitalist to close the transaction. Naturally, this situation creates divided loyalties among the co-founders. The post-closing status of each of the co-founders may put a damper on and confuse an already complex transaction, when it is necessary to either raise capital or to consummate the sale of the company.

10. **The "I think I am a co-founder" non-co-founder.** Often key employees (with or without stock options) are made to feel as if they are a co-founder (e.g., open-book management styles, phantom stock plans, stock appreciation rights, etc.) and then get downright "uppity" about it. When key employees are "made to feel like owners" you may suddenly find yourself needing to justify that new home, car, or adjustment in salary base to non-shareholders. Also, if a company with two co-founders grants stock to a key employee, the co-founders have just given away the key swing vote— probably not what they intended.

Common Complaints of Business Partners

- A partner feeling he is not getting his "fair share"
- Dissatisfaction with how one's role has "evolved"
- Lack of trust in a business partner's competence or intentions
- Personal and financial expectations not being met
- Feeling excluded from decision-making
- Being left out of important communications

Reasons Conflicts Happen, and Measures to Avoid Them

Conflicts arise between co-founders for many reasons, but there are steps to take to avoid them. We often don't take the time to really get to know the personality quirks of our co-founders until the business is well established. Instead, many of us rush into business relationships with the same excitement, gumption, and willingness to overlook character flaws as we do other kinds of personal relationships. Many business relationships start out as friendships, and, like a marriage, negotiating a business "prenuptial" agreement is an unpleasant thought. No one likes to look into the crystal ball and see bad things, and it can be very difficult to predict what problems may come up in the future.

Many entrepreneurs in the early stages of their venture don't have the capital to hire lawyers to draft the types of shareholders' and/or partnership agreements that are necessary to protect against certain kinds of problems, and to provide predetermined solutions to these problems when, and if, they occur. At the point when the company can afford to hire lawyers to draft these agreements, or to purchase insurance policies, it is already too late; the company is already too far along in its development. These time bombs must be diffused before the company blows up.

In rapidly growing, closely held companies, decisions may not be properly documented, researched, or communicated, and key strategic decisions are often made on an ad hoc basis. There can also be significant disparities between how decisions are supposed to be made and how they are actually made, as it is difficult to predict each co-founder's communication and decision-making styles. These problems can be avoided with documents such as shareholders' agreements as well as partnership agreements that set out a series of key decisions that may not be made on an ad hoc basis, and can provide the rules under which these decisions will be made.

Owners of small companies often find it hard to separate their roles as directors, officers, shareholders, and key employees because during the initial growth of a business the co-founders wear many hats. Entrepreneurs often do not delegate well, both among themselves and to key employees. This can lead to problems among co-founders, and stifle the company's ability to truly "departmentalize." In this situation, it is important to know when a meeting or decision has risen to the level of a board of directors meeting (which requires detailed minutes), or whether the meeting is more of a strategic meeting at the officer or manager level. In many growing companies, management systems are often not properly documented (either contractually or procedurally), and issues of control, authority, and approvals are handled on an ad hoc basis with little guidance among co-founders or in the management of key employees. In particular, small companies often fail to provide for procedures in case of a "deadlock" when there is an even number of founders/directors. The founder/director must identify at an early stage how a deadlock will be broken.

The old adage "failure to plan is planning to fail" is often true in the context of disputes among co-founders. The lack of a clear and concise strategic development plan (not the boilerplate type that gets used to raise capital) often leads to confusion and problems among co-founders. Entrepreneurs often tend to approach problem solving on a reactive instead of proactive basis. By not understanding certain preventive law techniques, such as the legal audits discussed later in Chapter 6, entrepreneurs fail to take heed of another old adage that "an ounce of prevention is worth a pound of cure."

The best measure to resolve these problems is *prevention*. The co-founder's willingness to openly communicate, prepare for the worst, and detect problems before they mature is at the heart of the solution. Valuations and formal agreements are the key measures to preventing co-founder disputes.

Periodic valuations of the company, although expensive, are critical and can provide the co-founders with a clear-cut and objective valuation

FIGURE 3.1   *The Path Leading to Destruction of Co-founder Relationships*

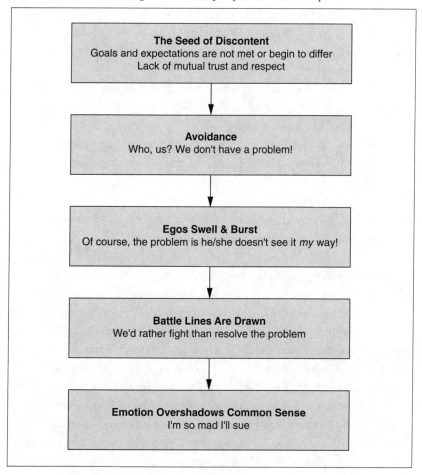

of the company. The timing of the valuations, usually annual, depends on the company's growth patterns and the industry trends. Occasional financial and legal audits will help lend insight into the company's value, and identify legal and financial problems before they mature.

It is critical to prepare a shareholders' and/or partnership agreement early in the development stages of the business in order to address decision-making procedures, restrictions on the transfer of stock, buy-out provisions, and when a shareholder stops participating in the business. *These documents should be updated periodically to reflect changes in law or circumstances. "Dust off" your old shareholders' and/or partnership agreement and ask:*

Does this still work for us? The co-founders can take mental comfort in knowing that these agreements are in place well in advance of a dispute. Here are some of the decisions that might require unanimous approval according to a shareholders' agreement:

1. Changes to the company's Articles of Incorporation and/or Bylaws
2. Increases or decreases in the company's number of authorized shares of any class of stock
3. The pledge of the company's assets (real or personal), or the grant of a security interest or lien that affects these assets
4. Creating, amending, or funding of a pension, profit-sharing, or retirement plan
5. Signing of any contract or agreement deemed to be major
6. Major changes in the nature of the company

Two other important preventative agreements are key-man insurance policies and employment agreements. Key-man insurance policies provide a source of capital for the buyout of a co-founder's shares in the event of departure, death, or disability. Employment agreements that are separate from the shareholders' and/or partnership agreements can be drafted for the co-founders. These agreements will provide for conditions of termination, which are especially critical in some of the more sensitive problems discussed above, such as alcohol and drug abuse, sexual harassment, or employment discrimination. These agreements should also clearly set forth each co-founder's duties and decision-making authority.

If these agreements are in place in the early stages of a company's growth, then co-founders can avoid having a third-party investor, venture capitalist, or investment banker setting forth these policies. Taking a dose of *preventive* medicine can go a long way in saving you legal fees, anxiety, and feeling as if you've wasted a productive effort. It also helps keep the relationship alive.

Managing the Inevitable Breakup

When the co-founders recognize that the working relationship is truly over and that all reasonable alternatives have been considered, the following are different scenarios for administering a smooth breakup.

Scenario #1: Once it has been decided that there are no solutions to the problems and that there is discord among the co-founders, the clearest and most obvious choice is for one or more of the co-founders to repurchase their equity in the company (perhaps on a lump-sum basis or over a period of time). The payment may be in cash, assets, contractual rights, intangibles, or a combination thereof. For sample buyout and arbitration provisions, see Figures 5.1 and 5.2 in Chapter 17.

Scenario #2: Several companies have resolved disputes among co-founders by splitting the business by function, essentially spinning off different operating divisions of the company based on each founder's interest. When proprietary technology is involved, there can be cross-licensing arrangements among the various companies (or joint-venture agreements between the now separate companies) that allow each co-founder to pursue his or her own interest and strategic objectives without losing some of the efficiencies and economies of scale created when the company was all under one roof. You should be as creative as possible. There may be ways to divide and subdivide the company by function, product line, market, territory, target customers, etc. that you may be unaware of. Ask yourself, How many different businesses are we *really* in?

Scenario #3: Selling certain key assets (or even the company) to a third party may include a co-founder transferring his or her interest to a separate company, providing a formal separation and an opportunity to pursue differing goals and objectives.

Scenario #4: Setting up a field office may create certain operational and overhead inefficiencies, but in the event that one or more of the co-founders feel the need to relocate, a field office might be an effective way for the business relationship to continue.

Scenario #5: If there is a suspicion of fraud or embezzlement, consider a court-ordered accounting of the books and records of the company.

Scenario #6: Seeking to dissolve the company through a judicial decree may also be an alternative. The court would have to be convinced that the company should be dissolved because of a major event affecting the company such as the insanity of a co-founder, or because the company may *involuntarily* go out of business, or because the company is operating at a financial loss.

Scenario #7: Consider arbitration, mediation, mini-trials, and other alternate dispute resolution techniques that may be less expensive, less time-consuming, and often less emotional than full-blown litigation. See Chapter 13 for a detailed discussion. One may also try a less legalistic situation by appointing an advisory board to resolve disputes.

Scenario #8: If the co-founders cannot reach an amicable solution (as described in the above scenarios), then formal litigation is inevitable. The co-founders should be prepared for a lengthy and expensive battle during which cost-benefit analysis at various stages of the litigation should be conducted. However, it is possible to ask the court to appoint a receiver or independent trustee to manage the affairs of the company during the time that the disputes are still pending.

Thoughts and Advice to Consider Prior to the Breakup

In more than 20 years of advising rapidly growing companies, I've found the following tips to be useful when facing a dispute with a co-founder:

- **Be creative in seeking and structuring solutions.** It's shortsighted to merely repurchase the shares when other types of strategic or creative types of solutions would be a better choice.
- **Be civil.** What goes around comes around. It is a small world.
- **Be reasonable and realistic regarding price and structure.** Whether you are the departing co-founder or the co-founder that will remain, it is important to structure the departure creatively, by asking such questions as how and when the payments are going to be made, and whether they are going to be made in cash, or with other assets or key licensing agreements. Some former co-founders have sued when they felt that information may have been wrongfully withheld from them concerning their buyouts, or the valuation used by their co-founders. These lawsuits are very difficult and complex, and can go on for some time at a significant cost

to both the co-founders (past and present), and the company. Consider an earn-out clause or some other participation right or post-sale adjustment to help avoid a future dispute.

- **Be sensitive to those around you when there are problems among the co-founders.** It is important to recognize that the media, key vendors, key customers, creditors, and even employees all must be treated with sensitivity when co-founders are having a problem. Do not lose sight of the impact of these disputes on company morale and leadership in the company. The rumor mill can be cruel, and lead to the eventual demise of the company if certain kinds of problems are not treated properly.

- **Never litigate over matters of principle.** Be sure that the potential rewards and remedies outweigh the many expenses and opportunity costs.

- **Be patient and disciplined in your breakup negotiations with your soon-to-be-former co-founder.** Be sure to deal with difficult issues such as notice to creditors, the extent of assumption by continuing co-founders of the liabilities of the company, the valuation of the withdrawing co-founder's equity in the company, indemnification, and protection from post-break-up obligations and liabilities. Do not let emotion or impatience interfere with your otherwise strong negotiating skills.

- **Keep your wits about you.** Remember that these problems and their solutions are as much psychological as they are legal, and as much strategic as they are contractual.

- **Do not hesitate.** If you see a problem such as those discussed earlier in this chapter, don't avoid the need for confrontations or an unpleasant set of negotiations. The longer you wait, the worse it typically becomes. Few problems go away or cure themselves by being ignored.

LEADERSHIP AND GOVERNANCE IN A POST–SARBANES-OXLEY WORLD

Effective leadership and governance are one of the key building blocks in the Grow Fast Grow Right Human Capital pillar for growth. The vision, success, and future path of the company's growth will be defined by the integrity of its leaders and the articulation and enforcement of its governance policies. Employees, as well as customers and shareholders, have the ability to "vote with their feet" if they do not agree with the vision, goals, and values of a growing company's leadership team. The leaders of today's growing companies must be able to communicate a clear and consistent vision to the employees and thus "walk the talk" when it comes to making decisions and formulating policies consistent with that vision. It is also critical that the leader is able to see the big picture *and* the minute details. Like a good pilot, the emerging-growth company leader must be competent, credible, and respected, and must have the ability to fly the plane safely at 30,000 feet and to land the plane smoothly when necessary.

Today's leaders must have the ability to recruit, retain, and develop talent within the company, understanding that loyalty and commitment are more conditional than ever before. The expectations of employees will continue to rise as the company grows, and the leaders of the company must keep pace, or employees will lose their willingness to follow.

Employees at virtually all levels want to feel that they are having some input into the future direction of the company—which also creates trust and buy-in as the company heads down the path selected.

Effective leaders of growing companies share the following characteristics:

- Ability to make decisions quickly (sometimes without the benefit of all the key facts)
- Ability to overcome confusion and skepticism
- A sense of urgency to accomplish measurable goals
- Ability to delegate effectively and communicate at all levels in the organization
- Passionate (but not wearing rose-colored glasses)
- Ability to clearly and effectively communicate goals and vision
- Ability to inspire and motivate employees, shareholders, customers, and market partners
- High tolerance for risk, along with an ability to admit mistakes and share praise and reward performance
- Keeping their ears close to the ground

GOVERNANCE STRATEGIES IN A POST–SARBANES-OXLEY WORLD

Since the collapse of Enron, the public's trust in our corporate leaders and financial markets—as employees, shareholders, or bondholders— has been virtually destroyed. In the late 1990s, corporate leaders such as Dennis Kozlowski of Tyco (who was convicted of tax evasion in connection with artwork purchases), John Rigas and family at Adelphia (who embezzled and misused corporate assets), and others, seem to have lost sight of their *responsibility* to those constituents that the laws dictate that they serve. In response, Congress acted relatively swiftly (and some say hastily) in passing the Sarbanes-Oxley Act, signed into law by the president on July 30, 2002. The SEC, NYSE, DOJ, Nasdaq, state attorney generals, and others also responded quickly to create more accountability by and among corporate executives, board members, and their advisors to shareholders and employees. Central themes include more objectivity in the composition of board members, more independence and autonomy for auditors, more control over financial reporting, stiffer penalties for those who abuse the laws and regulations pertaining to corporate governance, accounting practices, and financial reporting, and new rules to ensure fair and prompt access to the information and current events that affect the company's current status and future performance.

In this new environment, governance is the new leadership challenge for companies of all sizes and in all industries. Decisions need to be made *as if* they will be the lead story on the evening news. The corporate decision-making process must reflect a culture that puts the best interests of the shareholders first, and the protection of employees a close second.

At the heart of the solution to the irresponsible governance of the 1990s is a return to the fundamentals of what it means to serve as an executive or as a board member of a publicly traded or emerging-growth privately held company. Corporate governance laws, both in general, at the state level, and in connection with Sarbanes-Oxley, address duties of care, fairness (to avoid self-dealing and conflicts of interests), due diligence, loyalty, and the business judgment rule. The laws help ensure that *all* those who serve on boards, advisory councils, or committees do so primarily for the purpose of serving others—to help, to guide, to mentor, to be a fiduciary, and to look out for the best interests of the company's shareholders—not to perpetuate greed or fraud.

Yes, we have entered a new age of scrutiny—an era of *validation* and *verification*. The roles of the board and its committees are being redefined, re-examined, and retooled. A new set of best practices, procedures, and protocols are being written, and the costs of implementation are very costly. Internal controls and systems need to be designed to ensure compliance with these new rules of the game, and managers must be held accountable for enforcement and results. The CEO's new job description reads "Forget the gravy, where's the beef," and includes less pay, fewer perks, and less power in exchange for more performance and less tolerance for error or abuse. CEOs must live in a new era that will feature more accountability and shorter tenure.

In this new era of transparency, building shareholder value must be done the old-fashioned way—not via exaggerated revenues, the mischaracterization of expenses, the use of special-purpose entities to disguise debt obligations, or the use of creative accounting to inflate earnings. The recapturing of shareholder trust will be a costly and time-consuming process—both institutional and individual investors have to get past their disgust for the greed and negligence shown by some of our corporate leaders. A recent study by the Pew Forum demonstrated that Americans now think more highly of Washington politicians than they do of business leaders.

The Impact on Privately Held Companies

Why do privately held and emerging businesses need to be aware of the requirements of Sarbanes-Oxley? There are at least 12 reasons. The requirements of this legislation are likely to have a "trickle down" or indirect effect on nonpublic companies as follows:

1. There is a new emphasis on *accountability* and *responsibility* in corporate America that affects board members and executives of companies of all sizes as shareholders look for better and more informed leadership.
2. Some of the corporate governance provisions of Sarbanes-Oxley are likely to evolve into "best practices" in business management over the next decade, and other provisions merely reinforce the requirements of state corporate law that have been in place for many years that govern all corporations and limited liability entities in that state. Since corporate law is generally made at the state level, entrepreneurs and executives of privately held companies should keep a close watch on developments in their state of incorporation.
3. It is highly likely that *insurance companies* that issue D&O insurance and related policies will require Sarbanes-Oxley compliance as a condition of issuing new policies, or as a condition of obtaining favorable rates for both public and privately held companies.
4. Employees at all types of companies are generally placing a new focus on ethics and honest leadership as a condition of staying on board or maintaining their loyalty to the company. They are also looking for greater flexibility and fairness in their compensation and stock option plans.

5. Venture capitalist and other private equity key players have a tendency to mimic developments in the public equity markets when structuring deals, and may begin inserting Sarbanes-Oxley–type provisions into their term sheets and covenants regarding executive compensation, governance, auditor autonomy, and reporting and certification of financial statements. These may also become a condition of closing.

6. Privately held companies who may be positioning themselves for an eventual sale to a public company will want to have their governance practices, accounting reports, and financial systems as close to the requirements of Sarbanes-Oxley as possible in order to avoid any problems in these areas that may potentially serve as impediments to closing. (Be ready for a whole new level of due-diligence questions in M&A that focus on governance practices and dig deeper into financial, compensation, and accounting issues.)

7. Board member recruitment at all levels is likely to be more difficult even for privately held companies given that the perceived risk of serving as a director is higher and the general cost-benefit analysis seems to point away from accepting an offer. Once accepted, expect board members to be more focused, more vocal, more inquisitive, and more likely to ask the hard questions and to want detailed and substantiated answers.

8. Commercial lending practices for borrowers of all types are likely to change slightly in response to Sarbanes-Oxley. Be ready for the implementation of additional conditions to closing and loan covenants that focus on strong governance practices, board composition issues, certified financial reporting, and so on.

9. We are now in an era when it is critical to build systems and procedures for better *communications* by and between:
   - The board and its appointed executives
   - The board and the shareholders
   - The executives and the employees
   - The company and its stakeholders

   This is the case for companies of all types and sizes, whether or not your shares are publicly traded. There is a renewed emphasis on independence, autonomy, ethical leadership, open-book management (see *A Stake in the Outcome* by Jack Stack), accountability, responsibility, clarity of mission, and full disclosure that these systems and procedures need to create for all of corporate America.

10. The requirements of Sarbanes-Oxley must be *adopted* by publicly traded companies and *understood* by privately held companies, but they are also beginning to make their way into the management and governance practices at nonprofits, trade associations, business groups, academic institutions, cooperatives, and even government agencies where any form of poor management, corruption, embezzlement, or questionable accounting practices cannot be, and will not be, tolerated.

11. Sarbanes-Oxley was passed in part to help restore confidence in the public capital markets. Until these laws have their intended effect and the public markets begin to rebound, entrepreneurs and executives at privately held companies are likely to continue to run into strong barriers to capital formation. The shrinkage in public company valuations and the virtual shutdown of any exit strategies means that less venture capital and private equity capital will be provided, especially to a new project (e.g., versus follow-on investments to existing portfolio companies). When it *does* get provided, the entrepreneur needs to be ready for tougher terms and lower valuations.

12. Finalizing deals will be tougher in a post-Sarbanes-Oxley environment. Many of the highly acquisitive companies (e.g., Tyco, Sun, and Cisco) have had their accounting practices called into question, and some of the biggest mergers (e.g., AOL/Time Warner) do not appear to be working very well. The appetite for doing M&A deals seems to have faded, except for the value players, distressed company buyers, and bottom-fishers. The fraud behind Enron's many phony partnerships has made some larger companies hesitant to partner with smaller ones in a joint-venture or strategic alliance structure.

CORPORATE GOVERNANCE BEST PRACTICES AUDIT

A natural place to begin the review and analysis of current corporate governance practices is a legal audit that focuses on compliance with current laws, as well as the adoption of new procedures to ensure that systems and internal processes are in compliance with the new laws and regulations. The legal audit should include recommendations for improvement, as well as provide a series of compliance training program for officers, directors, and managers with significant or reporting responsibilities.

The topics and questions to be examined and discussed during the Corporate Governance Best Practices Audit are the following:

- The size and composition of the board, and the relationship of its composition to the performance of the company. There is a definite trend toward smaller boards with higher ratios of outside directors. It is now critical to have a written statement of corporate governance policy in place.
- The independence and objectivity of the audit committee that must meet the new Sarbanes-Oxley requirements.
- The knowledge, skills, and discipline of the Compensation Committee (*Note:* Many predict that the members of these committees will soon be forced to meet the more stringent independence requirements that audit committees already face.)
- The overall structure of executive and management compensation and stock option plans. Pay for performance, fairness issues, linking reward with the meeting of strategic objectives, the reduction of excessive perquisites, the board's ability/willingness to stand up to the CEO, and so on, are all current issues that will require examination.
- Internal control processes to ensure that the board is fully and promptly informed and adequately performing its oversight role, and that they are addressing "red flags" in a timely and proper manner. This is as good a time as ever to re-examine the efficiency and effectiveness of the internal controls at your growing company. An overhaul of these systems that takes advantage of current best practices and available technology may result in reduced costs, better decisional "checks and balances," and an improvement in the quality and integrity of the financial reports produced by the company.

- The level of scrutiny and efficiency of the way in which the board monitors the integrity and accuracy of the company's financial statements and reports (without micromanaging the process).
- The compensation system for the board members and the extent to which board compensation influences their objectivity. For example, are directors required (or not) to own a specific amount of company stock?
- The transparency of communications with shareholders and the financial markets. Are the requirements of Regulation FD (Fair Disclosure) being met?
- The effectiveness of the board's strategic and business planning skills. Have clear goals been set for the executive management team? How well is the team implementing these goals?
- The risk management procedures that are in place. The audit should include a comprehensive review of the officer and director liability insurance policies as well as other types of risk management, such as information/data security, physical security, and so on.
- The succession plans that are in place at both the board and executive management levels.
- The level to which the skills of the various board members match up with the company's current medium- and long-term strategy. Have changes to the company's business model caused shifts in its focus, triggering a need for new directors with different sets of skills? What procedures are in place for replacing directors?
- Any proactive steps the board is taking to maximize shareholder value, such as the leveraging of existing intellectual assets.
- Whether the board has a nominating committee. Are its policies and criteria clearly articulated? If yes, how closely are these policies followed? What due diligence is done on prospective candidates (and vice versa)?
- Whether there is a performance review process for board members. Why or why not? If yes, how effective have these reviews been in improving individual member or overall board performance?
- Whether board meetings are held both with and without the CEO present to encourage candor and objectivity. Who selects and appoints committee chairs and committee members? The board? The CEO? Do the by-laws allow for a nonexecutive chairman? If

yes, have the differences in the responsibilities between the Chairman and CEO been clearly articulated? Is there good chemistry between the Chairman and CEO? Why or why not? Are periodic meetings of only the independent directors held?

- The frequency of board meetings. Who sets the agenda? How effective are meetings? Are there minimal attendance standards? How often do the committees meet and how well do they function? Are they adequately reporting to the entire board? Are lines of authority between the committees and the entire board clearly established?
- The board's contingency plan in the event that the company becomes financially distressed. Does the board understand that its fiduciary responsibilities may extend to other types of stakeholders, such as creditors and vendors, as plans and strategies are developed?
- Whether the board has a formal orientation program for new members. If so, when was it last updated?
- Whether board composition reflects gender, ethnic, and racial diversity. How many international members are on the board? What is the average age of board members?

A corporate governance process must be put in place for both privately held and publicly held companies that restores the integrity of the company's leadership in the eyes of the shareholders and employees. The process must also create truly informed board members who have the power to act, based on timely and accurate information. It must protect the authority and foster the courage of the board to take whatever actions necessary to fulfill its fiduciary obligations. In re-examining the roles, functions, and responsibilities of board members, it is no longer sufficient to merely make a periodic meaningful contribution to the strategic direction of the company; rather, directors must now be proactive defenders of the best interests of the shareholders and to the employees, participants, and beneficiaries of pension, 401(k), and stock option plans. Board members and corporate leaders should assume that their meetings will be in "rooms with glass walls" and that their actions will be examined under a microscope.

5

RECRUITING, MOTIVATING, AND REWARDING YOUR TEAM

Ask any CEO of any sized company in any industry what his or her company's greatest asset is—the answer will almost always be "our people." Ask that same CEO what his or her greatest problem or challenge is—the answer will almost always be "our people." Why?

Why are recruiting, motivating, and rewarding the growing company's most critical asset so difficult and sometimes seemingly impossible to manage? Why is the process of motivating workers, keeping them focused on a shared vision, and instilling a culture of innovation and performance such a daunting task? How long has this been a challenge in our society?

As to the timelessness of the difficulty of effectively managing human capital, consider the following quote: "People can be stubborn and troublesome. Your job as a leader is to help them overcome their shortcomings."

Would you be surprised to learn that these were allegedly God's words when he handed Moses the Ten Commandments? Clearly, then, managing human capital has been a challenge for some time. Peter Drucker wrote extensively about the idea that it is the manager's job to provide the resources and the training that people need to build on their strengths. Jack Welch summarized his success at GE as follows: "My main job was developing talent. I was a gardener providing water and other nourishment to our top 750 people. Of course, I had to pull some weeds, too."

So, is the process of managing people as simple as first recognizing that we are human, and that all of us have our share of talents and flaws, and that a good leader's job is to nourish the talent and manage those flaws? Is building a performance-driven culture as simple as applying some of the basic lessons that we all learned as children, such as "treat people the way you want to be treated," "share toys in the sandbox," and "you get what you give"? Certainly it is more complex than that. Or is it?

In a recent *Fortune* magazine article that focused on how the most admired companies find the best talent, the Top Ten companies listed included firms as diverse as Procter & Gamble, BP, General Electric, UPS, Google, Nordstrom, Starbucks, PepsiCo, and Anheuser-Busch. So what did an oil company, a clothing retailer, a coffee-shop empire, and a beer brewer all have in common?

1. **Communication.** These companies communicate early and often, both up and down the ranks. Top management is accessible, and employees are engaged in the company's vision, understand its goals, and work toward achieving them.
2. **Excellence and versatility.** These companies expect excellence from employees at every level, and empower them with the tools, resources, and training that they need to achieve excellence. People are challenged regularly and are given the opportunity to move into different positions to avoid complacency and turfmanship.
3. **Opportunity for advancement.** These companies provide career tracks and opportunities *at all levels* for promotions and advancement. At UPS, more than 90 percent of the senior management started on the loading dock, often on the night shift, and came up through the ranks. Everyone has an opportunity to learn and to grow. Recruiting for top spots is always done from within wherever possible.
4. **Loyalty.** In classic "you get what you give" fashion, all these companies have a low turnover rate. Procter & Gamble's annual turnover rate is below 2 percent per annum. And when people do leave, they are treated like alumni, not as traitors or enemies. Since genuine and regular attempts to stay in touch with alumni are made

across the board, new relationships are forged. For example, at Procter & Gamble, three of its former managers, who have done fairly well since leaving, now sit on its board: Boeing CEO James McNerney; eBay CEO Meg Whitman; and Intuit Founder and Chairman Scott Cook.

If you are reading this chapter as the CEO or leader of a smaller company that is skeptical of whether you'll be able to mimic these best practices, or afford to be able to build a culture that will be competitive in the fight to recruit and keep great people, don't be. Let's turn to a June 2006 survey by *Fortune Small Business* magazine of the best small companies to work for and find out what *they* are doing to motivate and reward their human capital. Once again, clear and constant communication, a culture of honesty and trust, pride in their work, fun in the workplace, profit-sharing plans and camaraderie were characteristics shared by the award winners, which included small businesses as diverse as software development, government contracting, specialty retailing, financial services, and construction.

Each June, the Society for Human Resource Management (SHRM) releases a similar survey, its annual "Best Small and Medium Companies to Work For in America." Companies made the list not because they provide employees with fat paychecks and expensive country club and luxury car perquisites, but rather because they foster a culture in which performance is recognized, safety and training are top priorities, benefits are provided at low cost, and vacation time is encouraged and mandatory. And these benefits were provided cost-effectively and without adversely affecting the company's performance. All the top companies made annual retreats, quarterly town hall meetings, and weekly roundtables part of their communications best practices.

Your management's approach to developing employee-benefit and motivation programs can speak volumes by sending subtle messages about how your company views your employees. For example, an early-stage technology company recently replaced its free beer and pool tables program with free smoking-cessation programs, personal diet and fitness trainers, and complementary car seats for families with newborn babies. The change not only sent a message regarding its concern for the welfare of its team, but also reflected that the company was in tune with the evolving needs of its workforce, which had shifted from those of young, single, party-loving Gen Xers to those of married people with young families. At USAA, a rapidly growing insurance and financial services company based in San Antonio, Texas, employee health programs are a way to convey a positive message to employees. The company's female employees are offered free breast cancer screening tests via mobile mammogram machines, and male employees are encouraged to take advantage of free prostate cancer exams at the company's onsite infirmary. Other programs the company offers include five different child care assistance options, including an after-school educational program to cover children's after-school hours while their parents are still at work. As you strive to create programs for your employees, carefully consider their needs, as well as what your company's budget will permit.

FIRST STEP: RECRUITMENT

Growing companies must customize their recruitment programs to find employees who will be patient in their compensation expectations, or who will value noncompensation-based factors in evaluating different positions—factors such as leadership or management practices, corporate culture, flexible hours, training opportunities, or special rewards and incentives. However, if you choose to offer noncompensation-based incentives to attract employees, proceed carefully and avoid offering an excessive number of perks. Many dot.com companies in the late 1990s hired very young workers and devoted significant overhead to chill-out rooms, pool tables, vending machines, parties, and retreats. This sometimes created an environment in which little actual work got done, and some young workers were misled into thinking that they could play Ping-Pong all day and still become millionaires through their stock options. Many of these companies went out of business and their employees were left looking for jobs.

Focus your incentives on sharing the company's medium-term growth objectives and career-advancement opportunities, its leadership style, training opportunities, and respect for work/personal life balance. Be sure to clearly articulate the value proposition to prospective employees. Why is this *really* a better place to work? What does the medium- to long-term career path look like at your company? Emphasize any unique or general programs that are, or may soon be, in place that address quality-of-life issues, such as on-site childcare, health club memberships, casual-dress policies, or a willingness to support telecommuting. The candidates should understand and, at least in part, share the visions of the founder and the CEO of your company. This also means that the company's vision must be communicated early on to all candidates.

As an emerging growth company, your recruiting practices need to be very systematic. Prepare and share job descriptions, and, when appropriate, modify them with the input of the new employee, so that everyone's expectations are clear and realistic from the outset. It is also critical that new employees understand that your entrepreneurial growth company is not like big companies, and that the elements of their job descriptions and measurements of performance may change as different growth objectives are set and subsequently achieved. Think long-term in developing the key characteristics that you'll be looking for in a candidate, and how you will validate (through testing, interviewing, and otherwise) these skills. At Procter & Gamble, one million job applications are screened each year using a filter consisting of nine critical success drivers. These drivers include a willingness to embrace change, a knack for collaboration, the ability to execute a plan, and the ability to lead others and inspire them into action. This selection process is rigorously maintained and these same drivers have become training and development initiatives on a post-hiring basis.

The Role of Your Recruiting Process

The recruiting team for your emerging growth company must be well versed in your company's objectives and strengths. For small companies, the recruiters will not be able to attract talented candidates with big salaries and signing bonuses, so they must be armed with a strong knowledge of your company's intangible strengths.

In reviewing and evaluating potential candidates, your recruiting team must have an excellent ability to identify workers who have strong communication skills, who are willing to be flexible and take responsibility, and who have a positive attitude and a high energy level. In some cases, these intangible assets may need to compensate for a lack of direct experience or academic credentials.

Tailor the interview to ensure that the candidate has qualities that would enhance his or her ability to be comfortable and productive in a culture of rapid evolution and change. Candidates who are naturally curious, enjoy problem solving, and are creative and flexible will most quickly assimilate to the culture of an emerging growth company.

Your recruiters shouldn't waste time asking questions about the information that is contained on the written résumé, but instead spend a great deal of time learning what really drives the candidate. A standard interview and sloppy reference check may be sufficient for hiring by a local dry cleaning shop or a Fortune 500 company (where a poor hire can be easily absorbed). But for an emerging growth business, every hire is critical, and a bad hire can be very costly.

Finally, the role of a good recruiter does not end when a candidate accepts a position with your company. It also involves follow-up and assurances until the employee actually starts working for your company, and continues through the first few weeks on the job. These are critical to ensuring a smooth transition and integration into the company.

Beyond Conventional Recruitment Methods

Your recruiting team's approach to finding the right hires must be creative and aggressive. Merely relying on classified ads and employee-referral bonuses won't cut it. Even the use of headhunters and Web-based job sites won't meet your recruitment needs and hiring objectives. Many growth companies are turning to full-time, in-house recruitment teams that are totally focused on meeting the hiring needs of the company. Full-time recruiters can find the best and brightest talent by utilizing all possible hiring channels.

Some of the savviest recruiting techniques include studying a fellow traveler's luggage tags on airplanes to see if she or he works for a competitor, then striking up a conversation to see if the person would be interested in a position with your company. Similarly, a recruiter can strike up conversations at sporting events and parties when fellow attendees are wearing clothes or hats that bear the trademark of a competitor, to learn if they might make ideal candidates for your company. Successful recruiting is as much about marketing as it is about human resources management, and demands constant networking, schmoozing, and data gathering out-side of the confines of your company's human resource office.

Many companies are successfully using internship, mentoring, and apprenticeship programs as a fertile source for recruiting new workers. The more successful programs provide meaningful work assignments and some insights as to what life will really be like working at *this* company in *this* industry. In exchange, the on-the-job learning and future compensation opportunities are significant. These programs are especially critical in the technology, pharmaceutical, defense, and other technical industries, as recruiters are finding a shrinking pool of qualified graduates. It is important to provide some entertainment and fun activities during the summer, but internships that work best for both parties are those that feature lots of real-world experience and feedback. In a recent study by *Vault.com,* more than 80 percent of interns surveyed said that their internships were extremely important and insightful, and more than 60 percent had received job offers for full-time work from the companies where they had interned.

Alternatives to Permanent Hires

Up until this point, I have focused on the recruitment of traditional full-time employees. But what if even your well-planned recruitment program is not yielding results? Under what circumstances can, or should, your emerging growth company consider hiring free agents and temporary workers, outsourcing, or employee leasing as either short- or long-term solutions to your human-capital challenges? As your company and its staffing needs grow, you will have a number of options for filling those needs. Carefully consider the short- and long-term implications of each of the following options, and their impact on the continued growth of your company.

Free agents. Free agents are independent contractors who, rather than making a long-term commitment to an employer, prefer the flexibility of working on specific projects or working part-time for several employers simultaneously. Technology and networking solutions have spurred an increase in the use of free agents as a solution for emerging growth companies and the practice of using them instead of hiring permanent staff is growing steadily. Web sites and services such as *FreeAgentNation*

.com, bCentral.com, guru.com, and *PresenceWorks.com* were established to match the human resource needs of small and growing companies with free-agent talent. Although using free agents can be a very cost-effective and interesting solution to an emerging business's recruitment needs, it can also create ongoing concerns regarding such issues as loyalty, a genuine understanding of the company's objectives, protection of confidential information, quality control, and disputes over ownership of the work that has been created.

The outsourcing alternative. Outsourcing is the practice of using outside vendors to handle one or more of a business's operational, financial, or management functions. Like the hiring of free agents, outsourcing has become a popular solution for emerging growth companies, especially in the information technology (IT) areas, because of the pressure to keep up with emerging information technologies, and the severe shortage of skilled IT workers. For example, rather than hiring permanent IT personnel, an emerging growth company may turn to a vendor specializing in IT workers. This vendor acts as a middleman and provides IT workers for specific projects. Functions such as payroll and health-benefits management, accounting, insurance, training, and office administrative services may also be outsourced.

The use of an application service provider (ASP) is a common form of outsourcing that shifts the responsibility for installing, maintaining, and updating a company's software systems to a "host" that typically supports the same software for a number of different companies.

Although outsourcing can be a convenient and cost-effective staffing solution, it can also be very inefficient. A study by the MetaGroup in Stamford, Connecticut, estimates that in the year 2000 alone, more than $90 billion was wasted on poorly run outsourcing programs. Contributing to these excessive costs were vendors who sold either services that were inappropriate for the companies' needs, or products and service "suites" that their clients didn't want, need, or know how to use properly (rather like being forced to buy an option package you don't need when you buy a new car).

Your company's CFO and his or her team should carefully evaluate which functions should be handled externally. An internal specialist should carefully evaluate outsourcing proposals to ensure that the solutions proposed by the vendor are what your company really needs. Once you've selected a vendor, make sure that the outsourcing program is carefully managed and monitored to ensure that your company is truly getting value from the vendor. Finally, assign a point person to share new developments and relevant information with everyone within the company who may be affected by them.

Employee leasing. Employee leasing is provided by a professional employer organization (PEO) that, in essence, becomes the growing company's outsourced human resources department for some or all key functions. The PEO becomes a joint employer with the company, while contractually assuming substantial employer rights, responsibilities, and risks.

According to the National Association of Professional Employer Organization (NAPEO), when your company leases employees from a PEO, your company and the PEO contractually divide traditional responsibilities and liabilities. Typically, you retain full control over the operation of your business, and the PEO assumes responsibility for human resource issues, such as payment of wages, benefits issues, and the reporting and payment of employment taxes out of its own account.

STEP TWO: TIPS FOR KEEPING YOUR EMPLOYEES MOTIVATED

Each employee should understand how his or her role fits into the overall organization, and the role that his or her position plays in helping the company meet its goals. In my experience, people who *understand* their roles in relation to the company's overall goals tend to *enjoy* their positions much more. Recognition and reward programs should be balanced and built around both team and individual performance in order to reinforce the importance of teamwork, but at the same time not ignore the individual accomplishments of a particular superstar. Employees should be encouraged to be proactive, not merely reactive, when it comes to problem solving and finding ways to enhance the company's performance, and rewarded accordingly when their efforts and observations yield real results. The growing company should also ensure that employees feel secure in their positions with opportunities for advancement, but not to the point of complacency, when the employee begins taking his or her position for granted. People should be encouraged to smile and laugh often, and get along well with each other, but also understand that the primary purpose of the workplace is still actually to *get work done*. Here are some strategies and best practices for motivating your workforce.

Employees like to feel that they are working with others, not for others. They do not enjoy being micromanaged and welcome the flexibility, autonomy, and responsibility to make decisions for themselves and be accountable for the decisions that they make. Encourage your people to be proactive, not just reactive, when it comes to problem solving and finding ways to enhance the company's performance, and reward them when their efforts yield results.

Win the respect of your team. Most workers get caught up in the vision of the founder and the romantic heat of a company on a rapid ascent. But that passion can be fleeting, especially in a tight labor market, if the founders or leaders do not continue to share and communicate their vision and objectives, and reward only those who help the company meet those objectives. Leaders must avoid giving in to politics, red tape, favoritism, nepotism, and the "idea of the day" club, and must send clear and meaningful messages to workers so it is clear that they actually "walk the talk."

Don't use threats, guilt, or yelling to motivate your team. Fear will yield short-term results, but is not likely to be an effective long-term motivator.

Do not be afraid of a degree of employee turnover. Aiming for a zero-turnover rate may lead to complacency and mediocrity by keeping people in (or promoting them into) positions for which they are unqualified. Provided that your turnover rates stay below industry standards, a certain degree of turnover helps bring a new perspective and fresh ideas on how things are getting done, or how they ought to be done.

Take the time and effort to really ask what benefits the employees want. Offer options that reflect the diversity of your workforce and avoid a "one-size-fits-all" approach. Carefully monitor what benefits your competitors are offering to ensure that your programs keep pace. Remember to focus on more than just cash; often it is the intangible factors that make the real difference and yield the highest motivational results.

Technology is great, but don't forget the value of human interaction. Many emerging growth company leaders are so dependent on e-mail, voicemail, cell phones, and pagers that they don't spend enough face time with their team. To really listen to feedback, hear new ideas, and monitor performance goals, for example, you need to meet with your staff in person.

The way to hold on to quality people is not just to pay them well, but also to treat them well. A positive, challenging, high-energy workplace where everyone is treated with respect can be very hard to leave, even for the promise of more money.

Do what you say, and say what you do. Maintain open communication channels with your staff, and keep the promises you make to them.

Big bonuses and stock options are important, but they are not the only thing. A pat on the back, a big smile, a congratulatory company-wide e-mail, or small gift can go a long way in motivating and rewarding employees.

Be quick to celebrate and share achievements publicly, but give criticism privately. In a recent study, only 10 percent of the CEOs of growing companies felt as if they celebrated the company's overall success (or a particular division or team's success) often enough, yet a much higher percentage admitted to the mishandling of a disciplinary situation. Shouldn't those priorities be reversed?

Finally, don't fool yourself into thinking that you have what it takes to motivate people. People need to motivate themselves. Therefore, your role as an entrepreneur or leader of an emerging growth company is to create a culture that inspires and empowers people to motivate themselves, and properly rewards that self-motivation when results are achieved.

Motivation and Compensation Systems

A critical set of assets for a rapidly growing company is its human re-sources, which must be properly motivated and compensated if they are expected to stay around for the long term, and continue to stay focused on meeting the company's growth objectives. In an economy with very low unemployment rates and a severe shortage of well-trained technical and professional workers, it becomes hypercritical that the emerging-growth company take the appropriate, affordable steps to ensure that employees at all levels are motivated to come to work each day, be highly productive, and feel rewarded for their efforts with a competitive com-pensation package that includes a bundle of benefits and perks.

At one extreme, a motivation and compensation structure that re-volves around the co-founders and investors in the company getting very wealthy, and mid-level and lower-level workers getting a baseball cap at the company's annual picnic will not go a long way to instill long-term company loyalty, or provide a stimulus for performance. At the opposite extreme, I have seen some early-stage and emerging-growth companies go so far out of their way to make their employees feel comfortable and rewarded that it winds up putting them out of business.

The leadership of the emerging-growth company must strike a balance between these two extremes. They need to really talk to their employees to determine what benefits are feasible and affordable, and analyze the compensation and benefits being offered by their similarly situated com-petitors. As any experienced CEO or manager will tell you, motivating people is far from an exact science. There is no secret formula or bench-mark that can be developed and followed. Rather, it is an art form that can be as varied as the number of employees working at the company. There will always be the employee who is only motivated by money, an-other who is motivated by a flexible work schedule, another who places a high value on internal recognition, and still another who will only be truly motivated by the ability to earn an ownership position in the company.

Creating a Culture That Fosters Motivated Workers

Building a culture that fosters and yields motivated workers must also be custom-tailored not only to the needs of the employees, but also to the management styles of company leaders, which will vary from company to company. A charismatic leader may rely on company chants, songs, mission statements, and regularly scheduled motivational meetings that look more like a Tony Robbins seminar than an employee meeting as the basis for keeping employee motivation and loyalty at a high level. A financially focused leader may rely on periodic bonuses and other financial incentives to ensure that workers are happy. A "management by objectives" style leader may adopt techniques such as "open-book management," with rewards tied to the company's overall performance as a motivational technique. The motivational system and program ultimately selected should be consistent with, and reflective of, the company leadership's overall style and management practices, or it will be totally ineffective. A low-key executive's attempt to lead a company cheerleading meeting is likely to be a flop and serve as a strong demotivator.

There are certain steps that *all* leadership teams of emerging-growth companies can take to boost and maintain morale that will serve as motivators for *all* employees. These steps start with building a corporate culture

- that demands that personnel at all levels are treated with respect and dignity;
- that is relatively free from egotistical behavior, red tape, nepotism, and politics;
- that encourages open communication among employees at all levels;
- that is committed to teamwork, and that values working together toward organizational goals, not striving to achieve selfish personal objectives;
- where every employee feels valued;
- where employees feel secure in their positions and their opportunities for advancement, while never becoming complacent;
- where teamwork as well as individual performance are recognized and rewarded;
- where roles and performance targets are clearly articulated to each employee, especially if your company has adopted a goal-based compensation system;
- where each employee understands how his or her role fits into meeting the overall objectives of the organization; and
- where the employees trust the ability of the company's leadership to make the right decisions.

FIGURE 5.1   *Are You Reinforcing the Right Behaviors to Foster Growth?*

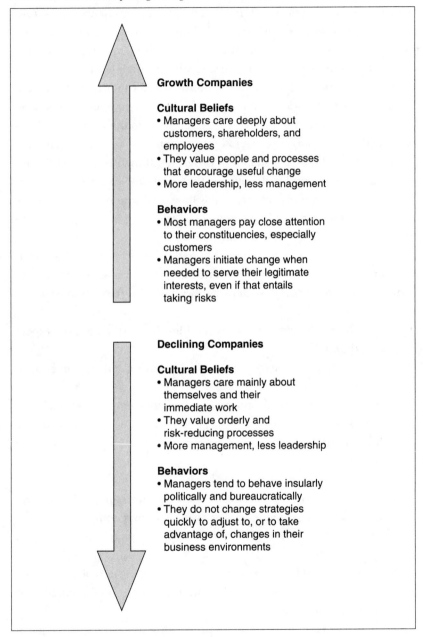

Growth Companies

Cultural Beliefs
• Managers care deeply about customers, shareholders, and employees
• They value people and processes that encourage useful change
• More leadership, less management

Behaviors
• Most managers pay close attention to their constituencies, especially customers
• Managers initiate change when needed to serve their legitimate interests, even if that entails taking risks

Declining Companies

Cultural Beliefs
• Managers care mainly about themselves and their immediate work
• They value orderly and risk-reducing processes
• More management, less leadership

Behaviors
• Managers tend to behave insularly politically and bureaucratically
• They do not change strategies quickly to adjust to, or to take advantage of, changes in their business environments

Source: Healthy Companies International

STEP THREE: DIVERSITY IN THE WORKFORCE

The emerging-growth company should strive to build a workplace that emphasizes, respects, and celebrates ethnic and racial diversity and that meets the needs of a multigenerational workplace, from Gen Xers, to baby boomers, to more senior workers. Diversity in the workplace can be a driver for business growth. In today's multicultural society, companies who do not embrace diversity at all levels, not just in hiring, are likely to be left behind.

Consider the following observation made by Anne Donnelon, associate professor of organizational behavior at Babson College, on the role and importance of diversity as a business growth driver:

> Research shows that innovation won't happen without a diverse work force. Then why do so many CEOs of entrepreneurial growth companies *clone themselves for every position?* Too many entrepreneurial companies are run by people cut from the same cloth, but these nondiverse teams are far less likely to meet growth objectives. *Homogeneity simply does not breed innovation.* [emphasis mine]

Terry Blum, Dean of the College of Management at Georgia Institute of Technology, had this to say:

> Diversity within a growing company will yield more, and better, ideas, and *supply a needed variety of perspectives to incorporate into an entrepreneurial company's vision.* Diversity can be a key counteracting force against organizational and creative inertia by providing cross-cultural norms and insights which support innovation, productivity, profitability and teamwork. [emphasis mine]

Diversity fits into the three Grow Fast Grow Right pillars of growth as follows:

Human Capital

- Improved productivity of workforce
- More effective governance and leadership

- Broader base of *relationships* with customers, vendors, and strategic partners that are reflective of today's multicultural marketplace
- Internal and external learning and training opportunities

Diversity as a component of Intellectual Capital:

Intellectual Capital

- Enhanced innovation and creativity
- Deeper understanding of market intelligence and trends/perspectives
- Facilitation and catalyst for global expansion
- Improvements to the quality of decision-making
- Diversity initiatives will lead to more effective channel partners, technology licensees, and alliance relationships

Diversity as a component of Financial Capital:

Financial Capital

- Private equity and VC firms are significantly increasing their focus on investment in minority-owned businesses and on diversity-driven market niches
- Commercial lenders are more aggressive in their pursuit of minority businesses as customers and borrowers
- Diversity in today's consumers is strongly and deeply impacting domestic and international financial markets (Selig Center at the University of Georgia projects that the combined buying power of African Americans, Asian Americans, and Native Americans will be more than 15 percent by 2008, and for Latin Americans, buying power will be at levels of 10 percent on a stand-alone basis by 2008)

Diversity is not about black or white, or grey. It must embrace all types of people, personalities, and cultural backgrounds: race, religion, age, gender, sexual preference, cultural background, physical and mental abilities, regional heritage, and personality type.

Physical characteristics and appearance (weight and height, for example), socioeconomic background and upbringing, and personality type or management style are all attributes that can be considered when striving

FIGURE 5.2 *Diversity Initiatives Must Penetrate Many Areas, Not Just Workforce*

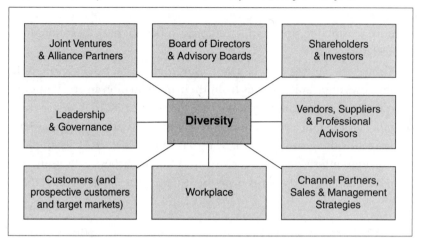

to achieve diversity. Diversity objectives must be linked to the company's strategic business plan, and woven into the fiber of the company's operations. It will fail as a strategic initiative if it is allowed or encouraged to be merely a stand-alone program or division within the human resources or procurement department.

STEP FOUR: DEVELOPING COMPENSATION AND BENEFIT PROGRAMS

The development of compensation and benefit programs over the past ten years has been a rapidly moving target. In the late 1990s, there was a severe shortage for qualified and experienced upper- and middle-level management talent and skilled technology workers. As a result, many companies felt that they had to offer well-into-six-figure salaries, aggressive stock option plans, country club memberships, chauffeur-driven limousines, executive dining rooms, and four-inch-thick plush carpeting in oversized corner offices. But in early 2000 and 2001, as the economy slowed and stock prices fell, the company's ability to offer or afford such a long list of executive perks became much more constrained, even though the need for qualified talent remained just as strong—putting even greater demands on the need to be creative and aggressive in structuring compensation and benefit programs. Today, the competition for qualified personnel and executive talent is fierce, but expectations are a bit more reasonable, and compensation and benefit packages should be tailored accordingly.

Today's executives and managers now realize that not everyone will become overnight millionaires from their participation in stock option programs, but at the same time, they are looking for more than just cash as a motivator to join a company and help it grow over the long term. The challenge for the growing company is to take the time to ask its employees (through interviews, periodic surveys, etc.) what they really want, develop the right mix of benefits from the list in Figure 5.3 below, and then

FIGURE 5.3 *Examples of Executive Perks and Employee Benefits an Emerging-Growth Company Might Offer*

- Life and disability insurance plans

- Drug and alcohol abuse counseling programs

- Comprehensive health care insurance plans

- On-site child care facilities, or child care assistance subsidies

- Dental/eye care/pharmaceutical reimbursement plans

- Casual dress policies

- Early eligibility for benefits

- Training costs and educational reimbursements (may be tied to grades)

- SERPs (supplemental/executive retirement plans)

- Seniority/tenure rollover from previous job

- Stock option plans

- Loans or partial payments on housing costs

- Laptops/cell phones/pagers provided at little to no cost

- Signing bonuses

- Pension and profit-sharing plans

- Reimbursement of moving or relocation expenses

- Waiver or dilution of noncompete clauses

- Car allowances

- Aggressive 401(k) and 403(b) retirement plans (including rollover features with employer contributions and matches)

- Stipends towards residential living costs

- Executive/employee dining rooms with free/ subsidized meals

- Transportation and commuting subsidies

- Executive mentoring of lower-level managers

- Employee innovation renewal programs

- Low/no interest consumer loan programs

- Reserved parking spots or parking subsidies

- Flexible work arrangements/job sharing programs

- Outplacement services

- Free transportation home when working late nights

- Flexible work hours

- Charitable contribution funds and directed giving programs

- Elder care assistance programs

- Golden parachutes (e.g., change-in-control agreements that provide for big severance packages if the company is involved in a merger or acquisition) including "gross-up" payments to cover tax liability

- Telecommuting options (allowing work from home)

- Prepaid legal services plans

- On-site facilities for doctor appointments

- Aggressive vacation policies (including a vacation stipend)

- Aggressive family and health leave policies

- College tuition subsidy program (for employers or their employees)

- Inexpensive take-home meals

- Financial planning, estate planning, and retirement planning seminars

- On-site health and fitness facilities (or arrangements for discounts with a nearby facility)

- Group home and automobile insurance programs

- Adoption assistance programs

- Executive and management training retreats

- On-site executive concierge, massage, custom tailors, dry cleaning, shoe shines, or spa/salon services

- Access to the corporate jet, vehicles, or apartments

- Tickets to local sporting events and theater

- Stress/time management and wellness seminars

- Half-day Fridays (summers only)

- First class air travel upgrades

- Employee appreciation days, picnics, and ice cream socials

- Be the CEO for a day/spend a day with the CEO program

find a cost-effective way of delivering these benefits and services. Some companies have focused on noncash benefits to reward certain behaviors or performance goals. For example, every six months, Continental Airlines gives away six Ford Explorers to six employees randomly selected from a pool of employees who have perfect attendance records for the previous six months. Many emerging-growth companies are recognizing that employees' lives are becoming busier and more complex, so they are offering ways to help the employees help themselves by offering key services at the workplace, such as travel services, concierge services, dry cleaning, and fitness and salon services, at a discounted or subsidized basis. Even if the services are offered at full cost, the employees still view the convenience as a benefit, and that typically results in greater workplace productivity as employees find it easier to balance work demands with life demands. A recent study by Mercer Management Consulting Services offers further proof that money is not everything. Mercer studied the reasons *why* information technology professionals stay at a given job. Among the top reasons were:

- The *opportunity to learn* and use new technology skills (training)
- Work environment (culture)
- Autonomy (management style)
- *Challenging work assignments* (innovation)
- *Career development opportunities* (growth)
- *High-quality supervision* and *leadership* (leadership); and, near the bottom of the list,
- Incentives provided under variable-pay arrangements (compensation)

STEP FIVE: DEVELOPING EFFECTIVE TEAMS

Once recruitment, motivation, and reward systems are in place, you must also make sure that the superstars you have hired and trained also function well *as a team.* Our "playing well with others and sharing toys with others in the sandbox" rule must be articulated and enforced if the company is going to meet its growth objectives. Recruiting all-stars and letting them take the floor without a unified agenda will not win championships. Allowing two superstars to clash regularly and maintain (or tol-

---

Successful Business Growth–Focused Teams Possess These Characteristics

---

1. Balance of complementary talents, styles *(dreamer, schemer, reamer)*, and ability to wear multiple hats (general utility infielders)
2. Truly shared vision and core values with a genuine sense of loyalty to the team
3. Communication channels that foster open dialogue, room for disagreement, and methods for resolving conflicts (without fear of repercussion, or a culture of revenge for speaking one's mind)
4. Accountability and willingness to share in the fruits of success, and taking responsibility for errors in judgment
5. Collaborative and empowered process for establishing (and modifying) goals and objectives
6. Egos parked at door
7. A track record of success (longer together is better) that builds "tacit" knowledge and confidence in each other (as long as it does not lead to complacency or a lack of long-term creativity)
8. Integrity, trust, fairness, and respect *by* and *among* team members
9. Strong, cooperative work ethic (imbalances in commitment lead to jealousy, infighting, and dysfunctional compensation systems)
10. Compensation and reward system which balances the need to reward the team for teamwork without defeating the need/benefit of recognizing individual accomplishment

(*Note:* The relationship between the "star" of the team and the other players will ultimately define the team's *overall* and *sustainable* success.)

---

erate) competing agendas on the same team like Kobe and Shaq during the Lakers era, or Michael Eisner and Michael Ovitz at Disney, will result in a diversion of focus and a dysfunctional culture. Undermining leads to underperformance.

Effective teams must be built on trust, respect, and a unified and mutually beneficial vision. The team must have a collective sense of purpose that is reinforced by the coach, the captain, and the players. Every team member must clearly understand his or her role as it relates to the team winning, and feel as though they have contributed in some meaningful way to the team's success. The challenge is that trust-building takes time and patience, and in today's fast-moving and transient marketplace, growth companies need to find ways to expedite the trust-building and mutual respect process.

Team building needs to follow the Dan Brooks model. The 1980 U.S. Olympic hockey team beat the Soviet Union in Lake Placid and made world history (and were the subject of the top-grossing Hollywood movie, *Miracle*) by focusing on personal chemistry and character. In building the team, Coach Brooks was criticized by the committee, and even his assistant coaches, for overlooking some of the big names in building his roster. His response to them was, "I'm not lookin' for the best players, I'm lookin' for the right players."

6

EFFECTIVE USE OF BOARDS AND PROFESSIONAL ADVISORS

Our discussion of Human Capital as the first pillar of the Grow Fast Grow Right foundation has focused to this point on recruiting and compensating the team as you meet growth targets. But whom does the senior management team turn to for advice and guidance? Who provides general policies and direction to the company's leaders and executives around which a specific growth plan is built and executed? For most growing companies, the answer is twofold: (1) a formal board of directors and (2) an informal advisory board (or a series of advisory boards for specific purposes).

These two boards are often confused, but actually play very different roles and have very different responsibilities. Publicly held companies are required to form a board of directors under virtually all applicable state corporate laws. The board owes very specific fiduciary duties to the shareholders of the corporation, as described below. The basic governance structure is that the shareholders elect the directors who, in turn, appoint the board's officers. It is the role of the directors to set broad goals and policy objectives for the company that will benefit and protect the interests of the shareholders. It is incumbent on the officers to develop and implement plans to meet these goals and objectives. A strong director has broad-based business experience, strong industry knowledge, a useful Rolodex, adequate time to devote to truly understanding the company's key challenges and weaknesses, and the objectivity to challenge decisions made by the management team. The director is a good listener and sounding board for the team, and is generally well-trained in the university of hard knocks. A good director does not get easily discouraged if the company gets off course, nor does he or she view the world through rose-colored glasses. The board members should take their responsibilities very seriously when it comes to critical tasks like board meeting preparation and attendance, guarding confidentiality, or avoiding what appears to be a personal agenda. Each board member, and the board as a whole, must be constantly guided by "What is in the best interest of our shareholders?"

On the other hand, an advisory board is not required by state corporate laws, does not owe the same levels of fiduciary duties to the shareholders (hence, it generally cannot be held as responsible for their acts or recommendations), and can be much more informal with regard to the number of meetings and agendas for meetings. The advisory board can be assembled for general purposes, or a series of advisory boards can be set up for very specific purposes, such as technical review, marketing strategy, recruitment and compensation, or research and development. An advisory board can also be an excellent way to get a second opinion on certain matters without interrupting existing relationships. For example, you may want access to a highly respected business lawyer, but be reluctant to terminate the relationship with your current law firm. Asking that lawyer to serve on your advisory board can be a good compromise. A growing company will often set up an advisory board in connection with the capital formation process in order to demonstrate to prospective investors in the business plan that the officers of the company have access to a credible and objective source of advice and contacts, without filling up precious board of director seats. Initially, these seats are usually set aside for co-founders and investors. Many prospective advisory board members may be reluctant to accept the responsibility that comes with a board of director seat, especially at the outset of the relationship. Of course, the "showcase value" of putting together a bunch of names that barely know you, and who will never show up for any meetings, dilutes the value of the credibility that you sought to establish when appointing the board of advisors. Prospective investors will put varying weights on the strength and composition of the board of advisors in making their final investment decisions, and will often want direct access to the advisory board members as part of their due diligence process, and to ascertain the depth of their commitment.

One critical difference between a board of directors and an advisory board is the management's ability to accept or ignore the recommendations of the advisory board, a worry they do not have when a mandate comes down from the board of directors. Also, because members of the advisory board do not owe the same duties to the company and its shareholders, they can be used to mediate disputes by, and among, the officers, or between the officers and the directors. The advisory board members can also help identify potential board of director candidates. It can also be a recruiting ground for the board of directors.

Since the rules governing the board of advisors are not set forth in a corporate law statute, it is critical to be very clear about your expectations of each advisory board member, and about how they will be compensated for their efforts. In the early stages of the company's development, the rewards to advisory board members should be structured in a fashion that encourages a long-term commitment, and encourages the members to be proactive, not merely reactive, contributors to the company's growth plans.

DUTIES AND RESPONSIBILITIES OF THE BOARD OF DIRECTORS

There are certain duties that the law imposes on a director that must be met during the candidate's service on the board. Each act or decision of the board must be performed in good faith, and for the benefit of the corporation. The legal obligations of the directors fall into three broad categories: a *duty of care*, a *duty of loyalty*, and a *duty of fairness*.

- **Duty of care.** The directors must carry out their duties in good faith with diligence, care, and skill in the best interests of the corporation. Each director must actively gather information to make an informed decision regarding company affairs and in formulating company strategies. In doing so, the board member is entitled to rely primarily on the data provided by officers and professional advisors, *provided that the board member has no knowledge of any irregularity or inaccuracy in the information.*

- **Duty of loyalty.** The duty of loyalty requires each director to exercise his or her powers in the interest of the corporation, and not in his or her own interest, or in the interest of another person (including a family member), or organization. The duty of loyalty has a number of specific applications, such as the duty to avoid any conflicts of interest in your dealings with the corporation, and the duty not to usurp personally what is more appropriately an opportunity or business transaction to be offered to the corporation. *For example,* if an officer or director of the company was in a meeting on the company's behalf, and a great opportunity to obtain the licensing or distribution rights for an exciting new technology was offered at the meeting, it would be a breach of this duty to try to obtain these rights individually, and not to offer them first to the corporation.

- **Duty of fairness.** The last duty a director has to the corporation is that of fairness. For example, duties of fairness questions may come up if a director of the company is also the owner of the building in which the corporate headquarters are leased, and that same director is seeking a significant rent increase for the new renewal term. It would certainly be a breach of this duty to allow the director to vote on this proposal. The central legal concern under such circumstances is usually that the director may be treating the corporation unfairly in the transaction, since the director's self-interest and gain could cloud his duty of loyalty to the company. When a transaction between an officer or director and the company is challenged, the individual will have the burden of demonstrating the propriety and fairness of the transaction. If any component of the transaction involves fraud, undue overreaching, or a waste of corporate assets, it is likely to be set aside by the courts. In order for the director's dealings with the corporation to be upheld, the "interested" director must demonstrate that the transaction was approved or ratified by a disinterested majority of the company's board of directors.

In order for each member of the board of directors to meet his or her duties of care, loyalty, and fairness to the corporation, the following general guidelines should be followed:

- The directors should be furnished with all appropriate background and financial information relating to proposed board actions well in advance of a board meeting. An agenda, proper notice, and a mutually convenient time, place, and date will ensure good attendance records and compliance with applicable statutes regarding the notice of the meetings.
- Remember that a valid meeting of the board of directors may not be held unless a quorum is present. The number of directors needed to constitute a quorum may be fixed by the articles or by-laws, but is generally a majority of board members.
- Work with your attorney to develop a set of written guidelines regarding the basic principles of corporate law for all officers and directors. Keep the board informed about recent cases or changes in the law.
- Work closely with your corporate attorney. If the board or an individual director is in doubt as to whether a proposed action is truly in the best interests of the corporation, consult your attorney immediately—*not* after the transaction is consummated.
- Keep careful minutes of all meetings and comprehensive records of the information upon which board decisions are based. Be prepared to show financial data, business valuations, market research, opinion letters, and related documentation if the action is later challenged as being "uninformed" by a disgruntled shareholder. Well-prepared minutes will also serve a variety of other purposes, such as written proof of the director's analysis and appraisal of a given situation, proof that parent and subsidiary operations are being conducted at arm's length and as two distinct entities, or proof that an officer did, or did not, have authority to engage in the specific transaction being questioned.
- Be selective in choosing candidates for the board of directors. Avoid the consideration or nomination of someone who may offer credibility, but is unlikely to attend any meetings, or have any real input to the management and direction of the company. It is often the case that the most high-profile business leaders are spread too thin with other boards and activities to add any meaningful value to your growth objectives. In my experience, such a passive relationship will only invite claims by shareholders of corporate mismanagement.

Avoid inviting a board candidate who is already serving on a number of boards in excess of five to seven, depending on their other commitments. Similarly, don't accept an invitation to sit on a board of directors of another company unless you're ready to accept the responsibilities that go with it.

- In threatened takeover situations, or in the event of friendly offers to purchase the company, be careful to make decisions that will be in the best interests of *all* shareholders, not just the board and the officers. Any steps taken to defend against a takeover by protecting the economic interests of the officers and directors (such as lucrative "golden parachute" contracts that ensure a costly exit) must be reasonable in relation to the threat.

- Any board member who independently supplies goods and services to the corporation should not participate in the board discussion, or vote on any resolution relating to his or her dealings with the corporation, in order to avoid self-dealing or conflict-of-interest claims. A "disinterested" board must approve proposed actions after the material facts of the transaction are disclosed, and the nature and extent of the board member's involvement is known.

- Questionnaires should be issued periodically to officers and directors regarding possible self-dealings or conflicts of interests with the corporation. Incoming board members and newly appointed officers should be provided with a more detailed initial questionnaire. These questionnaires should also always be circulated among the board prior to any securities issuances (such as a private placement or a public offering).

- Don't be afraid to get rid of an ineffective or troublesome board member. Don't let the board member's ego or reputation get in the way of a need to replace them with someone who is more committed or can be more effective. It may be best to avoid close friends on the board of directors who may be either difficult to terminate or become lazy in the execution of their duties because of the friendship. Maintain the quality of the board and measure it against the growth and maturity of the company. Emerging businesses tend to quickly outgrow the skills and experiences of their initial board of directors who then need to be replaced with candidates who have deeper and wider ranges of experiences. Try to recruit and maintain board members who bring "strategic" benefits to the company, but who are not "too close for comfort" in that their fiduciary duties prevent them from being effective because of the potential conflict of interests. Carefully consider recruiting candidates from your outside team of advisors, such as attorneys and auditors, who may not be able to render objective legal and accounting advice if they wear a second hat as a board of directors member. It may be easier for these professionals to sit on your advisory board, however, as this is less likely to cause conflicts.

- Board members who object to a proposed action or resolution should either vote in the negative and ask that such a vote be recorded in the minutes, or abstain from voting and promptly file a written dissent with the secretary of the corporation.

Following these rules can help ensure that your board of directors meets its legal and fiduciary objectives to the company's shareholders, and also provides strong and well-founded guidance to the company's executive team to help ensure that growth objectives are met.

GETTING SOLID GROWTH ADVICE—TIPS FOR HIRING EFFECTIVE OUTSIDE ADVISORS

One key critical success factor for growing companies is the need to build a team of attorneys, accountants, consultants, and other external professional advisors in a wide variety of business disciplines—such as marketing, sales, finance, administrative management, strategic planning, computer systems, manufacturing, production, advertising, operations, and personnel. When building this team of advisors, these relationships must be *managed* in order to ensure cost efficiency, and compatibility among team members, and that tasks and problems are assigned to an advisor with the appropriate background and expertise.

Identifying the Need for Professional Advisors

As a general rule, professional service providers and business consultants are hired to fill a particular need of the fast-track growth company, such as:

- Expert advice in a particular field of knowledge
- A readily available pool of human resources when you can't hire full-time employees
- Identification and solution of specific problems or barriers to growth
- Stimulation or implementation of new ideas, technology, or programs
- A sounding board (or even shoulder to cry on)
- Access to contacts and resources (the opening of the Rolodex)
- Insights on the successes and failures of other companies similarly situated

When the exact reason or specific project or problem has been identified, there are certain key questions that must be addressed during the selection process, such as:

- How does the background, education, and experience of the particular advisor relate to the task or problem at hand?
- How does the professional advisor charge for his or her services? What billing options, if any, are available? Does the firm offer any creative billing options, such as equity for services (see below), deferred fees, reduced rates, or project-specific discounts or contingencies? How do rates vary among various members of the firm? How much will it cost to accomplish this specific project to resolve the problem?
- Which staff members of the advisory firm will actually be assigned to this project? What is the expertise of these particular members of the firm? Will you be able to get access to other members of the firm with specialized expertise on an as-needed basis?
- What is the firm's anticipated timetable for completing the work? What progress reports will be provided? What input will the management team have to give to the service provider?
- What is the service provider's representative client base? What references can be provided? Does the firm have any actual or potential conflicts of interest? How does the company compare to the firm's existing client base?

In addition, there are certain key misperceptions and myths regarding the use of outside advisors which must be dispelled *prior* to the commencement of the relationship. The more common *myths* and *fears* include:

- The need for an outside consultant is a sign of the management team's inability, business weakness, or failure.
- The internal management team is *too busy* to have the time to work with external advisors.
- Consultants *never really understand* the special demands and problems of a company.
- Consultants are just too expensive, especially for what you get in return—a lot of advice about things already known.
- And the *classic:* If this consultant knew this industry so well, then why is he not running his own company?

You must, therefore, understand the exact reason *why* the advisor is being retained, ask the right questions before hiring the advisor, and enter into the relationship with the proper attitude.

Because of my nearly 20 years of experience as a corporate and transactional lawyer, I have devoted the balance of this chapter to the dynamics of the attorney-rapid growth company relationship; however, these insights and observations are equally applicable to relationships with accountants, business consultants, bankers, advertising agencies, and other key advisors.

Getting Advice from Unexpected Sources

Five years ago, Warren Coopersmith's family-owned distribution firm in Takoma Park, Maryland, was at one of those crucial "grow-or-die" junctures. Its biggest customers, movie theaters and video-rental outlets, were consolidating and looking for suppliers big enough to provide all popcorn, candy, soda pop, and cleaning supplies to their expanding empires.

Coopersmith decided that his company, Marjack, was going to be a survivor. He began to recruit experienced professionals to his management team. He made a few acquisitions, extended his business with existing customers such as Regal Cinema, and developed new lines, such as providing candy and snacks to Office Depot and Kinko's outlets. He even embarked on a bit of vertical integration when he bought his own popcorn company.

But as Marjack's revenue grew toward $150 million, five times what it had been, Coopersmith and his team realized that there were problems. Their profit margins weren't what they should have been, and their systems weren't up to handling the increase in volume. He needed help, but did not want to pay seven-figure consulting fees.

On a parallel track, General Electric's Commercial Finance unit had just financed Marjack's new warehouse in Landover. What Coopersmith didn't expect from the financing was that GE experts would be willing to use their rigorous Six Sigma statistical analyses of warehouse operations, and find ways to cut costs and improve quality at no cost to the company.

So why does a $25 billion division of a global corporate behemoth want to go through the time, hassle, and money of helping Marjack pick and pack Milk Duds and red licorice? The answer is pretty simple: For the $15 million that Six Sigma costs a year, GE Commercial Finance buys a ton of customer loyalty, and sets itself apart in what is otherwise a commodity-service business. Perhaps even more important, the program increases the odds that the mid-size firms to which GE is lending money will not only stay in business long enough to pay back the loans, but will be more likely to grow in the future—as will their need for capital. The lesson here for growing companies is that help may be available from unexpected sources and at very attractive pricing, but you don't know if you don't ask.

At Marjack, GE's experts meticulously analyzed the steps taken by the warehouse staff members as they moved their carts up and down the aisles, filling the weekly orders from movie theaters and retail outlets. As is often the case, there weren't any major fixes—just a whole bunch of little things, like collecting all the used carts in one place, clustering all the most-used items near the packing stations, and dispatching forklift drivers with walkie-talkies. The warehouse staff improved productivity by 35 percent, while cutting in half the number of customer complaints. As a result, Marjack now dispatches 500 boxes to customers each day with almost the same size staff that used to send out 350.

SELECTING A BUSINESS ATTORNEY

As your company grows, you are likely to undergo a wide variety of changes in structure, your products and services, markets, and capital requirements. Each change will raise a host of legal issues that must be considered prior to implementing your strategy to achieve your next level of growth. As a result, your outside legal counsel should serve as a key member of the external team, and as an active participant in the development of your company. When an experienced attorney is made an integral part of the management team, you will enjoy several benefits, including: (1) a genuine understanding of the legal hurdles and requirements raised by a particular proposed strategy or transaction *prior to* implementation or closing, (2) identification of the optimal legal structure and alternatives for achieving your objectives, and (3) cost savings that are the result of the attorney truly understanding your basic goals, internal politics, and trends affecting your industry. The costs of having legal counsel participate in the growth planning and decision-making process will be far outweighed by these benefits.

Entrepreneur-attorney relationships have changed significantly in the last ten years. No longer is the strength of a personal relationship enough to sustain a long-term working relationship, nor is the ability to draft an effective contract the measure of a good advocate. In recent years, entrepreneurs do not exhibit the loyalty they once did, and seem more willing than ever to leave a long-term relationship if true insight, efficient performance, and a wide array of value-added services are not brought to the table (and not just once in a while, but consistently). The pace of business has also become rapid fire, and the tolerance for mistakes, missed deadlines, exceeding budgets, or a lack of business acumen is gone. In this highly competitive legal services marketplace, the law firms that compete effectively for the business of entrepreneurs are ready to deliver services in a manner that is cost-effective, strategy-driven, technologically savvy, and focused on problem-solving and creative solutions.

These are the attorneys and firms that you should select to represent you and your business. No longer can business lawyers be selected on the basis of blood relationships, fraternity memberships, or golf skills. To the successful entrepreneur, today's attorney must be nimble, shrewd, and have a genuine understanding of the entrepreneur's goals and objectives. The attorney must do everything possible to help facilitate these goals and objectives every day. Today's business lawyer must understand how technology and the Internet impact the growth of smaller companies, have strong strategic-planning skills, and be willing to open his or her Rolodex of sources of capital and other helpful contacts within the community to the client.

The Selection Process

The process of selecting, retaining, and knowing how and when to use an attorney are among the more important business decisions that an entrepreneur must make, both initially and throughout the growth of the company. Yet, most entrepreneurs express frustration, dissatisfaction, and confusion when asked about the law firm selection and retention process. Many owners point to high fees, failure to meet deadlines, lack of business savvy, inaccessibility, inability to cut through red tape, and mountains of paperwork, inexperienced staff, and a general failure to understand the business ramifications of legal decisions as the sources of their ongoing problems with attorneys. As a result, attorneys are viewed as a necessary evil who don't understand the business considerations of proposed transactions. Therefore, the entrepreneur may take matters into his or her own hands, only to have the proposed agreement or strategy backfire—creating even larger legal problems than ever anticipated. An experienced attorney can, and should, be a key member of the management team of any company, but this does not mean that an attorney needs to be involved in every step of every transaction. The key to a prosperous and harmonious attorney-entrepreneur relationship is knowing how to select, and when to seek advice from, an attorney.

If your idea of an attorney with strong corporate legal skills and business acumen is the lawyer who was hired to keep your spouse away from key assets in a hotly contested marital dispute, then think again. The days when your divorce lawyer could also handle a complicated corporate transaction are long gone. Due to the increasing complexity of the law, and the ever-growing specialization of the legal profession, the division of family assets in a divorce or in estate planning, and the division of corporate assets in a merger, acquisition, or shareholders' agreement must be handled by two very different types of lawyers. Although it is more than likely that the attorney who prepared your will could also assist in the performance of routine corporate tasks during the formation of the company, many general practitioners are quickly outgrown as the business expands and legal needs become more complex. As a result, you must periodically assess whether your current attorney and/or law firm best meet their legal interests and requirements.

You are likely to have varying personal preferences with respect to the age, experience, and interests of the attorney you hire. Priority may be placed on experience and clout (which would tend to favor an older, more seasoned lawyer), or on aggressiveness and cost (which would tend to favor a younger lawyer). However, it is dangerous to place too great a priority either on experience or billing rates. For example, an older lawyer with time constraints is likely to assign the project to a younger, less experienced attorney, and a younger lawyer who offers lower billable rates may take twice as long to complete the assigned project. Similarly, age and reputation should be viewed with a grain of salt. An attorney who has only practiced for three years but who has devoted all of his or her attention to a given area of law will probably know more about that area of law than a general practitioner with 30 years of experience. Nonetheless, there are certain common denominators that a company should identify when selecting its legal counsel:

- **Responsiveness.** An attorney must be able to meet a client's timetable for accomplishing a particular transaction or implementing a particular strategy. An attorney with all the expertise in the world on a given legal topic is of no use to a company if the knowledge can't be communicated to the client in a clear and timely fashion. Make sure that deadlines are discussed and that the attorney has adequate resources set aside to meet those requirements in accordance with the schedule established.
- **Business acumen.** Many attorneys are criticized by their clients for being unable to comprehend the business ramifications of legal decisions. Although small companies need an independent and objective legal advisor, they also need an attorney with business acumen, management and marketing skills, and a genuine understanding of the industry in which the company operates. Attorneys with tunnel vision, who are unable to understand the impact of the law on the client's business goals and objectives, should not make legal decisions and strategies.

- **Reputation.** It goes without saying that a company will want to hire a law firm with a good reputation in the business community. However, reputation goes beyond a series of names on a door or letterhead. In considering the references of a prospective attorney, you should look closely at the *foundation* upon which the reputation has been built. Is the attorney's reputation primarily due to the accomplishments of named partners who have been dead for more than 20 years? Or, on the other hand, maybe the lawyer enjoys a fine reputation as a golfer and a philanthropist, but no one can really give you an opinion on the quality of his legal expertise. Be careful of attorneys who have built a reputation solely on the basis of heavy networking, but whose actual legal or strategic planning skills are uncertain.

- **Philosophy and approach.** You need to understand an attorney's or a firm's overall philosophy of practice and approach toward business. Are they more inclined to be "deal makers" or "deal breakers?" Will they act as trusted advisors, or a necessary evil? Do they understand the importance of value-added relationships; that is, bringing more to the table than just good documents or accurate advice? Are they an asset or a liability to your company's growth, and its ability to meet or exceed its business plan?

- **Representative client base.** Just because an attorney's list of clients reads like a "Who's Who" of the Fortune 500, it does not necessarily mean that the legal needs of a growing company will be understood. As has often been said, "A Small Business Is Not A Little Big Business." Many corporate lawyers assume that because they have handled a $5 billion acquisition, they can understand the legal needs of the parties to a $5 million transaction. Although some of the legal planning and documentation may be similar, the business goals and mindsets of the parties are likely to be very different. Growth companies should look for attorneys who represent businesses of a similar size and stage of development, and that are in an industry similar to their own. The attorney's client base should also be evaluated to determine whether there are any actual or potential conflicts of interest or complementary resources, or whether the attorney has experience in prior matters that are relevant to your company.

- **Billing rates and policies.** Managing legal costs is of especially great concern when your resources are limited. The good news is that increasing competition among lawyers for small business clients demonstrating growth potential has created a certain amount of flexibility in billing policies. At the same time, however, attorneys at firms of all sizes expect to be paid for quality services that have been rendered within a client's deadline. There is nothing more frustrating or offensive to any professional service provider than to work nights and weekends for a client who does not pay its bills. Therefore, it is important that any mystery or confusion concerning the billing rates and policies be clarified before any legal work is commenced. One effective means of controlling billing rates and policies (as well as defining related rights and obligations of the attorney and the client) is the use of a retainer agreement. A retainer agreement protects both parties because it resolves any mystery about the relationship before any work commences. The components of a well-drafted retainer agreement include:

1. Nature of the services to be provided
2. Compensation for services rendered
3. Use of initial retainers or contingent fees
4. Reimbursement of fees and expenses
5. Conditions for withdrawal of counsel or termination of the relationship
6. Counsel's duty to provide status reports
7. Time limitations or timetables for completion of work
8. Ceilings or budgets (if any) that have been set for legal fees
9. Any special provisions needed in the agreement as a result of the nature of the project (e.g., rules governing media relations, court appearances, protocol, etc.)

- **Knowledge and skills.** The specific tasks, assignments, or transactions for which assistance is needed will naturally influence the type of knowledge and skills that should be sought. If the task involves an adversarial dispute, then a skilled litigator will be more useful than a transactional attorney. Conversely, a litigator may be very inappropriate for a complex business deal for which the skills of a more diplomatic attorney would be more effective in negotiating and closing the transaction.
- **Creativity.** Identifying and analyzing various alternative methods of structuring a particular transaction or achieving a particular objec-

tive are among the most important tasks that an attorney performs for an emerging-growth company. The ability to develop creative legal solutions to a client's problems or disputes is one trait that should be sought when selecting legal counsel.

Controlling Legal Costs

As your company grows, an increasingly larger portion of the annual budget must be allocated for the cost of legal services. As a result, many owners have attempted to control this expense either by avoiding lawyers, *or* by avoiding the invoices sent by lawyers. Neither strategy is an effective way to manage a growing business. Completely ignoring lawyers is likely to result in problems that far outweigh the cost of retaining competent counsel. Similarly, ignoring the legal invoices will lead to tension in the relationship, resentment by counsel toward tasks assigned by the client, and, ultimately litigation. The most effective way to control the cost of legal services is to work with legal counsel in an efficient manner.

- **Be prepared before the call or meeting with the attorney.** Remember that time is money. Gather all the facts and review all documents before the telephone call or conference, and develop a specific agenda and list of questions.
- **Clearly define your goals and objectives.** Many entrepreneurs don't clearly tell (and lawyers don't ask) the goals and objectives of a given transaction or strategy. If counsel understands your key objectives and negotiating parameters, then your company is likely to get much better value for its legal dollars.
- **Do not rely on the attorney for basic tasks** that could be performed more quickly and cheaply by you or your staff. Basic forms, correspondence, renewal filings, etc. can probably be handled by a designated legal compliance officer within the company.
- **Do not let executed contracts collect dust.** Most contracts are living, breathing documents that must be consulted periodically. Your failure to understand or perform obligations under a contract will usually lead to expensive litigation.
- **Do not be afraid to request that your attorney set a ceiling on fees for a given project or transaction.** Attorneys experienced in a given

area of law should be able to predict the amount of time that it will take to accomplish a specific task, absent any special problems, facts, or circumstances.

- **Monitor administrative and incidental expenses.** Ask your lawyer about travel, photocopying, postage, and related expenses. If these extra fees or reimbursements are too steep for your budget, ask your lawyer to make alternative arrangements for these services.

- **Review all bills and invoices carefully.** Insist on an itemized account that adequately explains the nature of the services rendered, or out-of-pocket expenses incurred. Unfamiliar names or charges may be a sign that the legal firm's billing system is not functioning properly, or that the primary attorney for the matter has not been reviewing invoices carefully. Be certain that your company is only paying for services that were truly necessary, and were actually rendered.

- **Do not tolerate paying for the education of an inexperienced attorney.** Although virtually every legal matter will entail a certain amount of legal research, this does not mean that the company should have to foot the entire bill to train an attorney who is handling a matter of this nature for the first time. Therefore, check the bills carefully to monitor exactly which lawyers or paralegals are working on your behalf.

- **Take a proactive, not a reactive, role in the preparation and negotiation of legal documents.** Insist on participating in the process of identifying alternatives and developing solutions. Request that periodic progress reports be provided to managers who are responsible for the given project or transaction.

- **Establish controls within the company as to who may communicate with legal counsel and for what purposes.** As the company grows, it is likely that more employees will come into contact with legal counsel. If not properly controlled, this will result in mixed signals from the company to the attorney, unnecessary or duplicate tasks being assigned, or personal matters being handled at the company's expense.

The relationship between the entrepreneur and the attorney must be one of synergy, ongoing communication, mutual respect and understanding, and trust and confidence. A shared goal of planning, implementing, and monitoring actions will ensure that business objectives come to fruition in a cost-effective and trouble-free manner. The best interest of the company—its employees, shareholders, assets, products and services, and future—must be placed as the highest priority by legal counsel. Selecting the right lawyer and other key professionals to help your company grow is crucial to its long-term success.

The Practice of Preventive Law

Over the past few years, a concept known as "preventive law" has become very popular among rapid-growth companies and their legal counsel. Preventive law is a "two-way street" approach to the attorney-entrepreneur relationship that redefines its nature and purpose. Legal counsel *proactively* identifies potential problems and, conversely, companies' owners and managers (and when applicable, in-house legal counsel) to develop systems to work with their outside attorneys in order to recognize legal issues before they mature into more serious problems or conflicts.

Preventive law dictates that certain periodic steps are taken that enable legal counsel to properly assess the legal health of the rapidly growing company, and prescribe a set of strategies and solutions for any problems identified in the checkup. This legal checkup is often referred to as a "legal audit."

In a legal audit, the growing company's management team meets with outside legal counsel in order to: (1) discuss strategic plans and objectives, (2) review key documents and records, and (3) analyze and identify current and projected legal needs of the company. The legal audit also lays the groundwork for an ongoing legal compliance and prevention program in order to ensure that the growing company's goals, structure, and ongoing operations are consistent with the latest developments in business and corporate law. Finally, the legal audit helps managers identify the legal issues that are triggered by changes in strategies, goals, or objectives, and allows the planning for the legal tasks that must be accomplished as a result of the issues identified.

A comprehensive legal audit will examine a wide range of issues that may be as mundane as whether or not the company is qualified to do business in foreign jurisdictions, or as complex as an analysis of the company's executive compensation and retirement plans in order to ensure consistency with current tax and employment law regulations. The topics that must be addressed include:

- Choice and structure of the entity
- Recent acts of the board of directors and documentation (or lack thereof) relating to those decisions
- Protection of intellectual property
- Forms and methods of distribution and marketing
- Pending and threatened litigation
- Estate planning
- Insurance coverage
- Hiring and firing practices
- Employment agreements
- Securities law compliance
- Antitrust and related trade regulations
- Product liability and environmental law
- Review of sales and collection practices

Naturally, the extent and complexity of the legal audit will vary depending on the size and stage of growth of the company, the type of business (e.g., service vs. manufacturing), the number of shareholders and employees, the extent to which the company does business in a "regulated industry," and a host of other factors.

Mechanics of the Legal Audit

A legal audit may be performed on a periodic basis as part of an ongoing compliance program, or in connection with a specific event, such as a financial audit. It may also be performed in connection with a specific transaction, such as an acquisition or securities offering. There are also specialized legal audits in specific areas such as tax, labor and employment, estate planning/asset protection, government contracts, franchising compliance, and environmental law audits. The mechanics of the legal audit and a sample questionnaire are set forth below.

- **The preliminary questionnaire.** The first step in a legal audit is a comprehensive questionnaire that the growing company's management

team reviews and addresses prior to the arrival of the team of attorneys who are to conduct the legal audit. In the case of smaller
companies, a simple checklist of issues, or a formal agenda, will be
more than sufficient to prepare for the initial conference.

- **The on-site audit.** Once the documents and related materials requested in the questionnaire have been assembled, and problem
  areas preliminarily identified, a meeting should be scheduled between audit counsel and the designated officers of the company
  who are well-versed in the various aspects of its operations. Related
  members of the management team, such as the company's outside
  accountant, and other professionals who play key advisory roles to
  the company should be present during at least the portion of the
  audit that relates to their area of expertise. This initial conference,
  or series of conferences, is basically an information-gathering exercise designed to familiarize the legal auditor with the most current information about all aspects of the company. In addition to
  these conferences with key personnel, the audit team should perform some on-site observations of the day-to-day operations of the
  company. The legal audit team should also review the current financial statements of the company and spend some time with the
  company's accounting firm.

- **Implementation of the post-audit recommendations.** Once the legal audit team has issued its post-audit evaluation to the company's
  management team, you can implement the recommendations made
  in the report. What you choose to implement will vary, depending
  on the growth planned by the company, as well as the specific findings of the report. At a minimum, you should schedule meetings
  with key personnel to review and discuss the post-audit recommendations, prepare internal memos to inform the "rank-and-file" employees about the findings, conduct employee seminars to educate
  employees about proper procedures and compliance, and in certain
  cases, develop handbooks and operations manuals for continued
  and readily available guidance for the company's staff. If significant problems are discovered during the audit, counsel should be
  careful as to what is included in the final written report in order to
  avoid potential adverse consequences down the road under the
  federal or state rules of evidence. In addition, you can establish a

"tickler system" for periodic reporting and key dates/deadlines, as well as a time set for the next legal audit.

Topics covered in the legal audit questionnaire.

The following is a series of topics that should be covered in the legal audit questionnaire:

A. **Corporate matters.** Under what form of ownership is the company operated? When was this decision made? Does it still make sense? Why or why not? Have all annual filings and related actions, such as state corporate annual reports or required director and shareholder meetings, been satisfied? What are the company's capital requirements in the next 12 months? How will this money be raised? What alternatives are being considered? What issues do these strategies trigger? Have applicable federal and state securities laws been considered in connection with these proposed offerings? Will key employees be offered equity in the enterprise as an incentive for performance and loyalty? Is such equity available? Has the adoption of such plans been properly authorized? Will the plan be qualified or nonqualified? Up to what point? Has anyone met with the key employees to ascertain their goals and preferences? Have all necessary stock-option plans and employment agreements been prepared and approved by the shareholders and directors of the corporation? Will any of the founders of the company be retiring or moving on to other projects? How will this affect the current structure? If the company is a corporation, was an election under Subchapter S ever made? Why or why not? If the entity is a Subchapter S corporation, does it still qualify? Is such a choice unduly restrictive as the company grows (e.g., ability to attract foreign investment, taxation of undistributed earnings, etc.)? If the entity is not a Subchapter S corporation, could it still qualify? Is this a more sensible entity under the applicable tax laws? Or should a limited liability company (LLC) be considered as an alternative? Have by-laws been prepared and carefully followed in the operation and management of the corporation? Have annual meetings of shareholders and directors been properly held and conducted? Have the minutes of these meetings been properly and promptly entered into the corporate record book? Have transactions "outside the regular course of business" been approved or ratified by directors (or, where required, by shareholder agreements or by-laws) and resolutions been recorded and entered into the corporate records? Are there any "insider" transactions or other matters that might constitute a conflict of interest? What "checks and balances" are in place to ensure that these transactions are properly handled? Have quorum, notice, proxy, and voting requirements been met in each case under applicable state laws? To what extent does the company's organizational and management chart reflect reality? Are customers and suppliers properly informed of the limits of authority of the employees, officers, or other agents of the company?

B. **Business planning matters.** Has a business and management plan been prepared? Does it include information about the following key factors?

1. The company's key personnel
2. Strategic objectives
3. Realistic and well-documented financial statements
4. Current and planned products and services
5. Market data
6. Strategy and evaluation of competition
7. Capital structure and allocation of proceeds
8. Capital formation needs
9. Customer base
10. Distribution network
11. Sales and advertising strategies
12. Facility and labor needs
13. Risk factors
14. Realistic milestones and strategies for the achievement of these plans and objectives

How and when was the business plan prepared? Has it been reviewed and revised on a periodic basis? Has it been changed/supplemented to reflect any changes in the company's strategies, plans, or objectives? To whom has the plan been shown? For what purposes? Have steps been taken to preserve the confidential nature of the document? To what extent have federal and state securities laws been reviewed to prevent violations due to the misuse of the business plan as a disclosure document?

C. **Compliance with governmental and employment law regulations.** Have all required federal and state tax forms been filed (i.e., employer's quarterly and annual returns, federal and state unemployment tax contributions, etc.)? Are federal and state recordkeeping requirements being met for tax purposes? Have all payroll and unemployment tax accounts been established? Has the company been qualified to "do business" in each state where such filing is required? Have all required local business permits and licenses been obtained? Are the company's operational policies in compliance with OSHA, EEOC, NLRB, and zoning requirements? Has the company ever had an external environmental law compliance audit performed? Has the company developed smoking, substance abuse testing, child labor, family leave, or child care policies and programs in compliance with federal, state, and local laws? Does the workplace comply with the Americans with Disabilities Act? Have steps been taken to ensure compliance with applicable equal employment opportunity, affirmative action, equal pay, wage and hour, immigration, employee benefit, and worker's compensation laws? When was the last time the company consulted these statutes to ensure that current practices are consistent with applicable laws? Has an employment manual been prepared? When is the last time that it was reviewed by qualified counsel?

D. **Employee benefit plans.** Has the company adopted a medical reimbursement plan? Group life insurance? Retirement plans? Disability plans? If so, should they be adopted? If yes, have all amendments to the structure and ongoing management of these plans been made to maintain qualification? Have annual reports been filed with the U.S. Department of Treasury and U.S. Department of Labor for pension and profit-sharing plans? Have there been any changes in the administration of these plans? Have there been any recent transactions between the plan and the company, its trustees or its officers and directors?

E. **Contractual matters.** On which material contracts is the company directly or indirectly bound? Were these agreements drafted in compliance with applicable laws, such as your state's version of the Uniform Commercial Code? Is your company still able to meet its obligations under these agreements? Is any party to these agreements in default? Why? What steps have been taken to enforce the company's rights and/or mitigate damages? To what extent are contractual forms used when selling company products and services? When is the last time these forms were updated? What problems have these forms triggered? What steps have been taken to resolve these problems? Are employees who possess special skills and experience under an employment agreement with the company? When was the last time the agreement was reviewed and revised? What about sales representatives of the company? Are they under some form of a written agreement and commission schedule? Has the scope of their authority been clearly defined and communicated to the third parties with whom they deal? To what extent does the company hire independent contractors? Have agreements been prepared with these parties? Have the intellectual property law issues, such as "work for hire" provisions, been included in these agreements?

F. **Protection of intellectual property.** To what extent are trademarks, patents, copyrights, and trade secrets among the intangible assets of the business? What are the internal company procedures for these key assets? What agreements (such as ownership of inventions, nondisclosure, and noncompete) have been signed by key employees who are exposed to the company's intellectual property? What procedures are in place for receiving new ideas and proposals from employees and other parties? What steps have been taken to protect the company's "trade dress," where applicable? Have trademarks, patents, and copyrights been registered? What monitoring programs are in place to detect infringement and ensure proper usage by third parties? Are documents properly stamped with copyright and confidentiality notices? Has counsel been contacted to determine whether the new discovery is eligible for registration? Does the company license any of its intellectual property to third parties? Have experienced licensing and franchising counsel prepared the agreements and disclosure documents?

G. **Relationships with competitors.** How competitive is your industry? How aggressive is the company's approach toward its markets and competitors? What incentives are offered for attracting and retaining customers? To what professional and trade associations does the company belong? What types of information are exchanged? Does the company engage in any type of communication or have any cooperative agreements with competitors regarding price, geographic territories, or distribution channels that might constitute an antitrust violation or an act of unfair competition? Has the company established an in-house program in order to educate employees of the mechanics and pitfalls of antitrust violations? Has an antitrust action ever been brought or threatened by, or against, the company? What were the surrounding facts? What was the outcome? Have you recently hired a former employee of a competitor? How was he or she recruited? Does this employee use skills or knowledge gained from the prior employer? To what extent has the prior employer been notified? What steps are being taken to avoid a lawsuit involving misappropriation of trade secrets and/or interference with contractual regulations? Does the company engage in comparative advertising? How are the products and services of the competitor generally treated? Are any of your trademarks or trade names similar to those of competitors? Have you been involved in any prior litigation with a competitor? Have you ever been threatened with litigation?

H. **Financing matters.** What equity and debt financing have been obtained in the past three years? What continuing reporting obligations or other affirmative/negative covenants remain in place? What triggers a default and what new rights are created to the investors or lenders upon default? What security interests remain outstanding?

I. **Marketing and distribution issues.** Has the company clearly defined the market for its products and services? Who are the key competitors? What are their respective market shares, strengths, weaknesses, strategies, and objectives? What new players are entering this market? What barriers exist to a new entry? What is the saturation point of this market? What are the key distribution channels for bringing these products to the market? Have all necessary agreements and regulations affecting these channels been adequately addressed (i.e., labeling and warranty laws, consumer protection laws, pricing laws, distributorship agreements, etc.)? If the company is doing business abroad, have all import/export regulations been carefully reviewed? Has a system been established to ensure compliance with the Foreign Corrupt Practices Act? Is the company considering franchising as a method of marketing and distribution to expand market share? To what extent can all key aspects of the company's proven success be reduced to an operations manual and taught to others in a training program? To what extent are competitors engaged in franchising? If franchising is appropriate for distribution of the company's products or business, have all necessary offering documents and agreements been prepared by experienced franchise legal counsel? What initial franchise fee will be charged? Are there any ongoing royalties? Are these fees competitive? What ongoing programs and support are given to franchisees? What products and services must the franchisee buy from your company? Under what conditions may a franchise be terminated or transferred? Are any alternatives to franchising being considered? Has the company looked at dealer termination, multilevel marketing, or pyramid laws?

Legal audits offer the small and growing company an inexpensive, yet comprehensive, method of making sure that its plans and objectives are consistent with developments in the law. The process helps to identify problem areas, maintain legal compliance, and offers legal solutions and alternatives for the achievement of the company's short and long-term business objectives. It also forces owners and managers to re-evaluate the company's strategies in light of the legal costs, risks, and problems that have been identified in the audit.

7

DEVELOPING A CAPITAL FORMATION STRATEGY

Virtually all types of growth strategies, especially the organic growth strategies such as internal expansion, or mergers and acquisitions, will require capital to implement successfully. The growing company's ability to develop a capital formation strategy (or rather, the ability to raise money) will ultimately determine its long-term success.

Virtually all capital formation strategies revolve around a balancing of four critical factors: *Risk, Reward, Control,* and *Capital.* You and your source of venture funds will each have your own ideas as to how these factors should be weighted and balanced. Once a meeting of the minds takes place on these key elements, you'll be able to do the deal:

- *Risk.* The venture investment company wants to take steps to mitigate its risk, which you can do with a strong management team, a well-written business plan, and the leadership to execute the plan.
- *Reward.* The rewards desired may vary depending on the type of venture investor, and your objective is to preserve your right to participate in a significant share of the growth in the value of the company, as well as partake of any subsequent proceeds from the sale or public offering of your business.

- **Control.** It's often said that the art of venture investing is "structuring the deal to have 20 percent of the equity with 80 percent of the control." But control is an elusive concept that's often overplayed by entrepreneurs. Depending on the venture investment company's philosophy, and its lawyers' creativity, there are many different tools available to venture investors to exercise control and mitigate risk. Only you can dictate which levels and types of controls may be acceptable, but remember that the higher risk deals are likely to come with the higher degrees of control.
- **Capital.** Negotiations with the venture investor will often focus on how much capital will be provided, when it will be provided, what types of securities will be purchased (preferred stock, convertible notes, debt with warrants, for example), at what valuation, what special rights will be attached to the securities, and what mandatory returns will be built into the securities. You need to think about how much capital you *really* need, *when* do you really need it, and if there are any alternative ways of obtaining these resources.

Regardless of the current state of the economy, or whether your particular industry is in or out of favor at any given moment, there are certain key components of the company's game plan that must be presented to the prospective source of capital in a clear and concise manner. These components include:

- A focused and realistic business plan based on a scalable and defensible business and revenue model
- A strong and balanced management team that has an impressive individual and group track record
- Wide and deep targeted markets that are rich with customers that want and need (and can afford) the company's products and services
- Sustainable competitive advantage that can be supported by real barriers to entry. The best kind of barriers are those created by proprietary products or brands that are owned exclusively by the company.

Finally, there should be some sizzle to go with the steak. This may include excited and loyal customers and employees, favorable media coverage, nervous competitors who are genuinely concerned that you may be changing the industry, and a clearly defined exit strategy that allows your investors to be rewarded for taking the risk of investing within a reasonable period of time.

UNDERSTANDING THE DIFFERENT TYPES OF INVESTORS

Most investors fall into one or more of three categories: **Emotional Investors,** who invest in *you* out of a love or a relationship; **Strategic Investors,** who invest in the synergies offered by your business (based primarily on a nonfinancial objective, such as access to research and development, or a vendor-customer relationship—though financial return may still be a factor); and **Financial Investors,** whose primary or even exclusive motivation is a return on capital, and who invest to garner the financial rewards that your business plan (if properly executed) will produce. Your approach, plan, and deal terms may vary depending on the type of investor you're dealing with, so it's important for you to understand the investor and his or her objectives well in advance. Your goal is then to meet those objectives without compromising the long-term best interests of your company and its current shareholders. Achieving that goal is challenging, but can be easier than you might think, *if* your team of advisors has extensive experience in getting deals done properly and fairly so that everyone's objectives are met. The more preparation, creativity, and pragmatism your team shows, the more likely that the deal will get done on a timely and affordable basis.

CAPITAL FORMATION STRATEGIES

There are many different choices available to a growing company that's looking to raise capital, but basically your choices are limited to two flavors: **debt** or **equity.** Defining your "optimal capital structure"—a proper balance between the two—is a challenge, as is finding these sources of capital at affordable rates. What's considered "affordable" varies, depending on whether you're pursuing debt *or* equity. Affordability in the debt context refers to the term, the interest rate, the amortization, and the penalties for nonpayment. In the context of equity, affordability refers to the company's net worth (known as "valuation"), dilution of the shares, or control held by the current owners, as well as any special terms or preferences such as mandatory dividends or redemption rights.

Your first option is to issue securities. There are essentially three types of securities that you can issue: debt securities, equity securities, and hybrid (or convertible) securities. Each has certain characteristics, variable features, and attendant costs.

Debt securities. When you authorize the issuance of a debt security, it is usually in the form of a *bond*, a *note*, or a *debenture*. Typically, a bond is an obligation secured by a mortgage on some property of the company, while a debenture or note is unsecured (and usually carries a higher rate of interest), and, therefore, is issued on the strength of the company's reputation, projected earnings, and growth potential. The terms of the debt security and the earnings (referred to as "yield") to the holder will be determined by an evaluation of the level of the risk to the holder and the likelihood of default. Growing companies that lack a high bond or credit rating will often be faced with restrictive clauses, or covenants, in the debenture purchase agreement, or in the actual terms of the bond, that govern their activities during the term of the instrument. For example, the covenants might restrict management's ability to get raises or bonuses, or might require that the company maintain a certain debt-to-equity ratio at all times. You and your attorney should assess the direct and indirect costs of these terms and covenants before you choose this option.

Equity securities. Equity securities include *common stock, preferred stock,* and *warrants and options.* Each type of equity security carries a different set of rights, preferences, and potential rates of return, in exchange for the capital contributed to the company. For example, the typical growing company (whose value to an investor is usually greatly dependent on intangible assets such as patents, trade secrets or goodwill, and projected earnings) will tend to issue equity securities before incurring additional debt. This is because its balance sheet lacks the assets necessary to secure the debt, and additional debt is likely to increase the company's failure risk to unacceptably dangerous levels. The three types of equity securities are:

1. *Common stock.* An offering of common stock and the related dilution of their interest in the company is often traumatic for owners
   of growing companies that currently operate as closely held corporations. The need for additional capital for growth, combined
   with the lack of readily available personal savings or corporate retained earnings, causes a realignment of the capital structure and
   a redistribution of ownership and control. Although the offering
   of common stock is generally costly and will entail a surrender of
   some ownership and control, it does offer you an increased equity
   base, and a more secure foundation upon which to grow. It also
   increases your chances of getting loans in the future.

2. *Preferred stock.* Broadly speaking, preferred stock is an equity security that shares some characteristics with debt securities. Preferred stockholders are entitled to receive dividends at a fixed or
   even an adjustable rate of return (similar to a debt instrument),
   before dividends are distributed to holders of the common stock.
   Owners of preferred shares also participate ahead of common
   stock holders in the distribution of assets in the event of liquidation. The preferred stock may or may not have certain rights regarding voting and convertibility to common stock. The shares
   may also have antidilution or pre-emptive rights, or redemption
   privileges that may be exercised either by the company or the
   shareholder. Although the fixed dividend payments are not tax
   deductible (as interest payments would be), and company ownership is still diluted, the balance between risk and reward is still
   achieved because the principal investment need not be returned
   (unless there are provisions for redemption). In addition, the
   preferred stockholders' return on investment is limited to a fixed
   rate of return (unless there are provisions for convertibility into
   common stock), and preferred stockholders' claims are subordinated to the claims of creditors and bondholders in the event of
   the liquidation of the company. The use of convertible preferred
   stock is especially popular with venture capitalists.

3. *Warrants and options.* This option gives the holder a right to buy a
   stated number of shares of common or preferred stock at a specified price, and within a specific period of time. If that right isn't
   exercised, it lapses. If the stock's price rises above the option price,

the holder can essentially purchase the stock at a discount, thereby participating in the company's growth.

Convertible securities. In their most typical form, convertible securities are similar to warrants and options in that they provide the holder with an option to convert the security—such as a convertible note or convertible preferred stock—into common stock. The incentive is usually the same as for the exercise of a warrant. The conversion price (the price the company will receive for the common stock upon conversion) is more favorable than the current rate of return provided by the convertible security. Convertible securities offer your company several distinct advantages, including an opportunity to sell debt securities at lower interest rates and with less restrictive covenants (in exchange for the investor having a chance to participate in the company's success if it meets its projections and objectives).

UNDERSTANDING THE DIFFERENT SOURCES OF CAPITAL

There are many different sources of capital, each with its own requirements and investment goals. They include:

Commercial banks. Smaller companies are much more likely to obtain an attentive audience with a commercial loan officer *after* the start-up phase has been completed. In determining whether or not to "extend debt financing" (essentially "make a loan"), bankers look first at general credit rating, collateral, and your ability to repay. Bankers will also closely examine the nature of your business, your management team, competition, industry trends, and the way you plan to use the proceeds. A well-drafted loan proposal and business plan will go a long way in demonstrating your company's creditworthiness to the prospective lender.

Commercial finance companies. Many companies who seek debt financing but are rejected by banks turn to commercial finance companies for credit. These companies usually offer debt financing at considerably higher rates than an institutional lender, but they sometimes provide lower rates if you take advantage of their other services, such as payroll and accounts-receivable management. Because of fewer federal and state regulations, commercial finance companies have generally more flexible lending policies and more of a stomach for risk than traditional commercial banks. However, the commercial finance companies are just as likely to mitigate their risk with higher interest rates and more stringent collateral requirements for loans or credit to undeveloped companies.

Leasing companies. Leasing typically takes one of two forms: (1) *operating leases* that usually provide you with both the asset and a service contract for a fixed period of time that is usually significantly less than the actual useful life of the asset. As a result, the total payments under the lease contract aren't sufficient to recover the full value of the equipment. This usually means lower monthly payments for you. If negotiated properly, the operating lease will contain a cancellation clause that gives you the right to cancel the lease with little or no penalty. The cancellation clause provides you with more flexibility in the event that sales decline, or the equipment leased becomes obsolete; and (2) *capital leases* differ from operating leases in that they usually don't include any maintenance services and involve your use of the equipment over the asset's full useful life.

State and local government lending programs. Many state and local governments provide direct capital or related assistance through support services, or even loan guarantees to small and growing companies, in an effort to foster economic development. The amount and terms of the financing will usually be regulated by the statutes of the state or local development agency.

Trade credit/consortiums. Many growing companies overlook an obvious source of capital or credit when exploring their financing alternatives—suppliers and customers. Suppliers have a vested interest in the long-term growth and development of their customer base, and may be willing to extend favorable trade credit terms, or even provide direct financing to help fuel a good customer's growth. The same principles apply to the customers of a growing company who rely upon the company as a key supplier of resources. There's also an emerging trend in customer-related financing called a consortium. Under this arrangement, a select number of key customers finance the development of a particular product or project in exchange for a right of first refusal or territorial exclusivity for the distribution of the finished product. You should carefully examine applicable federal and state antitrust laws before completing the plans to structure a consortium.

Private investors. Many early-stage companies receive their initial equity capital from private investors, either individually or as a small group. These investors are called "angels" or "bands of angels"—and are a rapidly growing sector of the private equity market.

Institutional venture capital firms. In recent years, perhaps the best-known source of equity capital for growing companies is the traditional venture capital firm. These formally organized pools of venture capital helped create Silicon Valley and the high-technology industry, which is the fastest growing sector of the national economy. These funds do very few deals each year, in comparison to the total demand for growth capital, so be ready to expand your horizons.

Private placement offerings. Many growing companies turn to the exempt offerings provided by SEC Regulation D as a source of growth-equity capital. These offerings can be made in increments of as little as $10,000, and offer an opportunity to attract a variety of strategic investors. This option is discussed in more detail in Chapter 8.

Mergers and acquisitions. Mergers and acquisitions (M&As)—or even joint ventures—with cash- or asset-rich companies can provide a viable source of capital for your growing company. This kind of a transaction triggers many legal, structural, and tax issues that the seller and its counsel must consider. The number of deals made in the middle-market merger and acquisition sector may be increasing due to several factors, including: the consolidation impact of technology; the "trickle-down" of the mega-mergers of 2005 and 2006, and the need for mid-sized companies to remain competitive in an age of mostly mega-companies and small niche players.

Strategic investors and corporate venture capitalists. Many large corporations have established venture capital firms as operating subsidiaries that look for deal flow, not only to achieve financial returns, but also to achieve strategic objectives such as access to the technology that your company may have developed. Examples of companies that have a track record of making venture-capital-style investments include Intel, Motorola, Nokia, and General Electric.

Overseas investors. There are a wide variety of overseas investors, foreign stock exchanges, banks, and leasing companies that are interested in financing transactions with companies based in the United States. Naturally, you should consider cultural and management style differences before you engage in any international financing transaction.

HOW MUCH MONEY DO YOU *REALLY* NEED?

One mistake that leaders of growing companies often make in their search for capital is to raise too little or too much capital. The management team will lose credibility if, during a presentation to prospective investors, it becomes clear that they have misbudgeted or misjudged *actual* capital needs, *or* have failed to demonstrate creativity in exploring alternative ways to obtain the resources for which they are attempting to raise the capital. The issue of misbudgeting is problematic—if you ask for too little, the cost of capital will usually be much higher, and the process more painful when you need to go back to the well prematurely. However, if you ask for too much, it may be a turnoff to a prospective investor, lead to waste, or even worse, cause greater dilution of your ownership than was really necessary.

One way that investors will protect against "over-investing" is to invest capital in stages instead of in a lump sum. These stages (or "tranches") are often tied to specific business plan milestones or performance objectives, such as revenues, profits, attaining customers, recruiting team members, or obtaining regulatory approvals. Breaking the investment into tranches protects the investors against capital mismanagement and waste, and protects you against premature dilution or loss of capital. Your natural inclination will probably be to request that all the necessary capital be invested in a lump sum (to reduce the chances that future conditions will get in the way of receiving all the money you need), but bear in mind that there may be some real advantages to being more patient and allowing for a staged investment.

BUDGETING, FORECASTING, AND USE OF PROCEEDS

Before you develop specific equity and debt capital formation strategies, which are discussed in Chapters 8 and 9, it is critical that you are able to develop strong budgets, forecasts, and allocation of proceeds statements that will support your business growth strategy. All sources of capital, whether venture capitalists or commercial lenders, will want to know that you and your management team have taken the time to think through the capital that will be required to implement the growth strategy selected, and the financial impact that the capital infusion will have on the company from a cash flow and net worth perspective.

The best place to demonstrate that your team has thought through the financial components of the capital required to implement the growth strategy is in the Budgets/Allocation of Proceeds, and the Financial Projections sections of the Business Growth Plan.

Budgets and Allocation of Proceeds

This section of the Business Growth Plan should address *how much* money the company will need to implement its business growth strategy, and *why*. It should also demonstrate *when* the various capital levels will be required, since many investors and lenders will prefer to invest or lend in stages as milestones are met, rather than giving your company all of the money in a lump sum. The budgets section should also answer what you are going to buy, and why you believe that this expenditure is necessary at this stage in your company's growth. This section should be broken down into at least three different scenarios, reflecting differing funding levels at the bottom, middle, and upper ranges of the capital that you seek to raise, since it is unlikely that you will be able to raise the exact amount of money you require.

FIGURE 7.1 *The Capital Formation "Reality Check" Strategic Pyramid*

IPO	Initial Public Offerings (The few, the proud, the IPOs)	
Big-time venture capital (VC)	Large-scale institutional VC deals (4th or 5th round level—for the elite/pre-IPO or M&A deals)	
Institutional venture-capital market	Very competitive: Everybody wants them, few get them (In 1997, 625 VC funds at this level did 2,300 deals totaling $10.5 billion at an average deal size of $4.1 million) Usually 2nd or 3rd round money, and you'll need a track record or to be in a very hot industry. They see hundreds of deals and only do a handful per annum	
Early-stage venture capital/seed capital funds, SBICs	A small portion (less than 15 percent) of all VC funds; very competitive, very focused niche—typically more patient, with less aggressive return-on-investment (ROI) needs	
Informal VC—strategic alliances, Fortune 1000 Corp. VCs, global investors, etc.	Synergy-driven: more patient, more strategic (make sure you get what was promised)	
Larger-scale commercial loans	You'll need a track record, a good loan proposal, a banking relationship, and some collateral	
Private Placement Memoranda (PPM) under Regulation D (groups of angels that you assemble)	Understand federal/state securities laws, have a good hit list, and know the needs of your targeted group (relationship-driven)	
Bands of angels that are already assembled (syndicates, investor groups, private investor networks, pledge funds, etc.)	Find out what's available in your region and get busy	
Angels (wealthy families, cashed-out entrepreneurs, etc.) (Found by networking/by computer/smaller angels vs. super angels)	Rapidly growing sector of venture-investment market	
Small Business Administration/microloans/general small-business commercial lending	Very common but require collateral (tough for intangible-driven businesses	
The money/resources of your family, friends, key employees, etc.	Why should *we* give you money if *they* won't?	
Your own money/resources (credit cards, home-equity loans, savings, 401(k) loans, etc.)	A necessary precursor for most venture investors (Why should *we* give you money if *you're* not taking a risk?)	

Financial Projections/Forecasts

The financial projections, or forecasts, section of your business growth plan demonstrates to prospective lenders or investors that your team has thought through the financial performance impact that the infusion of capital will have on the company's growth plans. Financial projections predict what the company's sales, costs, profits, and net worth will be at various points in the future, if the capital is raised and the growth strategy is successfully implemented, at various levels of success.

While underlying detail should be available for further discussion, financial projections should include high-level figures, not line item detail, department by department. Present five-year projections at least monthly for the first year, but no longer than two, and quarterly or annually for the remaining years. The financial projections should also be presented in at least three scenarios, Worst Case, Expected Case, and Best Case, to demonstrate that sensitivity analysis has been conducted for the forecasting process.

As supporting documentation to the financial projects, notes should be included detailing assumptions, payment policies, receivable policies, depreciation utilized, and any other information used in generating the figures. Consider what key factors you relied upon to arrive at these numbers, and make sure these facts are documented.

TIPS AND COMMON MISTAKES TO AVOID WHEN PREPARING BUDGETS AND FORECASTS

The key to developing effective forecasts and budgets is to have clear and detailed footnotes that explain your underlying assumptions and the variables that affect these assumptions, and to explain the key factors and sources of data that you relied upon in arriving at these conclusions. If you can't back up the numbers, then prospective investors and lenders will tear them up and, worse, not do the deal.

- Costs projections are often grossly underestimated by emerging growth companies, especially in the area of personnel expenses. Be sure to include *all* costs associated with human resources, such as headhunter fees, benefits, resources, office space, and so on, not just salaries and projected bonuses.

- Understand your key revenue drivers and the variables that affect actual performances. If people/time is your chief revenue driver, do your projections match up with your current personnel? Are you sure you will be able to attract and retain additional personnel as you grow? Your strategy must match the numbers.

- Understand the financial and cash flow needs of the prospective lender or investor. For commercial lending, do your projections and cash flows match up with the schedule of debt service payments? Don't force-fit your projections into a third party's perceived cash flow needs, or their expected rates of return. Your numbers will either meet their needs, or they won't. A little bit of tweaking is fine, but don't do a major overhaul or get too aggressive just because you think that is the only way they will invest. In fact, your realistic projections will often help you narrow the field of prospective lenders or investors because your company's timing as to when it creates positive cash flow will help you select the appropriate source of capital.

- Know the numbers for your competitors and industry overall. Does your forecast fit with applicable and relevant key industry ratios? Why or why not? Where are you stronger than the norm? Where are you weaker, and why? Investors and lenders who regularly provide capital to your industry will be very familiar with these numbers, and you need to be as well.

- The text of the Business Growth Plan and the growth strategy articulated must match up consistently with the stated capital needs and projected cash flows. These are often called the "critical linkages" between the body of the plan and the forecasts, and they must fit together smoothly. For example, the sales forecast should fit with the marketing budget. The new product development must fit with the research and development budget. A sophisticated reader will quickly spot gaps between the words and the numbers. There must also be consistency among the senior team members on the key milestones and capital needs; any major differences of opinion should be resolved well *before* the meeting with the sources of capital.

- Don't rely too heavily on outside advisors or software programs when preparing budgets and forecasts. The prospective lenders and investors want to know how *you* arrived at these conclusions, not how some consultant or software program got you there. Use your advisors as editors and sounding boards but not as primary draftsmen.
- Give yourself plenty of working capital cushion. It is very costly to go back to the source of capital for additional funds prematurely, or "in between expected rounds." Leave room for error in your projections so that you do not run out of cash too soon.
- Don't overload the reader with too much information. Although most Business Growth Plans fall short in adequately explaining their assumptions, others that I have seen weigh the document down with unnecessary detail. Focus on the key information as needed, or that which was requested by the lender or investor.
- In budgeting your financial models, avoid some of the classic problems faced by emerging-growth businesses if at all possible. For example, many companies have experienced the classic "sideways V" where sales go up, but profits go down. Try to demonstrate that management will stay focused on controlling costs during the growth phase, so that as sales increase, expenses increase at a slower rate.
- The ability to measure costs and financial data is key to your ability to manage the company based on this data. The ability to contain and control costs, keep debt low on the balance sheet, experience rapid sales growth, increase profit margins, build multiple reserve

---

Sample Statement of Assumptions

The management of GrowCo believes that initial funding of $2.5 million will be adequate to carry the company through to initial profitability. It is anticipated that receivables and inventory financing from commercial bank sources will be available in the second quarter of year two.

The company anticipates being able to sustain a gross margin in the 40 percent range. This approximates industry average. On a net basis, GrowCo will turn approximately 9 to 11 percent of sales to the bottom line, beginning it its third year.

The company anticipates being able to sustain a gross margin in the 40 percent range. This approximates industry average. On a net basis, GrowCo will turn approximately 9 to 11 percent of sales to the bottom line, beginning it its third year.

Management has taken what it believes to be an extremely conservative approach in formulating its pro forma financial—no debt financing is shown until year two, and lease financing is not proposed as an option. Management is vigorously pursuing both avenues at this stage, and fully expects to arrange at least modest credit facilities in the short-term.

Assumptions underlying financial projections:

- Founders contribute $70,000 cash to GrowCo in month one (accomplished)
- Founders defer salaries and out-of-pocket expense of $42,500 indefinitely (accomplished)
- Depreciation is calculated on all fixed and capital assets, assuming five-year lives and straight line computation
- Receivables are 30 days in duration (industry standard is 30 days)
- Payables are 30 days (industry standard is 50–65 days), do not begin until month thirteen, and equal only to 50 percent of inventory costs during the period (trade support is expected much sooner)
- Inventories turn an average of seven times per year (on top of a fixed base of $40,000)
- Salaries through month 18 are approximately 50 to 75 percent of industry standard (higher at lower personnel levels in the company)
- Interest is earned at 8 percent per annum
- Interest is paid at 13 percent per annum
- Cash purchases are the sum of the period's cost of goods sold, 50 percent of inventory purchases, and capital acquisitions.
- Minimum cash on hand is $20,000 (under bank line when cash flow is negative for the period)
- Detail budgets underlying the financial data are available for further review and discussion

streams and strong earnings, and position your company for additional rounds of capital at higher valuations are all critical drivers for continued business growth that will depend on the systems and procedures you put in place to measure and monitor performance. Once this data is analyzed, the team needs to constantly tweak and fine-tune the operations to be managed toward maximum bouts of growth and profitability. *It is important not to confuse effort and activity with actual results.*

8

STRATEGIES FOR RAISING EQUITY CAPITAL

Virtually all types of growing companies raise some equity capital to continue to fuel their expansion. The two most common ways that a growing company raises equity capital are through an exempt (for regulation) offering known as a private placement memorandum (PPM Offering), or by raising capital from a venture capitalist, either a standalone venture capital fund, or a venture capital investing arm of a large corporation. This chapter will focus on these two strategies. It will also provide an overview of the initial public offering (IPO) process, though IPOs have been much less prevalent since their heyday in the late 1990s, dropping from 486 offerings in 1999 to only 68 in 2003, and 194 in 2005. In a June 2006 survey of more than 300 rapid growth companies conducted by PricewaterhouseCoopers, 29 percent of the company leaders surveyed said that they were considering private placements as their primary strategy for raising equity capital, in comparison to 18 percent who were pursuing angels or strategic investors, and 16 percent whose sights were set on institutional venture capital. Only 3 percent were considering an initial public offering over the next few years.

PRIVATE PLACEMENT OFFERINGS

Private placements generally refer to any type of offering of securities by a small or growing company. The offering of these securities does not need to be registered with the Securities and Exchange Commission (SEC). With loan criteria for commercial bankers and investment criteria for institutional venture capitalists tightening on both fronts, the private placement offering remains one of the most viable capital formation alternatives available for companies. In order to determine whether a private placement is a sensible strategy for raising capital, it is imperative that you: (1) have a fundamental understanding of federal and state securities laws affecting private placements (which are provided below as an overview); (2) are familiar with the basic procedural steps that must be taken before such an alternative is pursued; and (3) have a team of qualified legal and accounting professionals.

The private placement generally offers reduced transactional and ongoing costs because of its exemption from many of the extensive registration and reporting requirements imposed by federal and state securities laws. The private placement alternative usually also offers the ability to structure a more complex and confidential transaction, since the offerees will typically consist of a small number of sophisticated investors. In addition, a private placement permits a more rapid penetration into the capital markets than would a public offering of securities requiring registration with the SEC.

Federal Securities Laws Applicable to Private Placements

As a general rule, Section 5 of the Securities Act of 1933 (the Securities Act) requires the filing of a registration statement with the SEC prior to the offer to sell any security in interstate commerce, *unless* an exemption is available under Sections 3 or 4 of the act. The company offering the securities is referred to as the *issuer* or an *offeror.* The most commonly recognized transactional exemption is a private placement. The penalties for failing to register, or for disclosing inaccurate or misleading information under Sections 11 and 12 of the Securities Act, are quite stringent. Registration under Section 5 is an expensive and time-consuming process, and a network of underwriters and brokers or dealers must be assembled to make a market for the security. An issuer that registers under Section 5 is also subject to strict periodic reporting requirements.

To qualify for a private placement, you must work with legal counsel to structure the transaction within the various categories of exemptions available, such as: (a) Section 4(2), considered the broad "private offering" exemption and designed for "transaction(s) by an issuer not involving any public offering"; (b) Section 3(a)(11), an intrastate exemption; and (c), the most common, Regulation D, which specifies three specific transactional exemptions from the registration provisions within the framework of Sections 3(b) and 4(2) of the Securities Act.

Fast-track growing companies typically seek a transactional exemption from registration through one of three options offered by Regulation D:

1. **Rule 504** permits offers and sales of not more than $1 million during any 12-month period by any issuer that is not subject to the reporting requirements of the Securities Exchange Act of 1934 (the Exchange Act), *and* that is not an investment company or a blank check company. The aggregate offering price for an offering under Rule 504 may not exceed $1 million, less the aggregate price for all securities sold (a) in the 12 months before the start of, and during, the Rule 504 offering; (b) in reliance on any exemption based on Section 3(b) of the Securities Act; or (c) in violation of Section 5 of the Securities Act. Rule 504 places virtually no limit on the number or the nature of the investors that participate in the offering. The issuer may use general advertising and solicitation, and there are no restrictions on resales of securities issued pursuant to Rule 504. **But even if accreditation is not required, it is strongly recommended that certain baseline criteria be developed and disclosed in order to avoid unqualified or unsophisticated investors.** Even though no formal disclosure document (also known as a "prospectus") needs to be registered and delivered to offerees under Rule 504, there are many procedures that still must be understood and followed, and a disclosure document is nevertheless strongly recommended. An offering under Rule 504 is still subject to the general antifraud provisions of Section 10(b) of the Exchange Act, and Rule 10b-5 thereunder; thus, every document or other information that is actually provided to the prospective investor must be accurate and not misleading by virtue of its con-

tent, or its omissions in any material respect. The SEC also requires that its Form D be filed for all offerings under Regulation D within 15 days of the first sale. Finally, a growing company seeking to raise capital under Rule 504 should examine applicable state laws very carefully because, although many states have adopted overall securities laws similar to Regulation D, many of these laws do not include an exemption similar to 504, and as a result, a formal memorandum (discussed later in this chapter) may need to be prepared.

2. **Rule 505** is selected over Rule 504 by many companies because its requirements are consistent with many state securities laws. Rule 505 allows an issuer that is not an investment company to sell up to $5 million of the issuer's securities in a 12-month period to an unlimited number of "accredited investors," and up to 35 non-accredited investors (regardless of their net worth, income, or sophistication). For purposes of Regulation D, an "accredited investor" is a person or entity that is considered able to withstand the economic risks involved in securities transactions. An individual is considered to be an accredited individual if he or she falls into one of the eight categories set out in Rule 501(a) of Regulation D. A director, executive officer, or general partner of an issuer; an individual whose net worth, or joint net worth with a spouse, exceeds $1 million at the time of purchase, or who had an individual income in excess of $200,000 in each of the last two years (joint incomes in excess of $300,000), and who has a reasonable expectation of reaching the same income level in the current year, are considered accredited investors pursuant to Rule 501(a). The $5 million cap is calculated by aggregating (1) the offering price of all securities sold pursuant to Rule 504 or 505, plus (2) the offering price of all securities sold within the previous 12 months in reliance on any Section 3(b) exemption, plus (3) the offering price of all securities sold in the previous 12 months that were in violation of the Section 5 registration requirement. Included in these categories are officers and directors of the company who have "policy-making" functions, as well as outside investors who meet certain income or net worth criteria. Rule 505 has many of the same filing requirements and restrictions imposed by Rule 504 (such as the need to file a Form D), in addition to an absolute prohibition on advertising and general solicitation for offerings.

Any company that is subject to the "bad boy" provisions of Regulation A is disqualified from being a 505 offeror, and applies to persons who have been subject to certain disciplinary, administrative, civil, or criminal proceedings, or sanctions which involve the company or its predecessors.

3. **Rule 506** is similar to Rule 505; however, the issuer may sell its securities to an unlimited number of accredited investors and up to 35 nonaccredited investors. For those requiring large amounts of capital, this exemption is the most attractive because it has no maximum dollar limit. The key difference under Rule 506 is that any nonaccredited investor must be "sophisticated." A "sophisticated investor" (in this context) is one who does not fall within any of the eight categories specified by Rule 501(a), but is believed by the issuer to "have knowledge and experience in financial and business matters" that render him capable of evaluating the merits and understanding the risks posed by the transaction (either acting alone or in conjunction with his "purchaser representative"), or the issuer reasonably believes that the purchaser meets this description. If the purchaser employs a purchaser representative, the representative must be unaffiliated with the issuer, knowledgeable in business matters, and must be acknowledged by the purchaser in writing. The best way to remove any uncertainty over the sophistication or accreditation of a prospective investor is to request that a comprehensive Confidential Offeree Questionnaire be completed before the securities are sold. Rule 506 does eliminate the need to prepare and deliver disclosure documents in any specified format if exclusively accredited investors participate in the transaction. As with Rule 505, an absolute prohibition on advertising and general solicitation exists. States cannot impose their registration requirements on securities issued pursuant to Rule 506. States can only demand notification that they are going to sell securities under Rule 506.

State Securities Laws Applicable to Private Placements

Regulation D was designed to provide a foundation for uniformity between federal and state securities laws. This objective has been met in some states, but still has a long way to go on a national level. Full compliance with the federal securities laws is only one level of regulation that must be taken into account when developing plans and strategies to raise capital through an offering of securities. Even if the offering is exempt under federal laws, registration may still be required in the states where the securities are to be sold under applicable "Blue Sky" laws, the state laws that govern securities offerings. You must consider the expense and requirements on both the federal and state level.

Overall, there are a wide variety of review levels among the states, ranging from very tough "merit" reviews (designed to ensure that all offerings of securities are fair and equitable), to very lenient "notice only" filings (designed primarily to promote full disclosure). The securities laws of each state, where an offer or sale will be made, should be checked very carefully prior to the distribution of the offering documents. You must also be keenly aware of the specific requirements of each state. Although a comprehensive discussion of the state securities laws is beyond the scope of this chapter, be advised that every state in the nation has some type of statute governing securities transactions and securities dealers. When drafting the offering, these laws should be carefully reviewed in order to determine

- whether the particular limited offering exemption selected under federal law will also apply in the state;
- whether pre-sale or post-sale registration or notices are required;
- whether special legends or disclosures must be made in the offering documents;
- what remedies are available to an investor who has purchased securities from a company that has failed to comply with applicable state laws; and
- who may offer securities for sale on behalf of the company.

Preparing the Private Placement Memorandum

You should work with legal counsel to prepare the document and exhibits that will constitute the Private Placement Memorandum (known as the PPM). The PPM describes the background of the company, the risks to the investor, and the terms of the securities being sold. In determining the exact degree of "disclosure" that should be included in the document, there are several factors that affect the type of information that must be provided, and the format in which the data must be presented, such as the following:

- Minimum level of disclosure that must be made under federal securities laws (depending, in part, on the exemption from registration being relied upon)
- Minimum level of disclosure that must be made under an applicable state's securities laws (naturally dependent upon *in* which state or states an offer or sale of the securities is to be made)
- Sophistication and expectations of the targeted investors (e.g., some investors will expect a certain amount of information presented in a specified format regardless of what the law may require)
- Complexity or nature of the company, and the terms of the offering (e.g., many offerors should prepare detailed disclosure documents, whether or not they are required to do so, in order to avoid liability for misstatements, fraud, or confusion, especially if the nature of the company and/or the terms of its offering are very complex)

Legal counsel must carefully review each transaction or proposed offering of securities to first determine the *minimum* level of disclosure that must be provided to prospective investors under applicable federal and state laws. Once this is established, the costs of preparing a *more detailed* document than may be required should be weighed against the benefits of the additional protection provided to the company by a more comprehensive prospectus. The key question will always be, "What is the most cost-effective vehicle for providing the targeted investors with the information that they require, and that both applicable law and prudence dictate they must have?" *There are no easy answers.*

The specific disclosure items to be included in the PPM will vary depending on the size of the offering and nature of the investors, as categorized under federal securities laws and any applicable state laws. The text should be *descriptive, not persuasive* and allow the reader to reach his or her own conclusions as to the merits of the securities being offered by the company. Use the following as a checklist in preparing your PPM.

- **Introductory materials** introduce the prospective investor to the basic terms of the offering. A *cover page* should include a brief statement about the company and its core business, the terms of the offering (often in table form), and all "legends" required by federal and state laws. The cover page should be followed by a *summary of the offering*, which serves as an integral part of the introductory materials, and as a cross-reference point for the reader. The third and final parts of the introductory materials are usually a *statement of the investor suitability standards*, which includes a discussion of the federal and state securities laws applicable to the offering, and the *definitions of an accredited investor* as applied to the offering.

- **Description of the company** is obviously a statement of the company's history (as well as its affiliates and predecessors) and should include a discussion of its principal officers and directors; products and services; management and operating policies; performance history and goals; competition; trends in the industry; advertising and marketing strategy; suppliers and distributors; intellectual property rights; key real and personal property; customer demographics; and any other material information that would be relevant to the investor.

- **Risk factors** is usually the most difficult section to write, yet it's viewed by many as one of the most important to the prospective investor. Its purpose is to outline all the factors that make the offering or the projected business plans risky or speculative. Naturally, the exact risks posed to the investors by the offering will depend on the nature of the company and the trends within that industry.

- **Capitalization of the issuer** should discuss the capital structure of the company both before and after the offering. For the purposes of this section in the PPM, all authorized and outstanding securities must be disclosed (including all long-term debt).

- **Management of the company** should include: a list of the names, ages, special skills or characteristics, and biographical information on each officer, director or key consultant; compensation and stock option arrangements; bonus plans; special contracts or arrangements; and any transactions between the company and individual officers and directors (including loans, self-dealing, and related types of transactions). The role and identity of the company's legal and accounting firms should also be disclosed, as well as any other "expert" retained in connection with the offering.

- **Terms of the offering** should describe the terms and conditions, the number of shares, and the price. If the securities are to be offered through underwriters, brokers, or dealers (to the extent permitted by federal and state laws), then the names of each "distributor" must be disclosed, as well as (1) the terms and nature of the relationship between the issuer and each party; (2) the commissions to be paid; (3) the obligations of the distributor (e.g., guaranteed or best efforts offering); and (4) any special rights, such as the right of a particular underwriter to serve on the board of directors, and any indemnification provisions or other material terms of the offering. *Note:* **The terms and structure of the offering should be based on a series of preliminary and informal meetings with possible investors (without those discussions qualifying as a formal "offer," as that term is defined by the securities laws), as well as research on current market conditions, and recently closed similarly situated offerings.**

- **Allocation of proceeds** must state the principal purposes for which the net proceeds will be used, and the approximate amount intended to be used for each purpose. You should give careful thought to this section because any material deviation from the use of funds as described in the PPM could trigger liability. If no exact breakdown has been prepared, then try to describe why additional capital is being raised, and what business objectives are expected to be pursued with the proceeds.

- **Dilution** should include a discussion of the number of shares outstanding prior to the offering, the price paid, the net book value, and the effect on existing shareholders of the proposed offering, as well as dilutive effects on new purchasers at the completion of the offering. Often the founding shareholders (and sometimes their key advisors, or the people who will help promote the PPM) will have acquired their securities at prices substantially below those in the prospective offering. As a result, the book value of shares purchased by prospective purchasers pursuant to the offering will be substantially diluted.

- **Description of securities** should explain the rights, restrictions, and special features of the securities being offered, and any applicable provision of the articles of incorporation or by-laws that affect its capitalization (such as preemptive rights, total authorized stock, different classes of shares or restrictions on declaration, and distribution of dividends).

- **Financial statements** to be provided by the issuer will vary, depending on the amount of money to be raised, applicable federal and state regulations, and the company's nature and stage of growth. Provide a discussion and explanation of these financial statements, and an analysis of its current and projected financial condition.
- **Exhibits** such as the articles of incorporation and by-laws, key contracts or leases, brochures, news articles, marketing reports, and résumés of the principals may be appended as exhibits to the PPM. These documents will generally be examined by attorneys and accountants during the due diligence process.

Subscription Materials

Once the prospective investors and their advisors have made a decision to provide capital to the company, in accordance with the terms of the PPM, there are a series of documents that must be signed as evidence of the investors' desire to "subscribe" to purchase the securities offered by the PPM. There are two key documents of this type, which are known as subscription materials:

- **Offeree and/or purchaser questionnaire** is developed in order to obtain certain information from prospective offerees, and then serves as evidence of their required sophistication level, and their ability to fend for themselves as required in a PPM. You may also wish to attempt to obtain information regarding the prospective purchaser's background, citizenship, education, employment, and investment and/or business experience.
- **Subscription agreement** is the contract between the purchaser (investor) and the issuer for the purchase of the securities. It should, therefore, contain acknowledgments of
  1. the receipt and review by the purchaser of the information given about the offering and the issuer;

2. the restricted nature of the securities to be acquired, and that the securities were acquired under an exemption from registration;

3. any particularly significant suitability requirements (such as amount of investment or passive income, tax bracket, and so forth) that the issuer feels may be crucial to the purchaser's ability to obtain the benefits of the proposed investment;

4. an awareness of specific risks disclosed in the information furnished; and

5. the status of the purchaser representative (if one is used).

The Subscription Agreement should also contain a reconfirmation by the purchaser of the accuracy and completeness of the information contained in the offeree, or purchaser, questionnaire; the number and price of the securities to be purchased and the manner of payment; and agreement to any special elections that may be contemplated (such as "S" corporation elections, accounting methods, and any relevant tax elections). The Subscription Agreement often contains an agreement on the part of the purchaser to indemnify the issuer against losses or liabilities, resulting from any misrepresentations on the part of the prospective purchaser, that would void or destroy the exemption from registration that the issuer is attempting to invoke. The Subscription Agreement should also contain representations on the part of the purchaser with respect to its authority to execute the agreement.

NEGOTIATING VENTURE CAPITAL TRANSACTIONS

The term "venture capital" has been defined in many ways, but refers generally to relatively high-risk, early-stage financing of young emerging-growth companies. The professional venture capitalist is usually a highly trained finance professional who manages a pool of venture funds for investment in growing companies on behalf of a group of passive investors.

Owners and managers of growing companies often have mixed views toward the institutional venture capital industry. On one hand, they welcome the money and management support they desperately need for growth, but fear the loss of control and various restrictions that are typically placed on the company by the investment documents. In order to achieve the delicate balance between the needs of the venture capitalist and the needs of the company, business owners and managers must understand the process of obtaining venture capital financing.

Three Types of Venture Capitalists

In general, there are three types of traditional institutional pools of venture capital, though in recent years the lines between the three have started to blur. These include:

1. **Public and private international venture capital firms.** These firms are typically organized as limited partnerships that seek capital from venture investors, trusts, pension funds, and insurance companies, among others. They, in turn, manage and invest in high-growth companies. Venture capital firms tend to specialize in particular niches, either by the business's *industry, territory,* or *stage of development.* Their investors expect a certain success rate and return on investment (ROI), which is critical to the firm's future ability to attract additional capital and track record.

2. **SBIC/MESBIC.** The Small Business Investment Act, enacted in 1958, established a national program for licensing privately owned small business investment companies (SBIC). Minority-Enterprise SBICs were added by a 1972 amendment to the act. Although the SBIC program has experienced some difficulty, it currently remains an integral part of the organized venture capital community. The program allows the SBA to grant licenses to certain types of venture capital firms that are eligible to borrow money from the federal government at very attractive rates, in exchange for certain restrictions on deal structures, as well as the types of businesses to which the SBIC can provide capital.

3. **Corporate venture capital divisions.** These include venture capital divisions of large corporations such as Intel, Nokia, and Motorola, usually established in hopes of funding small companies that have technology or resources that larger companies want or need. The investment is often structured more like a quasi-joint venture, because corporate venture capital often brings more to the

table than just money, such as access to the resources of these large companies. Corporate venture capital efforts typically revolve around the corporation's goals to incubate future acquisitions; gain access to new technologies; obtain intellectual property licenses; provide work for unused capacity; inspire technology and entrepreneur thinking in current corporate staff; find usages for excess cash; and break into new markets.

The Importance of Preparation

Preparation is the key to obtaining an initial meeting with the institutional venture capitalist. There are three central components to the preparation process: business and strategic planning; effective networking; and research.

A well-written business plan and financing proposal is a necessary prerequisite to serious consideration by any sophisticated source of capital. Effective networking means using professional advisors, commercial lenders, investment bankers, and consultants who may be able to assist you in getting the business plan into the hands of the appropriate venture capitalists. Institutional sources of capital are often flooded with unsolicited, "nonintroduced" plans that are likely to end up in a wastebasket instead of before an investment committee. Remember that the average venture capital firm will see thousands of business plans per year, make a return phone call to only a few dozen candidates, and may actually close only four to six deals per annum, so you need to find ways to increase your chance of survival, as the field of choices rapidly narrows. Finally, most venture capitalists have certain investment preferences regarding which companies they will include in their investment portfolio. These preferences may be based on the nature of the company's products and services, geographic location, projected rates of return, stage of development, or amount of capital required. Rather than waste precious resources by blindly sending business plans to any and all venture capitalists in your region, take the time to research the venture capital industry to match the characteristics of the proposed investment with the investment criteria of the targeted firm.

If your business plan submission survives the rigid initial review of most institutional venture capital firms, then the key to your first meeting and success thereafter is MORE PREPARATION. Keep in mind the following points:

Have a dress rehearsal. You need to rehearse your presentation many times, using a "moot court." This involves giving your presentation to different audiences who ask different questions. Make sure your rehearsal audiences (such as lawyers, accountants, business school professors, and entrepreneurs who have raised venture capital) have the background and the training to ask the right questions (including the tough ones), and are able to critically evaluate your responses. Do your homework on the venture capital firm and learn what their "hot buttons" may be so that you can address key issues in your presentation. As the saying goes, "You never get a second chance to make a first impression." The rehearsals will help you survive the first meeting and get to the next steps. Be prepared for the tough questions, and don't be scared, intimidated, or upset when the really hard ones start flying at you. If the venture capital firm's team doesn't ask tough questions, then they are not engaged with your presentation. If they are not engaged enough to beat you up a little, then there will probably be no next steps and no deal.

Have a mentor. It's always helpful to have a venture capitalist coach or mentor who has himself either raised venture capital, or been an advisor on—or negotiated—venture capital transactions. The mentor or coach can help you stay focused on the issues that are important to the venture capitalists so you do not waste their time. The mentor can reassure you during the difficult and time-consuming process, and teach you to remain patient, optimistic, and levelheaded about the risks and challenges that you face.

Have a detailed game plan. Prepare a specific presentation that isn't too long or too short (usually 15 minutes is about right). Don't attempt to "read" every word of your business plan or put every historical fact of your company on a PowerPoint slide. Keep it crisp and focused, and be prepared for questions, and to defend your key strategic assumptions and financial forecasts. Remember that every minute counts. Even the small talk at the beginning of the meeting is important because the seasoned venture capitalist is sizing you up, learning about your interests, and looking for the chemistry and the glue that is key to a successful relationship.

Have your team available to meet the venture capitalist. Don't overlook the "personal" component of the evaluation. In many cases, it can be the most important factor considered in the final decision. The four Cs—camaraderie, communication, commitment, and control (over your ego)—may make or break the outcome of the meeting. Any experienced venture capitalist will tell you that, at the end of the day, the decision depends on the strength of the people who will be there day-to-day to execute and manage the future of the company. The venture capitalist will look for a management team that's educated, dedicated, and experienced (and ideally has experienced some success *as a team* prior to this venture). The team should also be balanced, with each member's skills and talents complementing each other so that all critical areas of business management are covered—from finance, to marketing and sales, to technical expertise.

Have passion but don't wear rose-colored glasses. Many entrepreneurs fail to make a good impression in their initial meeting with the venture capitalist because they come on too strong or not strong enough. The experienced venture capitalist wants to see that you have a passion for—and commitment to—your company, and to the execution of the business plan. However, he or she does not want to be oversold, or have to deal with an entrepreneur who is so enamored with an idea or plan that he or she can't grasp its flaws, or understand its risks.

Have a way to demonstrate your personal commitment to the project. All venture capitalists will look to measure your personal sense of commitment to the business and its future. Generally, venture capitalists won't invest in entrepreneurs whose commitment to the business is only part-time, or when their loyalty is divided among other activities or ventures. In addition to fidelity to the venture, the investor will look for a high energy level, a commitment to achievement and leadership, self-confidence, and a creative approach to problem solving. You will also have to demonstrate your personal financial commitment by investing virtually all of your own resources into a project before you can ask others to part with their resources. Remember, any aspect of your personal life, whether it's good, bad, or seemingly irrelevant, may be of interest to the venture capitalist in the interview and due diligence process. Don't get defensive or be surprised when the range of questions is as broad as it is

---

How the Venture Capitalist Interprets Your Presentation

WHAT YOU SAY:	WHAT YOU MEAN:
Product is 90 percent complete	We've got a name for it
Leading-edge technology	We can't make it work
Limited downside	Things can't get much worse
Possibility of shortfall	We're 50 percent below plan
Proven technology	It nearly worked once before
We're repositioning the company	We're lost
Upside potential	It stopped breathing

---

deep—venture capitalists are merely trying to predict the future by learning as much as possible about your past and current situation.

Have an open and honest exchange of information. One sure deal killer for venture-capital firms is if you try to hide something from your past or downplay a previous business failure. A seasoned venture capitalist can, and will, learn about any skeletons in your closet during the due diligence process, and will walk away from the deal if they find something that should have been disclosed to them at the outset. A candid, straightforward channel of communication is critical. A previous business failure may be viewed as a sign of experience, provided that you can demonstrate that you've learned from your mistakes and figured out ways to avoid them in the future. On a related note, you must demonstrate a certain degree of flexibility and versatility in your approach to implementing your business plan. The venture capitalists may have suggestions on the strategic direction of the company, and will want to see that you are open-minded and receptive to their suggestions. If you're too rigid or too stubborn, they may view this as a sign of immaturity, or that you're a person with whom compromise will be difficult down the road. Either one of these can be a major deal "turnoff" and a good excuse to walk away.

Have a big market and a big upside. Make sure your business plan and your presentation adequately demonstrate the size of your potential market(s) and the financial rewards and healthy margins that strong demand will bring to the bottom line. A venture capitalist who suspects that your product or service has a narrow market, limited demand, and thin margins will almost always walk away from the deal. If your target market is too mature with established competitors, then the venture capitalist may feel the opportunity is too limited and will not produce the financial returns that they expect. They're looking for a company that has a *sustainable competitive advantage,* demonstrated by a balanced mix of products and services that meet a *new* market need on both a domestic and overseas basis. Remember that most venture capitalists want a 60 to 80 percent return for seed and early-stage or post-launch deals, and at least a 25 to 35 percent return on latter-stage and mezzanine level investments. When the S&P 500 offers 30 percent returns, and when the average investor can double his or her money with investments in lower-risk companies like General Electric and Intel, then your business plan and presentation had better demonstrate that the venture capitalists' money will be better served in your company.

Have an understanding of what really motivates the venture capitalist's decision. David Gladstone, a seasoned venture capitalist and author of the *Venture Capital Handbook,* writes: "I'll back you if you have a good idea that will make money for both of us." That one sentence captures the essence of the venture capitalist's decision-making process. You must have a *good idea*—one that's articulated in a business plan that truly expresses the risks and opportunities, and how your management team will influence the odds of success and survival. But then, it must make money for *both* of you. The venture capitalist wants deals in which both the investors *and* the entrepreneurs can enjoy the upside, and the scale is not weighted in favor of one over the other. Finally, the *I'll back you* component reminds you that in exchange for capital and wisdom, the venture capitalists expect to have some controls and "checks and balances" built into the structure of the deal, the governance of the company, and documented protection to ensure that their investment and ability to participate in the growth and success of the company are protected.

Have an exit strategy. The saying "Begin with the end in mind" clearly applies to venture capital deals. Investors aren't looking for a long-term marriage; they will be very focused on how you intend to get their original investment and return on capital back to them within four to six years. Your business plan and oral presentation should include an analysis and an assessment of the likelihood of the three most common exit strategies, namely: an initial public offering, a sale of the company, and a redemption of the venture capitalists' shares of the company by the company directly. Other exit strategies include: restructuring the company, licensing the company's intellectual property, finding a replacement investor, or even liquidating the company.

Central Components of the Venture Capitalist's Investment Decision

Regardless of a company's stage of development, primary products and services, or geographic location, there are several variables that all venture capital firms will consider in analyzing any business plan presented for investment. The presence or absence of these variables will ultimately determine whether they will commit capital to the project. These variables generally fall into four categories: management team, products and services, markets, and return on investment. Your team must be prepared to answer the following questions:

Management team.
- What is the background, knowledge, skills, and abilities of each member of the management team?
- How is this experience relevant to the proposed business plan or project?
- How are risks and problems identified, managed, and eliminated by the members of the management team?
- To what extent does each member of the management team exhibit certain entrepreneurial personality traits, such as self-confidence, leadership skills, tenacity, drive, and unbounded energy?

Products and services.
- At what stage of development are your products and services? What is the specific opportunity that you have identified? How

long will this "window of opportunity" remain open? What steps are necessary for you to exploit this opportunity?

- To what extent are your products and services unique, innovative, and proprietary? What steps have you taken to protect these proprietary features?
- To what extent do you control the means of production of the products and services, or is it dependent on a key supplier or licensor?
- To what extent do your products or services represent a "technological breakthrough," or are the products and services more "low-tech," with less risk of obsolescence?

Markets.

- What is the stage in the life cycle of the industry in which the company plans to operate?
- What is the size and projected growth rate of your targeted market?
- What marketing, sales, and distribution methods will you use to bring your products and services to the marketplace?
- What are the strengths and weaknesses of each of your direct, indirect, and anticipated competitors?
- Will the development of your products and services create new markets? If yes, what are the barriers to entry in these markets?
- What are the characteristics of the typical consumer of the company's products and services? What has consumer reaction been thus far?

Return on investment.

- What is your current and projected valuation and performance in terms of sales, earnings, and dividends? To what extent have you substantiated these budgets and projections? Have you over- or underestimated the amount of capital you'll require?
- How much money and time have you—and your managers—already invested? How much more time and money are you willing to commit before realizing a return on your own personal investments? How well are you managing your current assets and resources?
- How much capital will you require both currently and as projected, in order to bring your business plans to fruition? Could this capital be invested in stages tied to the performance of the company, or is the capital required all at once? What types of securities

are being offered? To what extent will additional dilution be necessary to meet these growth objectives?

- What is the projected return on the proposed investment? How will this projected return be affected if you fail to meet your business plans or financial projections? What rights, remedies, and exit strategies will be available to us as investors if problems arise?

Naturally, you should answer all these questions in the business plan you and your advisors have prepared because the plan will be further explored in any initial and subsequent meetings that you may have with the venture capitalist. There are also certain *negative* factors that you should avoid at all costs because they often disqualify what might otherwise be a workable deal. These factors include:

- Unqualified family members filling key management positions
- Projections that provide for excessive management salaries, company cars, and other unnecessary executive benefits
- An unwillingness to provide a personal guaranty for debt financing
- Incomplete, or overly slick, business plans
- Business plans that project overly optimistic or unrealistic goals and objectives

Negotiating and Structuring the Venture Capital Investment

Negotiating and structuring most venture capital transactions depends less on "industry standards," "legal boilerplate," or "structural rules-of-thumb," and more on striking a balance between your needs and concerns and the venture capitalist's investment criteria. Negotiations regarding the *structure* of the transaction will usually revolve around the types of securities involved and the principal terms of the securities. The type of securities ultimately selected and the structure of the transaction will usually fall into one of the following categories:

- **Preferred stock.** This is the most typical form of security issued in connection with a venture capital financing of an emerging growth company. This is because of the many advantages that preferred stock offers an investor—it can be converted into common stock, and it has dividend and liquidation preference over common stock. It also has antidilution protection, mandatory or optional redemption schedules, and special voting rights and preferences.

- **Convertible debentures.** This is basically a debt instrument (secured or unsecured) that may be converted into equity upon specified terms and conditions. Until converted, it offers the investor a fixed rate of return, and offers tax advantages (for example, deductibility of interest payments) to the company. A venture capital company will often prefer this type of security for higher-risk transactions because they'd prefer to enjoy the position of a creditor until the risk is mitigated, *or* in connection with bridge financing, whereby the venture capitalist expects to convert the debt to equity when additional capital is raised. Finally, if the debentures are subordinated—commercial lenders will often treat them as equity on the balance sheet—it enables the company to obtain institutional debt financing.

- **Debt securities with warrants.** A venture capitalist will generally prefer debentures or notes in connection with warrants often for the same reasons that convertible debt is used: namely, the ability to protect downside by being a creditor, and the ability to protect upside by including warrants to purchase common stock at favorable prices and terms. A warrant enables the investor to buy common stock without sacrificing the preferred position of a creditor, as would be the case if only convertible debt was used in the financing.

- **Common stock.** Rarely do venture capitalists initially choose to purchase common stock from a company, especially at early stages of its development. Straight common stock offers the investor no special rights or preferences, no fixed return on investment, no special ability to exercise control over management, and no liquidity to protect against downside risks. One of the few times that common stock *might* be selected would be if you wish to preserve your Subchapter S status under the Internal Revenue Code, which would be jeopardized if you authorized a class of preferred stock. Finally, you should be aware that common stock investments by venture capitalists could create "phantom income." This would have adverse tax consequences for employees if stock is subsequently issued to them at a cost lower than the price per share paid by the venture capital company.

Once you and the venture capitalist have selected the type of security you'll use, you must take steps to ensure that the authorization and issuance of the security is properly carried out under applicable state laws. For example, let's say that your corporate charter doesn't currently provide for a class of preferred stock. You must then prepare articles of amendment, get them approved by your board of directors and shareholders, and file them with the appropriate state corporation authorities.

The nature and scope of the various rights, preferences, and privileges that will be granted to the holders of the newly authorized preferred stock will be the focus of negotiation between you and the venture capitalist. Specifically, the terms and conditions of the voting rights, dividend rates and preferences, mandatory redemption provisions, conversion features, liquidation preferences, and the antidilution provisions (sometimes referred to as "ratchet clauses") are likely to be hotly contested. In addition, if any portion of the financing from the venture capitalist includes convertible debentures, then negotiations will also focus on term, interest rate, and payment schedule, conversion rights and rates, extent of subordination, remedies for default, acceleration and prepayment rights, and underlying security for the instrument.

UNDERSTANDING THE BASICS OF AN INITIAL PUBLIC OFFERING (IPO)

An initial public offering (IPO) is the legal process whereby a company initially registers its securities with the Securities and Exchange Commission (SEC) for sale to the general investing public. Many entrepreneurs view the process of "going public" as the epitome of financial success and reward, and it can be a critical crossroad and milestone for a company following a rapid growth path. The decision to go public, however, requires considerable strategic planning and analysis from both a legal and business perspective. The planning and analysis process involves weighing the costs and benefits, understanding the process and costs, and understanding the obligations of the company, its advisors, and shareholders once the company has successfully completed its public offering, including the obligations under Sarbanes-Oxley discussed in Chapter 4.

For the rapidly expanding privately held company, the process of going public represents a number of benefits, including:

- Significantly greater access to capital
- Increased liquidity for the shares
- Market prestige
- Enhancement of public image
- Flexibility for employee ownership and participation
- Improved opportunities for mergers, acquisitions, and further rounds of financing
- An immediate increase in the wealth for the founders and current stockholders

However, the downside of being a public company must be strongly considered in the strategic planning process. Among these costs are:

- Dilution in the founders' and current stockholders' control of the entity
- Pressure to meet market and shareholder expectations regarding growth and dividends
- Changes in management styles and employee expectations
- Compliance with complex regulations imposed by federal and state securities laws
- Stock resale restrictions for company insiders
- Vulnerability to shifts in the stock market
- Sharing the company's financial success with hundreds, even thousands of other shareholders

Hidden Expenses of Going Public

In addition to some of the more obvious business costs, the most expensive aspect of registering the securities is often the hidden costs that are imposed by federal and state securities laws. The rules and regulations imposed by the SEC make going public a time-consuming and expensive process that, in reality, begins several years before the public offering, and continues (through the SEC periodic reporting process) for as long as the company remains public. From a legal perspective, the following costs and factors should strongly be considered:

Planning and preparing the business for the IPO. From the day that the company is formed, there are a host of legal and structural pitfalls that must be avoided if an IPO is in your company's future. Some of these pitfalls, if not avoided early on, will serve as a significant impediment to a successful IPO, and will be expensive to remedy once the damage has been done. In addition, being a public company will require a more formal management style from a legal perspective that normally entails more regular meetings of the board of directors, and that all formalities imposed by state corporate laws be followed. From a systems, controls, leadership, and governance perspective, it is best to operate the company as if it were public right from the start.

Due diligence and housecleaning. Many owners (and their managers) who take their companies public complain that they feel as though "their company and personal lives are conducted in a fishbowl." Federal and state securities laws dictate that a prospective investor must have access to all material information about the company offering its securities to the public. As a result, *well before* you are ready to file a registration statement with the SEC, you must go through the due diligence process. The corporate charters, bylaws, shareholder agreements, employment agreements, leases, licenses, accounting methods, and related documents and procedures may need to be formalized, amended, or even terminated before you're ready to operate in the "public fishbowl."

The registration process. The time, effort, and expense required to prepare the registration statement should not be underestimated. In fact, the 6- to 12-month time frame and the out-of-pocket expenses alone make the cost a prohibitive capital formation strategy for many growing businesses. Although costs will vary depending on a number of factors, a company planning to offer its securities to the public should be prepared to spend anywhere from $300,000 to $500,000 (and above) in legal and accounting fees, appraisal costs, printing expenses, consulting, and filing fees. This amount does not include the underwriters and broker commissions that many run as high as 10 percent or more of the total offering. As discussed later in this chapter, however, the SEC has implemented new regulations for small business owners that will create cost savings in legal and accounting fees. You must remember, however, that few, if any, of these costs will be contingent on the success of the offering and, therefore, must be paid regardless of how few, or how many, shares are actually sold.

In addition to the registration statement, exhibits and attachments that document major business transactions (such as plans of acquisition, reorganization, liquidation, etc.), customer and vendor arrangements, and financial statements must be filed *prior* to the offering. These required disclosures will result in a loss of confidentiality that may be costly, especially as competitors, creditors, labor unions, suppliers, and others will have access to these documents once they become available to the public.

Periodic reporting and ongoing compliance. Most public companies are subject to the ongoing periodic reporting requirements imposed by the SEC, such as quarterly financial reporting (Forms 10-Q and 10-QSB), annual financial reporting (Forms 10-K and 10-KSB), reporting of current material events (Form 8-K), and related reporting requirements, such as those for sale of control stock and tender offers. The ongoing costs of being a public company also include an increased use of attorneys, accountants, and other advisors; a dedication of staff time to meet with securities analysts and financial press; the implementation of a shareholder and media relations program; and the significantly greater cost of annual reports, shareholder meetings, and solicitations of proxies when shareholder approval is needed for major corporate transactions.

Preparing for the Underwriter's Due Diligence

Prior to preparing the registration statement, the proposed underwriter and their financial analysts and attorneys will conduct extensive due diligence on the company to ensure the viability of the offering. The due diligence process means the growing company's corporate records, personnel, business plans, industry trends, customer data, pricing and business models, products, key agreements, and financial data will be viewed under a microscope. You should begin preparing for the due diligence process well in advance to avoid the significant expenses incurred by being unprepared, or the embarrassing situations encountered when factual or strategic weaknesses or problems are unexpectedly revealed. *Remember* that the underwriter's legal counsel will be looking for any problems that may be impediments to the offering, such as excessive compensation or expenses, a weak management team, nepotism, problems with the company's underlying intellectual property or business model, and so on. The sooner these problems are addressed, the better. The best way to begin the preparation process is to have the company's counsel conduct a legal audit, as discussed in Chapter 6.

In a legal audit, the company's management team meets with corporate counsel in order to: (1) discuss strategic plans and objectives; (2) review key documents and records; and (3) analyze and identify current and projected problem areas that may be identified by the underwriter's team. In the context of preparing for an IPO, the key goal of the legal audit is to identify and solve these problems well in advance of the first meeting with the underwriting team. The legal audit also lays the groundwork for an ongoing legal compliance and prevention program that will ensure that the company's goals, structure, and ongoing operations are consistent with the latest developments in business and corporate law. Finally, the legal audit helps managers identify the legal issues that are triggered by changes in strategies, goals, or objectives, and allows managers to plan for the legal tasks that must be accomplished as a result of the issues identified.

Additional Preparation Tips

In addition to the legal audit, you should immediately plan, adopt, and implement a more clearly defined management structure that will include formal board meetings on a monthly or quarterly basis. In addition to maintaining complete and accurate corporate minutes and resolutions, and preparing periodic reports to existing shareholders, the company should begin recruiting an experienced and independent board of directors who will be acceptable to the investing public. You should begin acting like you are already a publicly traded company from a management, record keeping, shareholder reporting, and financial controls perspective well before your first meeting with an underwriter. Demonstrating the discipline that it takes to put these practices in place while still privately held will expedite the process, and will likely enhance your valuation, and your attractiveness, to prospective underwriters.

Deal Breakers to Avoid

Here are a few items that will have a negative effect on the company's valuation and the underwriter's willingness to participate in the public offering:

- Inefficient management structure or major holes in the management team
- Unprofitable business model or weak revenue base
- Overly restrictive shareholder agreements that affect the company's control
- Operating in a market with low barriers to entry
- Self-dealing among the board of directors and key stockholders
- Weaknesses in the company's key intangible assets, such as brand or operating technology
- Inadequate corporate records
- Capital structure with excessive debt
- Series of unaudited and uncertain financial statements
- Poor earnings history

The Mechanics of a Public Offering

After the company has taken all the necessary preparation steps to conduct an IPO, and has made its selection of the lead underwriter, an organizational meeting must be scheduled with all the key members of the registration team (attorneys, accountants, lead underwriter, chief executive officer, chief financial officer, etc.). The focus of the organizational meeting will be to establish a timetable for the preparation of the registration statement, and a delegation of the initial responsibilities for preparing the first draft. Several preliminary tasks must also be completed in connection with the preparation of the registration statement, such as:

- Dealing with the underwriter's counsel, due diligence concerns, and questions
- Meetings of the board of directors to authorize the offering
- Preparation and completion of the confidential questionnaire for the officers and directors

- Legal research as to compliance with applicable state blue sky laws
- NASD Regulations (the National Association of Securities Dealers is a self-regulatory body that reviews the underwriting and distribution agreements prepared in connection with the public offering, in order to ensure that the terms and conditions are consistent with industry practices)
- Establishment of marketing and distribution strategies, including planning and preparing for the meetings around the country, or even the world, with large institutional investors and other brokers, otherwise known as the Road Show

Choosing a Disclosure Format

The registration statement consists of two distinct parts: the *offering prospectus* (used to assist underwriters and investors in analyzing the company and the securities being offered), and the *exhibits and additional information* (provided directly to the SEC as part of the disclosure and registration regulations). The registration statement is part of the public record, and is available for public inspection.

There are a variety of alternatives to the registration statement. The appropriate alternative depends on the company's history and the size and nature of the specific offering. The most common form used is the Form S-1. The S-1, however, is complicated, as it has several requirements that must be fulfilled *before* going public. The S-1 requires the description of the company's business, properties, and material transactions between the company and its officers, pending legal proceedings, plans for distribution of the securities, and the intended use of the proceeds from the IPO. However, the Forms S-2 and S-3 (subject to certain requirements) are available for companies that are already subject to the reporting requirements of the Securities Exchange Act of 1934 (the Exchange Act). Form S-4 is limited to corporate combinations including mergers, reorganizations, and consolidations. The S-1 through S-4 forms are filed and processed by the Division of Corporate Finance at the SEC's headquarters in Washington, DC.

The SEC's "Small Business Initiatives"

In 1992, the SEC implemented the Small Business Initiatives (SBIs), significantly modifying its special provisions for offerings by small businesses (Regulation S-B) not already subject to the reporting requirements of the Exchange Act. SBIs were designed to streamline the federal registration process in connection with IPOs to encourage investment in small businesses. A "small business issuer" (as defined in Rule 405 of the Securities Act of 1933) is a company meeting all of the following criteria:

- Revenue of less than $25 million
- U.S. or Canadian issuer
- Not an investment company
- If a majority-owned subsidiary, parent corporation also a small business issuer

Small business issuers can use the Forms SB-1 or SB-2 to register their securities to be sold for cash with the SEC. The SB-1 can *only* be used to register up to $10 million of securities to be sold for cash (the old predecessor S-18 had a ceiling of $7.5 million). Also, the company must not have registered more than $10 million in any continuous 12-month period (including the transaction being registered). In addition, it allows for financial statements (which must be audited by an independent party) that are in accordance with generally accepted accounting principles (commonly referred to as GAAP), and not the detailed requirements of the SEC.

The SB-2 (this predecessor to the S-1 was the form typically used by small businesses prior to 1992) allows small business issuers to offer an unlimited dollar amount of securities, therefore allowing companies that meet the SEC's definition of a small business to sell more securities without having to undergo the same extensive disclosure process of larger companies. The advantages to using the SB-2, in addition to those afforded by using the SB-1, include: (1) repeated use; (2) location of completed forms in a central depository; (3) allowing the filing with either the SEC's regional offices or headquarters in Washington, DC. These advantages have translated into economic benefits. For example, the average cost of the legal and accounting fees for small businesses registering to make an IPO were previously in the range of $200,000 to $500,000, but now range from $75,000 to $150,000.

9

EFFECTIVE USE OF DEBT CAPITAL

No small or growing company survives and prospers without some debt component on its balance sheet. Whether it's a small loan from family or friends, or a sophisticated term loan and operating line of credit from a regional commercial lender, most companies borrow some amount of capital along their path to growth.

The use of debt in the capital structure (commonly known as leverage) will affect both your company's valuation and the overall cost of capital. The proper debt-to-equity ratio for your business will depend on a wide variety of factors:

- **The impact** that your obligation to make payments under the loan will have on the cash flow of your business
- **Your costs** relating to obtaining the capital
- **Your need for flexibility** in the capital structure so you can respond to changing economic or market conditions
- **Your access** to alternative sources of financing
- **The nature and extent** of your company's assets (tangible or intangible) that are available as collateral
- **The level of dilution** of ownership and control that your shareholders (and managers) are willing to tolerate

- **Certain tax considerations** (interest payments are a deductible expense, but dividends are not)

The maximum debt capacity that a growing company will ultimately be able to handle will usually be determined by balancing the costs and risks of defaulting on a loan against the owners' and managers' desire to maintain control. Many entrepreneurs want to maintain control over their company's affairs, so they'll accept the risk inherent in taking on additional debt. Your ability to make payments must be carefully considered in the company's financial projections.

Only a handful of fast-growing businesses use bank financing as fuel for growth. According to a June 2006 study by PricewaterhouseCoopers, among "trendsetter" companies (312 private firms who are among the fastest growing in the United States) only 12 percent of fast-growing firms obtained bank financing in the first quarter of 2006. This proportion has dropped from 2005, but it has remained fairly consistent (in the range of 10–13 percent) over the past few years. Lines of credit and self-financing are the most commonly used financing tools. The critical observation of the survey, however, is that fast-growing companies who use debt as part of their growth fuel, grew faster (32 percent) than the counterparts who did not leverage their balance sheet (20 percent), a differential of nearly 50 percent.

A key issue in debt financing is *timing*. It is critical to start the process of looking for debt capital early, and not wait until you are in a real cash-flow crunch, because you will lose your negotiating leverage and weaken your company's financial position—a major turnoff to most lenders.

If your business plan and cash-flow projections reveal that making loan payments will strain your company's financial condition (or that you don't have sufficient collateral), then you should explore equity alternatives. It's simply not worth driving your company into bankruptcy solely to maintain maximum ownership and control. Remember the saying, 60 percent of *something* is worth a whole lot more than 100 percent of *nothing*.

You should also compare the level of debt financing you are planning to obtain against the typical ratios for businesses in your industry (such as those published by Robert Morris Associates or Dun & Bradstreet). Once you've figured out your optimum debt-to-equity ratio, you can look into the sources of debt financing, and the business and legal issues involved in borrowing funds from a commercial lender.

THE BASICS OF COMMERCIAL LENDING

Traditional bank loans from commercial lenders are the most common source of capital for small growing companies. The frenzy of mergers and acquisitions by, and among, large regional banks has made it somewhat more difficult for small business borrowers to build relationships with a commercial loan officer, who may be more focused on the bigger borrowers and customers. As a result, entrepreneurs often turn to small neighborhood banks that may be more receptive to winning their business, but may offer a limited range of services and have smaller lending limitations.

Things may be changing rapidly, however, as larger banks seek to establish relationships with high-tech start-ups in hopes of getting in on the ground floor of a fast-growing company. Many large commercial lenders, such as Chase Manhattan, Wells Fargo (through its acquisition of Norwest, which has an active venture-capital subsidiary), and JPMorgan, have established or beefed up their early-stage venture-capital equity funds so that they can offer both debt and equity financing alternatives. This broader range of options creates the convenience of "one-stop shopping" for the qualified emerging-business borrower, who may also be receptive to an equity investment.

Important Questions to Ask When Seeking Debt Capital

- How large a loan do you need?
- How will you use the money?
- Why will this type of capital benefit your business?
- When can you pay it back?
- How will you pay it back?
- Why are you and your company a good credit risk?
- What if the business fails or you can't repay the loan?
- Are you growing too fast, or in a manner that will jeopardize your ability to repay?

UNDERSTANDING THE LENDER'S PERSPECTIVE

Before you look at the types of loans available from commercial banks, it is important to understand the perspective of the typical commercial loan officer when he or she analyzes a loan proposal. There's often a lot of confusion and resentment about the relationship between bankers and entrepreneurs. The entrepreneur believes the banker doesn't understand or appreciate his business requirements, while the loan officer may have had bad experiences with entrepreneurs who expect to borrow more than a million dollars (collateralized only by a dream), or the loan officer has had to foreclose on a small business.

Banks are in the business of selling money, and capital is the principal product in their inventory. Bankers, however, are often personally risk-averse, and have internal controls and regulatory restrictions affecting their risk tolerance. The bank's shareholders and board of directors expect loan officers to take all steps necessary to minimize the bank's risk in each transaction, and obtain the maximum protection against default. As a result, the types of loans available to growing companies, the terms and conditions, and the steps the bank takes to protect its interest, all have a direct relationship to the loan officer's assessment of risk.

The management team assigned to obtain debt financing from a commercial bank must embark on an immediate risk-mitigation management program to prepare for negotiating the loan documentation.

Preparing for Debt Financing

A company's ability to minimize and manage risk will always have a direct impact on the attractiveness and affordability of traditional debt financing. For a small and growing company, this will mean a loan proposal package that demonstrates the presence of a strong management team; an aggressive internal-control and accounts-receivable management program; financial statements and projections that demonstrate both the ability to meet your repayment obligations and solid relationships with suppliers, distributors, and employees; and an understanding of industry trends. In addition, many commercial loan officers will apply the test of the traditional four Cs of creditworthiness: *character* (reputation and honesty), *capacity* (business acumen and experience), *capital* (ability

Questions Bankers Ask Themselves When Evaluating Your Proposal

- Have you shown sound business judgment in the past? Have you always had a written plan with a timeline for specific business goals (accompanied by a backup contingency plan)?
- Have you gone to see your banker only when you were in a tight spot and needed immediate help, indicating a lack of planning?
- Do you inform the banker monthly of good news and bad (including steps taken to mitigate the effects of the bad)?
- Do you show your banker that you have proper financial controls in place?
- Do you discuss suppliers, pricing strategies, marketing plans, and sales results?
- Do you send customer mailings and samples of new products to your banker?
- Do you exhibit a clear understanding of your company's assets and liabilities, and the trends in your industry?
- Have you invited your banker to visit your business? Do you arrange for him or her to meet with your employees?
- Do you have a strong five-year strategic plan for your business? Is it updated in a timely manner and shared with your banker?
- Are you maintaining a strong growth plan for your business, including its involvement in community projects? Have you considered co-sponsoring community causes with your financial institution?
- Do you invite input from your banker as part of your future planning activities?
- Are you actively addressing safety and environmental concerns within your business?
- Are you seen as a strong community leader?

to meet debt-service payments), and *collateral* (access to assets that can be liquidated in the event of a default). Loan officers will assess all of these elements to determine your creditworthiness and the relative risk to the bank in making the proposed loan. Loan officers will also assess whether your company and proposal present an opportunity to build a long-term banking relationship, in which you will need additional services and larger loans down the road. Be sure to help the loan officer understand your long-term needs as well as your desire to build a relationship.

THE LOAN PROPOSAL

Although the exact elements of a loan package will vary depending on a company's size, industry, and stage of development, most lenders will want the following fundamental questions answered:

- Who are you?
- How much capital do you need, and when?
- How will the capital be allocated, and for what specific purposes?
- How will you service your debt obligations (application and processing fees, interest, principal, or balloon payments)?
- What protection (collateral) can you provide the bank in the event that you are unable to meet your obligations?

These questions are all designed to help the loan officer assess the risk factors in the proposed transaction. They are also designed to provide the loan officer with the information necessary to persuade the loan committee to approve the transaction. You must understand that the loan officer (once convinced of your creditworthiness) will serve as an advocate on your behalf in presenting the proposal to the bank's loan committee, and shepherding it through the bank's internal processing procedures. The loan documentation, terms, rates, and covenants that the loan committee will specify as conditions to making the loan will be directly related to how you demonstrate your ability to mitigate and manage risk, as described in your business plan and formal loan proposal.

The loan proposal should include the following categories of information, many of which you can borrow or modify from your business growth plan:

- **Summary of the request.** A brief overview of the company, the amount of capital needed, the proposed repayment terms, the intended use of the capital, and the collateral available to secure the loan.

- **Borrower's history.** A background of your company's history; its capital structure; its founders; its stage of development and plans for growth; a list of your customers, suppliers and service providers; management structure and philosophy; your main products and services; and an overview of any intellectual property you own or have developed.
- **Market data.** An overview of trends in your industry; the size of the market; your market share; an assessment of the competition; your sustainable competitive advantages; marketing, public relations, and advertising strategies; market research studies; and relevant future trends in your industry.
- **Financial information.** Multi-scenario financial statements (best case/expected case/worst case); federal and state tax returns; company valuations or appraisals of key assets; current balance sheet; credit references; and a two-year income statement. The role of the requested capital in your plans for growth, an allocation of the loan proceeds, and your ability to repay must be carefully explained and supported by a three-year projected cash-flow statement broken out in a monthly format.

The Most Common Reasons Loan Proposals Are Rejected

- Unrealistically low expense forecasts
- Incomplete loan proposal
- Inability to take constructive criticism
- Underestimated capital requirements
- Little or no experience in the business field
- Overstated revenue projections
- Attempts to play one lender against another
- Lack of adequate collateral
- Poor communication skills
- Cash-flow projections that do not demonstrate an ability to repay the loan
- Cash-flow projections without adequate supporting documentation
- Lack of understanding of the loan proposal and approval process

- **Schedules and exhibits.** As part of the loan proposal, you should also assemble certain key documents such as agreements with strategic vendors or customers, insurance policies, leases, and employment agreements to be attached as exhibits. Résumés of your company's principals, recent news articles about the company, a picture of your products or site, and an organizational chart should also be appended as exhibits to the loan proposal.

TYPES OF COMMERCIAL BANK LOANS

There are a number of types of loans available from a commercial bank, one or more of which could be tailored to meet your specific requirements. Loans are usually categorized by the term of the loan, the expected use of proceeds, and the amount of money to be borrowed. The availability of various loans will depend on both the nature of your industry and the bank's assessment of your creditworthiness. The types of loans traditionally available include:

1. **Short-term loans.** These are ordinarily used for a specific purpose with the expectation by the lender that the loan will be repaid at the end of the project. For example, a seasonal business may borrow capital in order to build up its inventory in preparation for the peak season; when the season ends, the lender expects to be repaid immediately. Similarly, a short-term loan could be used to cover a period when the company's customers or clients are in arrears; when the accounts receivable are collected, the loan is to be repaid.

   A short-term loan is usually made in the form of a promissory note payable on demand. It may be secured by the inventory or accounts receivable that the loan is designed to cover, or it may be unsecured (that is, no collateral is required). Unless a company is a start-up, or operates in a highly volatile industry (increasing the risk in the eyes of the lender), most short-term loans will be unsecured, thereby keeping the loan documentation and the bank's processing time and costs to a minimum.

   Lenders generally view short-term loans as "self-liquidating," in that they can be repaid by foreclosing on the current assets that the loan has financed. Because the bank's transactional costs are low, and it perceives a lower risk, short-term loans can be easier for a growing business to obtain. Short-term borrowing can also serve as an excellent means for establishing a relationship with a bank and demonstrating creditworthiness.

2. **Operating lines of credit.** Lines of credit consist of a specific amount of capital that is made available to a company on an "as needed" basis over a specified period of time. A line of credit may be short term (60 to 120 days) or intermediate term (one to three years), renewable or nonrenewable, and at a fixed or fluctuating rate of interest. Be especially careful to negotiate ceilings on interest rates; to avoid excessive processing, application, and related "up-front" fees (such as origination and commitment fees); and to ensure that repayment schedules won't present an undue strain. You should also ensure that your obligations to make payments against the line of credit are consistent with your anticipated cash-flow projections.

3. **Intermediate-term loans.** These loans are usually provided over a three- to five-year period for the purposes of acquiring equipment, fixtures, furniture, and supplies; expanding existing facilities; acquiring another business; or providing working capital. The loan is almost always secured, not only by the assets being purchased with the loan proceeds, but also with the company's other assets, such as inventory, accounts receivable, equipment, and real estate. This arrangement usually calls for a loan agreement that typically includes restrictive covenants that govern the company's operation and management during the term of the loan. The covenants are designed to protect the lender's interests and ensure that all payments are made on time, before any dividends, employee bonuses, or noncritical expenses are paid.

4. **Long-term loans.** These are generally extended for specific, highly secured transactions, such as the purchase of real estate or a multi-use business facility, in which case a lender will consider extending a long-term loan to a small company for 65 percent to 80 percent of the appraised value of the land or building. (As a general rule, commercial banks don't provide long-term financing to small businesses. The risk of market fluctuations and business fail-

ure over a 10- or 20-year term is simply too high for the commercial lender to feel comfortable.)

5. **Letters of credit.** These are issued by commercial banks, solely in connection with international sales transactions to expedite the shipping and payment process. In a typical letter-of-credit scenario, the seller demands that payment be made in the form of a letter of credit, and the buyer must then make arrangements with its bank to issue the letter of credit. The buyer's bank, often in conjunction with a corresponding bank, will then communicate with the seller of the goods, explaining the documents that it requires (such as a negotiable bill of lading) as a condition to releasing the funds.

   It is important to understand that the bank issuing the letter of credit may be liable to the seller for payment if the bill of lading and related documents are properly presented, *even if* there are problems in the performance of the underlying contract between the buyer and the seller. Any defenses available to the buyer relating to the underlying contract are generally not available to the bank issuing the letter of credit.

NEGOTIATING THE LOAN DOCUMENTS

Negotiating the financing documents requires a delicate balance between the lender's requirements and your needs. The lender will want to protect all of the rights and remedies that may be available to mitigate the risk of loan default, while you will want to minimize the level of control the lender exercises, and achieve a return on your assets that greatly exceeds your debt-service payments.

Before examining each document involved in a typical debt financing, you'll need to understand some general rules of loan negotiation:

1. **Interest rates.** These will generally be calculated in accordance with prevailing market rates, the degree of risk inherent in the proposed transaction, the extent of any preexisting relationship with the lender, and the cost of administering the loan.

2. **Collateral.** You may have to secure the loan by pledging assets that have a value equal to or greater than the proceeds of the loan. Under such circumstances, try to keep certain assets of the business outside the pledge agreement, so that they are available to serve as security in the event that you need more money later. Beyond the traditional forms of tangible assets that may be offered to the lender, also consider intangibles (such as assignment of lease rights, key-man insurance, or intellectual property) as candidates for collateral. Naturally, these assets could be very costly to a firm in the event of default, and should be pledged only when you're able to repay the loan easily.

3. **Restrictive covenants.** These provisions are designed to protect the lender's interests, and the typical loan agreement will contain several kinds.

   Affirmative covenants encompass your obligations (and your subsidiaries, except as otherwise provided) during the period that the loan is outstanding, and may obligate you to perform the following affirmative acts:

   - Furnish audited financial statements (income and expenses and balance sheets) at regular intervals (usually quarterly and annually with the annual statement to be prepared and certified by an independent certified public accountant)
   - Furnish copies of all financial statements, reports, and returns that are sent to shareholders or to governmental agencies
   - Provide access to your properties, books of accounts, and records
   - Keep and maintain proper books of accounts
   - Comply with all applicable laws, rules, and regulations
   - Maintain your corporate existence (as well as that of any subsidiaries) and all rights and privileges
   - Maintain all property in good order and repair
   - Maintain any agreed dollar amount of net worth (or any agreed ratio of current assets to current liabilities)
   - Keep and maintain proper and adequate insurance on all assets
   - Pay and discharge all indebtedness and all taxes as and when they are due
   - Purchase and pay premiums due on life insurance on named key personnel (wherein the company is named as beneficiary)

Negative covenants (generally negotiable) encompass certain actions for which you must obtain the lender's consent, and depend in large part on your company's financial strength and economic and operational requirements. You must obtain the lender's consent in order to:

- Engage in any business not related to your present business
- Create any mortgage, lien, or other security other than pending security on the property securing the loan
- Create any mortgage, lien, or other encumbrance, including conditional sales agreements, other title-retention agreements, and lease-purchase agreements on any property of the company or your subsidiaries (unless excepted)
- Incur any new indebtedness, except for trade credit or renewals, extensions, or refunding of any current indebtedness. Your right to incur indebtedness may be conditioned on compliance with a specified ratio (actual or pro forma) of pretax income to interest expense for a designated period
- Enter into leases of real or personal property as lessee, in excess of a specified aggregate amount. (Your right to make leases may be conditioned on compliance with a specified ratio—actual or pro forma—of pretax income to fixed charges for a designated period.)
- Purchase, redeem, or otherwise acquire (or retire for cash) any of the company's capital stock in excess of a specified amount, or for reserves set aside to redeem preferred stock
- Pay any cash dividends (with stated exceptions), such as those from after-tax earnings earned subsequent to a specified date or in excess of a specified amount
- Make loans or advances to, or investments in, any person or entity other than your subsidiaries
- Merge or consolidate with any other corporation, sell, or lease substantially all of your assets. There may be exceptions in cases where your company is the surviving corporation.
- Permit net worth or current assets to fall below a specified level
- Permit capital expenditures to exceed a specified amount (which may be on an annual basis, with or without right to cumulate)
- Permit officers' and directors' remuneration to exceed a specified level

- Sell or dispose of all the stock of a subsidiary (subject to permitted exceptions), or permit subsidiaries to incur debt (other than trade debt)

    Covenants may be serious impediments to your company's ability to grow and prosper over the long run. Review covenants carefully for consistency in relation to other corporate documents, such as your bylaws and shareholders' agreements. However, under the rapidly changing area of lender-liability law, some commercial bankers are backing away from the level of control that has traditionally been imposed on a borrower.

4. **Prepayment rights.** Regardless of the actual term of the loan, negotiate for the right to prepay the principal of the loan without penalty or special repayment charges. Many commercial lenders seek to attach prepayment charges that have a fixed rate of interest in order to ensure that a minimum rate of return is earned over the projected life of the loan.

5. **Hidden costs and fees.** These might include closing costs, processing fees, filing fees, late charges, attorneys' fees, out-of-pocket-expense reimbursement (courier, travel, photocopying, etc.), court costs, and auditing or inspection fees in connection with the loan. Another way commercial lenders earn extra money on a loan is to impose depository restrictions, such as a restrictive covenant to maintain a certain balance in your company's operating account, or to use the bank as a depository as a condition to closing on the loan.

UNDERSTANDING THE LEGAL DOCUMENTS

Anytime you borrow money, you have to sign documents delineating the terms of the loan—how much is being borrowed; what collateral you'll be using; what the lender's interest is; and your promise to repay the debt, including guarantees.

The Loan Agreement

The loan agreement sets forth all the terms and conditions of the transaction between you and the lender. The key provisions include the amount, term, repayment schedules and procedures, special fees, insurance requirements, special conditions to closing, restrictive covenants, the company's representations and warranties (with respect to status, capacity, ability to repay, title to properties, litigation, and so on), events of default, and remedies of the lender in the event of default. Your attorney and accountant should carefully review the provisions of the loan agreement and the implications of the covenants. They should also analyze the long-term legal and financial impact of the restrictive covenants. You should negotiate to establish a timetable under which certain covenants will be removed or modified as your ability to repay is clearly demonstrated.

The Security Agreement

The security agreement identifies the collateral you will pledge in order to secure the loan, usually referencing terms of the loan agreement, as well as the promissory note (especially with respect to restrictions on the use of the collateral and procedures upon default). The remedies available to the lender in the event of default range from selling the collateral at a public auction to taking possession of the collateral. The proceeds of any alternative chosen by the lender will be used principally to repay the outstanding balance of the loan.

The Financing Statement

The financing statement records the lender's interests in the collateral, and is filed with the state and local corporate and land-records authorities. It is designed to give notice to your company's other potential creditors that a security interest that will take precedence over any subsequent claim has been granted in the collateral specified in the financing statement. Specific rules regarding this document and the priority of competing creditors can be found in your state's version of the Uniform Commercial Code (UCC).

The Promissory Note

The promissory note serves as evidence of your obligation to the lender. Many of its terms are included in the more comprehensive loan agreement (such as the interest rate, the length of the term, the repayment schedule, your ability to prepay without penalty, the conditions under which the lender may declare default, and the rights and remedies available to the lender upon default).

The Guaranty

The guaranty, which you personally execute, serves as further security to mitigate the risk of the transaction to the lender. You and your legal counsel should carefully review and negotiate the conditions of the guaranty, especially with respect to its term, scope, rights of the lender in the event of default, and type of guaranty provided. For example, under certain circumstances, the lender can be forced to exhaust all possible remedies before proceeding against you, or may be prevented from proceeding against certain of your assets. Similarly, the extent of the guaranty can be negotiated so that it is reduced annually as the company grows stronger, and your company's ability to meet its repayment schedule becomes more evident.

Although bankers understand and acknowledge an entrepreneur's resistance to providing a personal guaranty, they will often seek this protection from the company's principals to further mitigate their risk. This is especially true if your business is highly leveraged, has operated for fewer than three years, or pays bonuses that absorb most of its profits. Why do lenders usually insist on these protections? The lender's primary goal is to influence management to treat the funds borrowed from the bank prudently. In essence, the guaranty is a psychological tool, designed to keep pressure on the principals of the company to ensure prompt and regular repayment.

PERIODIC ASSESSMENT OF BANKING RELATIONSHIPS

Recognizing the importance of growing businesses to the economy, many commercial lenders have begun to fiercely compete for the trade of smaller companies. In general, this has resulted in greater access to debt capital for growth companies, as well as more variety in services that banks offer. It is wise to periodically assess your banking relationship to ensure that you're getting the best rates and services available to businesses of your size within your industry. That doesn't mean that you should discard a long-standing and harmonious banking relationship over a one-percentage-point difference in an interest rate, but it does mean that you shouldn't remain loyal to a bank that doesn't offer a full range of services meeting your needs just because you've "banked there for years." In periodically assessing the relationship, ask yourself:

- When did you last hear from your designated loan officer?
- What was the bank's reaction to your most recent request for another term loan or an increase in your operating line of credit?
- How well does the bank know and understand your industry?
- How strict has the bank been in enforcing loan covenants, restrictions, or late charges?
- What support services has the bank offered you?
- How do the bank's interest rates and loan terms compare with those from other local commercial lenders?
- What is the bank's general reputation in the business community? Has it done anything lately to enhance or damage its reputation?
- Is the bank itself basically operating on a solid financial foundation?
- Is the bank large enough to grow with your financial needs as your business expands and you require additional capital? (This should be considered early on in the company's development so that the relationship is not outgrown just at the time when you need it the most.)
- Does this bank *really* want your company as a customer? What has it done for you lately to demonstrate this?

In this age of "relationship banking," bankers understand that if they are armed with a thorough understanding of your company's operations, they are in a better position to structure commercial loan arrangements capable of satisfying your needs. Conversely, banks unfamiliar with your business operations tend to become fair-weather lenders. This lack of understanding perpetuates the myth that bankers are willing to provide funding only when there is little need for it.

10

MERGERS AND ACQUISITIONS
AS GROWTH DRIVERS

Mergers and acquisitions are among the most effective ways to implement a rapid-growth plan quickly. There are now countless examples of companies in all industries, from Cisco to General Electric to Microsoft, that have grown at lightning speed in part due to a very aggressive merger and acquisition strategy. The total value of merger and acquisition activity is predicted to reach $1.3 trillion in the United States in 2006, and about the same for 2007.

Buyers of all shapes and sizes have many of the same strategic objectives—to build long-term shareholder value, and to take advantage of the synergies that the combined firms will create—yet many post-closing objectives fail to come to fruition. Examples of failed mergers include the AOL/Time Warner transaction, and many of the large telecommunications deals from 2001 to 2005. Despite these notable exceptions, mergers and acquisitions continue to be an important strategy for growth. Deals in the defense industry have been driven by the swelling defense and federal budgets attributed to the post–9/11 Department of Homeland Security, and the ongoing war in Iraq. Deregulation in the energy and financial services industries has just begun to spawn deals that are driven by the new ability to offer a more diversified range of services, such as the Citicorp-Travelers Group's $37.4 billion merger to create CitiGroup, or the Deutsche

Bank AG's takeover of BankersTrust Corp. for $10.1 billion. In telecommunications and media, AT&T Corp's $52.2 billion takeover of TCI was driven by the competition to find faster ways into more households that offer an integrated package of long-distance services, Internet access, and cable television. The trends toward consolidation, globalization, deregulation, strong and accessible capital markets, and rapid improvements in technology and communications during the battle for efficiency and synergy are likely to continue into the year 2007 and beyond. The mega-merger activity is also likely to trickle down toward the middle-market and smaller companies.

As mergers and acquisitions continue to be important growth drivers, it is important to understand the *process* of doing deals the right way. The merger and acquisition frenzy has created intense competition for the same target companies, placing a premium on price and speed. The fear in many boardrooms is that the company will be left out or left behind if it doesn't move quickly to make acquisitions, which has reduced the time taken to complete deals from months to a matter of days, especially if there are no regulatory approvals to obtain, or shareholder battles to fight. In this environment, deals are moving so fast and prices are being bid up so high, that the likelihood of problems and errors has increased dramatically. You need to be armed with as much knowledge, and as many tools as possible, to be an effective financial professional in this marketplace.

MERGERS VERSUS ACQUISITIONS

The terms *merger* and *acquisition* are often confused and used interchangeably by business and financial executives.

At the surface level, the difference between a merger and an acquisition may not really matter since the net result is often the same: two companies (or more) that had separate ownership are now operating under the same roof, usually to obtain some strategic or financial objective. Yet, the strategic, financial, tax, and even cultural impact of the deal may be very different, depending on whether the transaction is structured as a *merger,* typically referring to two companies coming together (usually through the exchange of shares) to become one, versus an *acquisition,* which typically refers to one company, the *buyer,* who purchases the assets or shares of the *seller*, with the *form of payment* being cash, the securities of the buyer, or other assets of value to the seller. In a *stock purchase transaction*, the seller's shares in his own company are not necessarily combined with the buyer's existing company, but often kept separate as a new subsidiary or operating division. In an *asset purchase transaction*, the assets that the seller conveys to the buyer become additional assets of the buyer's company, with the hope and expectation that the value of the assets purchased will exceed the price paid over time, thereby enhancing shareholder value.

WHAT'S ALL OF THE FUSS ABOUT?

What has driven the merger mania of recent years? What factors have fueled the current resurgence of merger and acquisition activity? There is no one explanation, and the full impact on the economy is complex, and remains to be seen. However, there are certain themes and trends that have emerged. The key reasons deals are getting done are:

1. Mergers and acquisitions are clearly more strategically motivated than their 1980s and 1990s counterparts. Jobs are often being added, not lost, as a result of these deals. Companies are more likely to be built up, not busted up.
2. The financing that fuels M&A activity is more abundant than ever, with the S&P 500 firms (exclusive of banks and utilities) sitting on $640 billion in cash to do deals as of June 2006. Buyers are also using their stock as currency, and sellers are gladly accepting this form of payment in lieu of, or in addition to, cash which forces both parties to work together on a post-closing basis to truly enhance shareholder value. In addition, more than $800 billion in private equity fund overhang continues to be available to fund M&A deals as of June 2006.
3. Mergers and acquisitions are being driven in many cases by a key trend within a given industry, such as (1) rapidly changing technology that is driving many of the deals in the computer industry; (2) fierce competition that is driving many of the deals in the healthcare, telecommunications, and banking industries; (3) changing consumer preferences that are driving many of the deals in the

food and beverage industry; (4) the pressure to control costs, which is another factor driving many of the deals in the health-care industry; and (5) an increase in demand, such as the growing federal defense and Homeland Security budgets, that are driving the appetite for acquisitions of new capabilities in the aerospace and defense contractor industries.

4. Some deals are motivated by the need to transform corporate identity, following a crisis of negative publicity regarding the company and its leadership.

5. Many deals are fueled by the need to spread the risk and cost of: (1) developing new technology, such as in the communications and aerospace industries; (2) researching new medical discoveries, such as in the medical device and pharmaceutical industries; or (3) gaining access to new sources of energy, such as in the oil and gas exploration and drilling industries.

6. The global village has forced many companies to explore mergers and acquisitions as a means to develop an international presence, and expand market share. This market penetration strategy is often more cost-effective than trying to build an overseas foothold from scratch. One such recent merger was made between the wireless network equipment divisions of Nokia and Siemens.

7. Many recent mergers and acquisitions have been the result of the recognition that a complete product or service line may be necessary in order to remain competitive, or to balance against seasonal or cyclical market trends. Transactions in the retail, hospitality, food and beverage, entertainment, and financial services industries have been in response to the consumer's demand for "one-stop shopping."

8. The IPO boom of the late 1990s in the technology and Internet sector contributed to the merger and acquisition frenzy. The proceeds from the IPOs created large pools of cash that were earmarked for acquisitions, and the sellers were willing to take the buyer's stock as currency in the transaction.

9. In some cases, deals are motivated by multiple objectives and/or previous failed attempts at growth. For example, Johnson & Johnson paid $16 billion for Pfizer's consumer healthcare business, which included well-known products such as Listerine, Sudafed, and Rolaids, in order to consolidate its position as the world's larg-

est supplier of over-the-counter medicines, whereas, Pfizer needed the cash to boost its stock price that had been flat for several years, and announced plans to repurchase as much as $18 billion in stock in 2006 and 2007. Another factor was that Johnson & Johnson had just lost an expensive battle to buy Guidant, a medical devices company, to a rival bidder, Boston Scientific, which badly needed the Guidant line to diversify its *own* limited product pipeline. So, multiple factors were at play in driving this series of transactions.

10. Finally, many transactions are driven by the market need, or strategic desire, to achieve horizontal or vertical integration, such as a manufacturer buying some of its suppliers of critical materials, or in an attempt to capture the business or personal consumer in a "fuller cycle" of their spending. My favorite recent example is the May 2006 acquisition of the Jenny Craig weight-loss company by chocolate-giant Nestlé. Hey, why not grab market share as the scales tip upward, and then help them melt the pounds away?

As leaders of growing companies, your goal should be to closely monitor the trends and types of deals that the larger companies are doing, and then steal a page out of their playbook. What small-scale acquisitions could you be planning to help maximize shareholder value and meet growth objectives?

WHY BAD DEALS HAPPEN TO GOOD PEOPLE

Nobody ever plans to enter into a bad deal. Many entrepreneurs and business executives have entered with good intentions into mergers and acquisitions that they later regret because they make classic mistakes, such as inadequate planning, an overly aggressive timetable to closing, overlooking possible post-closing integration problems, or, worst of all, that the intended synergies are illusory. As discussed above, the underlying theme of the M&A boom is the goal of post-closing synergy. Everyone says that they want synergy when doing a deal, but few take the time to develop a transactional team, a joint mission statement of the objectives of the deal, or solve post-closing operating or financial problems on a timely basis.

In fact, a recent study by McKinsey found that 61 percent of 116 major acquisitions failed to earn back their invested capital over a three-year period following closing. These transactions not only failed to significantly enhance shareholder value for the buyer, but wound up being costly strategic and financial mistakes.

There are many reasons why M&A transactions fail to meet their pre-closing objectives, including poor post-closing integration planning, technological misfits, clashing cultures, overestimation of market demand for post-closing product and service offerings, miscalculation of post-closing efficiency estimates, leadership and management style problems, communication and vision articulation breakdowns, overpayment for a seller's company (when the markets are supporting inflated valuations), and a weak platform for the buyer (e.g., proving "quick fixes" rarely are successful).

WHAT MOTIVATES BUYERS, SELLERS, AND MERGERS?

Let's take a look at the basic reasons and strategies that motivate why a buyer buys and why a seller sells in the context of an acquisition, and why two companies decide to merge. Our goal is twofold: (1) to educate you as a leader of an emerging-growth business whose growth strategy is likely to include at least one and probably several acquisitions, and (2) to provide some insight into the genuine motivations of the seller in the transaction that will usually facilitate a more successful and mutually rewarding transaction.

Motivators in an Acquisition

The key motivators from the buyer's perspective in an acquisition usually include one or more of the following: revenue enhancement, cost reduction, vertical and/or horizontal operational and financial synergies or economies of scale, growth pressures from investors, underutilized resources, intrapreneurs with a large appetite, reducing the number of competitors (increasing market share), gaining a foothold in new domestic and international markets (especially if current markets are saturated), or diversification into new products and services.

The key motivators from the seller's perspective in an acquisition usually include one or more of the following: the owner is nearing retirement or is ready for an exit, the inability to compete as an independent, the desire to obtain cost savings, and access to the greater resources of the acquiring company.

Motivations in a Merger

It is important to note that a *merger* is a different animal, and thus a different set of objectives, shared by both parties, will typically emerge, such as: (1) to improve process engineering and technology; (2) to increase scale of production in existing product lines; (3) to acquire capability to produce subassemblies internally; (4) to find additional uses for existing management talent; (5) to redeploy excess capital into profitable/complementary uses; and (6) to obtain tax benefits. In a classic merger, there is not a buyer or a seller (though one party may be quarterbacking the transaction, or have initiated the contract) and therefore the "culture" and "spirit" of the negotiations are different than a classic acquisition. In a merger, data gathering and due diligence are two-way and mutual, with each party "positioning" its contribution to the post-merger entity to justify its respective equity share, management, and control of the post-merger company.

TAKING THE FIRST STEPS

Business strategists often say that it is "cheaper to buy than to build" a business. This approach, together with the low interest rates and the large pools of capital that have flowed into large- and medium-sized companies through initial public offerings both in the United States and abroad, has created a buying frenzy that is likely to continue into the next millennium. Our domestic market has clearly experienced major industry consolidation via acquisition and roll-up strategies. Notwithstanding all the excitement, the purchase of an existing business is a complex and challenging task. This section will lead the buyer through the process, with a focus on preparation and preliminary negotiation tips, as you begin to understand the seller's perspective.

FIGURE 10.1 *Common Motivators in an Acquisition*

Common Seller Motivations	Common Buyer Motivations
• The desire to retire	• The desire to grow
• Lack of successors	• Opportunity to increase profits
• Business adversities	• Desire to diversify
• Lack of capital to grow	• Buying up competitors
• Inadequate distribution system	• Using excess capital
• To eliminate personal guaranties or other personal obligations	• Achieving new distribution channels or efficiencies
• No ability to diversify	• Diversify new distribution channels or efficiencies
• Age and health concerns	
• Particular amount of money is needed for estate planning	• Particular people, existing business or assets are needed
• Irreconcilable conflict among owners	• Access to new or emerging technologies
• Losing key people or key customers	• Need to efficiently deploy key people or resources
	• Stategic fit between buyer and seller's current operations

Assembling the Team

Every buyer will need to develop an internal working team, as well as an experienced set of external advisors (such as lawyers, accountants, investment bankers, valuation experts, and, in some cases, insurance/employee benefits experts). As the quarterback, the CEO or appointed leader of the team must clearly define both responsibilities and authority, including who has the authority to speak on behalf of the buyer, who may contact prospective sellers, who may negotiate with the selected seller, and so on. Your internal team should probably include representatives from the finance, marketing, strategic planning, and operations departments, particularly those individuals who will be critical during the four critical stages for the buyer.

One interesting decision for a growing company as a buyer, with respect to assembling the team, is whether to use a "buyer's broker" or investment banker to find and evaluate candidates for acquisition, or whether "deal flow" will be generated internally, through networking, industry contacts, and so on. In many cases, the sellers (or at least those who have declared their eligibility for sale) may have already hired an intermediary. In these cases, when both sides are paying finder's fees to two different brokers, it can get expensive. Nevertheless, using a broker can save the buyer valuable time, and the expense of chasing after the wrong candidates, or trying to figure out which companies have expressed an interest in selling.

There are many different ways to structure your relationship with intermediaries, investment bankers, or business brokers. Although most relationships will be driven by the payment of a commission contingent on a successful transaction (generally in the 5–12 percent range, and often paid by the seller), many intermediaries will want a monthly retainer, or the option of billing for certain services, such as their assistance in preparing the acquisition plan, as well as certain expenses, such as trips to, or phone calls with, prospective candidates. These fees and expenses are not usually contingent upon a successful transaction (though some will credit the aggregate of the fees paid toward the ultimate commission), and therefore should be negotiated carefully. If you do retain an intermediary for smaller deals, be sure that you have hired a "buyer's" broker, who has the experience and the orientation to meet your needs.

Developing an Acquisition Plan

Mergers and acquisitions often play a key role in the ongoing growth planning process. External acquisition of assets and resources needed for growth may be a more efficient means of achieving certain corporate goals and objectives than internal expansion. As set forth below, a growing company considering an acquisition should always begin with an acquisition plan that identifies the specific objectives of the transaction and the criteria to be applied in analyzing a potential target company.

Identify objectives. The first step in developing an effective acquisition plan is to identify key objectives. Although the reasons for considering growth through acquisition will vary from industry to industry and from company to company, the following *strategic advantages* provided by acquisitions should be considered. The buyer may seek to acquire another company in order to:

- Achieve certain operating and financial synergies and economies of scale with respect to production and manufacturing, research and development, management, or marketing and distribution
- Obtain rights to develop products and services owned by the target company
- Provide growth opportunities for a surplus of strong managers who are likely to leave unless the company acquires other businesses, which these managers can operate and develop. The target company may stand to lose a talented management team due to the lack of career growth potential, unless it is acquired by a growing business that may offer higher salaries, increased employee benefits, and greater opportunity for advancement.
- Stabilize its earnings stream and mitigate its risk of business failure by diversifying its products and services through acquisition, rather than internal development
- Deploy excess cash into a tax-efficient project, such as an acquisition, since both distribution of dividends and stock redemptions are generally taxable events to its shareholders
- Achieve certain production and distribution economies of scale through vertical integration that would involve the acquisition of a key supplier or customer
- Be able to exploit residual assets left by the target company's management team that may be ready for retirement, or a key manager who may have recently died
- Strengthen key business areas, such as research and development or marketing, when it is more efficient to fill these gaps through an acquisition, rather than attempting to build these departments internally
- Gain recognition in the marketplace for superior products and services that lack customer loyalty and protected trademarks. The acquisition of an older, more established firm becomes a more efficient method of establishing goodwill.

- Penetrate new geographic markets. It is cheaper to acquire firms already doing business in target markets rather than establishing market diversification from scratch.
- Use existing resources to fill a gap in the target company's technical expertise, or capital needed to grow to the next likely stage in its development
- Acquire excess plant or production capacities that can be utilized by the buyer to achieve greater economies of scale
- Take advantage of a company available at a distressed price due to a death or divorce affecting the company's founders
- Acquire certain patents, copyrights, trade secrets, or other intangible assets that will be available to the buyer only by means of an acquisition

In essence, the statement of the objectives should be a reality check, answering the key questions "Why are we doing this, and are we convinced that growth via acquisition makes sense, as compared to other forms of growth strategies, such as internal expansion, joint ventures, franchising, licensing, or capital formation?" and "Are we really enhancing our shareholder value and competitive position as a result of this deal?"

DRAFTING THE PLAN

The next step for a growing company as buyer is to draft an acquisition plan. The acquisition plan defines the objectives of the buyer, the relevant trends in the target's industry, the method for finding candidates for acquisition, the criteria to be used to evaluate candidates, the targeted budgets and timetables for accomplishing the transaction, the price ranges to be considered, the past acquisition track record of the company, the amount of external capital that will be required to accomplish the transaction, and related issues. One of the overriding goals of the plan is to "narrow the field" as much as possible. The field is initially narrowed by choosing acquisitions as a growth strategy, over franchising or strategic alliances, narrowed again by selecting the targeted industries, and narrowed further by the development (and enforcement) of specific criteria to screen the possible candidates. In most cases, this narrowing process, if carefully followed, will yield a viable field of attractive candidates who can be approached. Other benefits to having a well-prepared Acquisition Plan include:

- Providing a road map for the company's leadership to follow
- Informing shareholders of key objectives
- Reducing professional and advisory fees
- Mitigating the risk of doing a transaction you'll later regret
- Identifying post-closing integration challenges well in advance
- Informing sellers of your plans for the company on a post-closing basis

In today's marketplace, with its trend toward roll-ups and consolidation strategies, it is particularly important to the seller (especially where the lion's share of their consideration will be stock of the buyer) to understand, accept, and respect the buyer's acquisition strategy and growth plans for the consolidated companies on a post-closing basis. The well-prepared acquisition plans will be valuable negotiation tools for the buyer when approaching sellers who will naturally be concerned with the value and continued growth of the buyer's stock.

The acquisition plan also identifies the value-added efficiencies and cost savings that will result from the proposed transaction(s), and answer the fundamental question: How will the buyer's professional management or brand equity enhance the performance or profitability of the seller's company? The objectives may vary, but they generally include a desire to accelerate growth in revenues and profits, strengthen the buyer's competitive position, broaden existing product lines, or break into new geographic markets or market segments as part of a diversification strategy. The heart of the plan will identify the *targeted industries* and the *criteria for evaluating candidates* within these targeted industries. The acquisition plan will also identify:

- Targeted *size* of the candidates
- Source of acquisition financing (including the logistics for obtaining the capital, when necessary, and the targeted amount and method of payment to the seller)
- Method for bringing candidates to the buyer's attention (e.g., internal search versus use of intermediaries versus dealing with unsolicited offers, etc.)

- Desired financial returns and/or operating synergies to be achieved as a result of the acquisition
- Minimum/maximum ranges and rates of revenues, growth, earnings, net worth, and so on, of the seller that would be acceptable to you and your board of directors
- Impact on existing shareholders of the company
- Likely competing bidders for qualified candidates
- Members of the acquisition team, and each of their roles
- Nature and types of risks that you are willing to assume (versus those that will be unacceptable)
- Desired geographic location of the target companies
- Desired demographics and buying habits of the seller's customers
- Plans to retain or replace the management team of the target company (even though this policy may vary on a target-by-target basis, it is recommended to include a section addressing your preliminary plans in the acquisition plan)
- Willingness to consider turnaround or troubled companies (again, each buyer will have a different tolerance level as to what condition it wants the seller to be in. Some want and prefer the cost savings of buying a "fixer-upper," and others prefer matters to be pretty well intact when they "move in")
- Tax and financial preference for asset versus stock transactions
- Openness to full, versus partial, ownership of the seller's entity or willingness to consider a spin-off sale, such as the purchase of the assets of an operating division, or the stock of a subsidiary
- Interest or willingness to launch an unfriendly takeover of a publicly held company, or buy the debt from the largest creditor of a privately held company

Communicating your vision and performance expectations is key to obtaining a commitment from the seller's management. A good way to do this is to have the seller's current management team play a role in developing the post-closing integration and communication plans. Here are other more tangible ways of demonstrating your long-term commitment to them, and thereby relieving any personal career anxieties:

- **Propose** salary and wage adjustments, if appropriate, to bring compensation up to your company or industry levels

- **Establish** an incentive bonus plan tied to realistic, attainable goals
- **Provide** employee contracts to key members of the management team
- **Review** benefit plans and assure employees that the transfer will be orderly and fair

APPLYING THE CRITERIA: HOW TO NARROW THE FIELD

Once the buyer's team has completed the preparation and analysis of its acquisition plan, it should be relatively easy to begin the process of identifying potential candidates and preliminary screening of them against the established criteria. Typical buyer's criteria may include some combination of the following:

- History of stable financial and growth performance during different market cycles and conditions
- Market leader in industry niches and geographic regions (recognized brand names with established market share)
- Products with life cycles that are not too short-term or susceptible to obsolescence or rapid technological change
- Strong management team with research and development capability and technological know-how
- Stable and economically favorable relationships with customers, vendors, lenders, and lessors
- Room for growth (or excess) capacity in manufacturing or production
- Current or potential claims or litigation in the $_____ to $_____ range
- Sales range in the $_____ to $_____ million level with minimum EBIT at $_____ million, with an aggregate set of post-closing obligations (e.g., liabilities, union contracts, other post-closing obligations, etc.) not to exceed $_____
- Purchase price range from $_____ to $_____. Seller must be willing to accept up to _____ percent of its consideration in buyer's stock, and an additional _____ percent of the consideration will be contingent on the performance of the seller's company on a post-closing basis (exact method, such as earn-out, to be determined)

- Geographical location within certain desired states, or within a certain range of miles, from the buyer's principal headquarters
- Existing management team must agree to remain in place for up to _____ years

Naturally, unless you are very lucky, not all your candidates will meet *all* your criteria, and if they do, there will likely be multiple bidders. Rather, the buyer and its team must be ready to mix and match, accept some compromise in the rigid criteria, but also be careful not to overlook "too many warts" that will result in a deal that you will regret later.

Again, the goal is to compare the acquisition objectives described in the acquisition plan with the strengths and weaknesses of each seller to ensure that the acquisition team has a clear idea as to *how* the targeted companies will complement the buyer's strengths, and/or mitigate the buyer's weaknesses. The specific qualitative and quantitative screening criteria help assist the buyer and its team to ensure that the right candidates are selected. They are intended to "filter out" the wrong deals, and mitigate the chances of post-closing regrets and problems.

THE LETTER OF INTENT AND OTHER PRELIMINARY MATTERS

At this stage of the transaction, both the seller and buyer (and their respective advisors) have developed a strategic plan, and hopefully have taken the time to understand each other's perspective and competing objectives. The field of available candidates has been narrowed, the preliminary "get to know each other" meetings completed, and a tentative selection has been made. After the completion of the presale review, the next step involves the preparation and negotiation of an interim agreement that will govern the conduct of the parties up until closing.

Although there are certain valid legal arguments against the execution of any type of interim document, especially since some courts have interpreted them to be binding legal documents (even if one or more of the parties did not initially intend to be bound), it has been my experience that a letter of intent that includes a set of binding and nonbinding terms as a road map for the transaction *is* a necessary step in virtually all mergers and acquisition transactions. I have found that most parties prefer the organizational framework and psychological comfort of knowing that there is some type of written document in place before proceeding further, and before significant expenses are incurred.

There are many different styles of drafting letters of intent, which vary from law firm to law firm and business lawyer to business lawyer. These styles usually fall into one of three categories: (1) binding, (2) nonbinding, and (3) hybrids, like the model at the end of this chapter. In general, the type selected will depend upon:

- Information to be released publicly concerning the transaction
- Degree that negotiations have been definitive, and necessary information has been gathered
- Cost to the buyer and the seller of proceeding with the transaction, prior to the making of binding commitments
- Rapidity with which the parties estimate a final agreement can be signed
- Degree of confidence in the good faith of each party and the absence (or presence) of other parties competing for the transaction

In most cases, the hybrid is the most effective format to protect the interests of both parties and to level the playing field from a negotiations perspective.

Although formally executed by the buyer and the seller, a letter of intent is often considered an agreement *in principle*. As a result, the parties should be very clear as to whether the letter of intent is a binding preliminary contract, or merely a memorandum from which a more definitive legal document may be drafted upon completion of due diligence. Regardless of the legal implications involved, however, by executing a letter of intent, the parties make a psychological commitment to the transaction, and provide a road map for expediting more formal negotiations. In addition, a well-drafted letter of intent will provide an overview of matters that require further discussion and consideration, such as the exact purchase price. Although a purchase price cannot realistically be established until due diligence has been completed, the seller may hesitate to proceed without a price commitment. Instead of creating a fixed price, however, the letter of intent should incorporate a price range that is qualified by a clause or provision that sets forth all the factors that will influence the calculation of a final fixed price. A well-drafted letter of intent will have a series of nonbinding, proposed terms, and a second section of covenants that will be binding on the parties.

Nonbinding terms. The first section addresses certain key deal terms, such as price and method of payment, but these terms are usually nonbinding, so that the parties have an opportunity to conduct due diligence, and have room for further negotiation, depending on the specific problems uncovered during the investigative process.

Binding terms. The letter of intent also includes certain binding terms that will *not* be subject to further negotiation. These are certain issues that at least one side, and usually both sides, want to ensure are binding, whether or not the deal is actually consummated. These include:

- **Legal ability of seller to consummate the transaction.** Before wasting too much time or money, the buyer will want to know that the seller has the power and authority to close the deal.
- **Protection of confidential information.** The seller in particular, and both parties in general, will want to ensure that all information provided in the initial presentation, as well as during due diligence, remains confidential.
- **Access to books and records.** The buyer will want to ensure that the seller and its advisors will fully cooperate in the due diligence process.
- **Break-up or walk away fees.** The buyer may want to include a clause in the letter of intent to attempt to recoup some of its expenses if the seller tries to walk away from the deal, either due to a change in circumstances, or the desire to accept a more attractive offer from a different potential buyer. The seller may want a reciprocal clause to protect against its own expenses if the buyer walks away, or defaults on a preliminary obligation or condition to closing, such as an inability to raise acquisition capital.
- **No-shop/standstill provisions.** The buyer may want a period of exclusivity during which it can be confident that the seller is not entertaining any other offers. The seller will want to place a limit,

or "outside date," to this provision in order to allow it to begin entertaining other offers if the buyer is unduly dragging its feet.

- **Good faith deposit, refundable versus nonrefundable.** In some cases, the seller will request a deposit or option fee, and the parties must determine to what extent, if at all, this deposit will be refundable, and under what conditions. There are often difficult timing problems with this provision. For example, the buyer will want the deposit to remain 100 percent refundable if the seller is being uncooperative, or at least until the buyer and its team complete the initial round of due diligence to ensure that there are no major problems discovered that might cause them to walk away from the deal. The seller will want to set a limit on the due diligence and review period, at which point the buyer forfeits all or a part of its deposit. The end result is often a progressive downward scale of refundability as the due diligence and the deal overall reach various checkpoints toward closing. To the extent that the buyer forfeits some or all of the deposit, and the deal never closes, the buyer may want to negotiate an eventual full or partial refundability if the seller finds an alternative buyer within a certain period of time, such as 180 days.

- **Impact on employees.** If an announcement is not made directly to the employees of the target company, then the employees may get the unmistakable message that their jobs are unimportant, or in jeopardy, or both. Supervisory personnel should be briefed first, and all their questions should be answered, so that they can inform their subordinates. After the closing, it is imperative that the top management of the acquiring company assures the employees of the target company of the continuation of beneficial policies, and welcomes them into a larger and better organization, if that is their intent. Employees who do not feel they are part of a team will have poor morale, and poorer productivity. It is essential that lines of communication be kept open at the time of the acquisition.

- **Key terms for the definitive documents.** The letter of intent will often provide that it is subject to the completion of definitive documents, such as the purchase agreement, and that those definitive documents will address certain key matters or include certain key sections such as covenants, indemnification, representations and warranties, and key conditions for closing.

- **Conditions to closing.** Both parties will want to articulate a set of conditions, or circumstances, under which they will not be bound to proceed with the transaction. Be sure to articulate these conditions clearly, so that there are no surprises down the road.
- **Conduct of the business prior to closing.** The buyer usually wants some protection that what he or she sees today will be there tomorrow. Thus, the seller will be obligated to operate its business in the ordinary course to guarantee that assets will not start disappearing from the premises, equipment won't be left in disrepair, new customers not pursued, bonuses magically declared, personal expenses paid the night before closing, and to avoid other steps that will deplete the value of the company prior to closing. These. "negative covenants" help protect the buyer against unpleasant surprises at, or after, closing.
- **Limitations on publicity and press releases.** The parties may want to place certain restrictions on the content and timing of any press releases or public announcements of the transaction, and in some cases may need to follow SEC guidelines. If either, or both, of the parties to the transaction are publicly traded, then the general rule is that once the essential terms of the transaction are agreed to in principle, such as through the execution of the letter of intent, there must be a public announcement. The timing and content of this announcement must be weighed carefully by the parties, including an analysis as to how the announcement will affect the price of the stock. The announcement should not be made too early, or it may be viewed by the Securities and Exchange Commission ("SEC") as an attempt to influence the price of the stock.
- **Expenses/brokers.** The parties should determine, when applicable, who shall bear responsibility for investment bankers' fees, finders' fees, legal expenses, and other costs pertaining to the transaction.

KEEPING M&A TRANSACTIONS DEALS ON TRACK: MANAGING THE DEAL KILLERS

Deal killers—we have all seen them, and have had to manage through them. They come in all shapes, sizes, and styles with different reasons, justifications, and rationalizations. They can emanate from the buyer, the seller, or any number of third parties, such as lenders, investors, key customers or suppliers, professional advisors, or all of the above. There are some deals that deserve to die, and there are some deal killers that are emotional, financial, or strategic in nature. They can be very costly to all parties to the transaction, especially when significant costs have already been incurred. For certain advisors and investment bankers, it means not getting paid. Clearly, deal killers inflict a lot of pain.

Most deal killers can be put into one of the following major categories:

- Price and valuation
- Terms and conditions
- Allocation of risk
- Third-party challenges

Common Reasons Why Deals Die at an Early Stage

- Seller has not prepared adequate financial statements (e.g., going back at least two years and reflective of the company's current condition)
- Seller and its team uncooperative during the due diligence process
- Buyer and its team discover a "deal breaker" in the due diligence (e.g., large, unknown, or hidden actual or contingent liabilities, like an EPA clean-up matter)
- Seller has "seller's remorse," "cold feet," or has not properly thought through its after-tax consideration or compensation
- Seller suffers from "don't call my baby ugly" syndrome and becomes defensive when the buyer and its team find flaws (and then focus on them in the negotiation) in the operations of the business, the valuation, the loyalty of the customers, the quality of the accounts receivable, the skills of the personnel, and so on
- A strategic shift (or extenuating set of circumstances) affecting the acquisition strategy or criteria of the buyer (e.g., a change in buyer's management team during the due diligence process)
- Seller is inflexible on price and valuation when buyer and its team discover problems during due diligence

Communication and Leadership

The first step in keeping a transaction on track (and greatly increasing the chance of completing the deal) is to have strong communication and leadership by, and among, all parties and key players to the transaction. As in football, each team (e.g., buyer, seller, source of capital, etc.) should appoint a quarterback, who will be the point person for communication and coordination. Too many lines of communication, like too many chefs in one kitchen, will create confusion and misunderstanding—which are fertile conditions for deal killers to breed. The more that the quarterbacks coordinate, communicate, and anticipate problems with the various members of their team, and promptly discuss key issues with the quarterbacks of the other teams, the greater the chances that the transaction can and will close.

Some of the key tasks that the transactional quarterback and each team must do to keep the transaction on track toward closing include:

- Put a master strategic plan in place (with realistic expectations regarding financial and post-closing objectives)
- Build the right team
- Establish open communication and functional teamwork
- Facilitate orchestration and leadership
- Maintain momentum and timetable accord
- Stay unemotional
- Start early on governmental and third-party appeals
- Encourage creative problem solving
- Ensure co-operation and support from financing sources
- Secure agreement on the key value drivers of the seller's business/ intellectual capital issues

Diagnosing the Source of the Problem

When a potential deal killer does arise, each quarterback should first diagnose the source of the problem. Where is the issue coming from, and what can be done to fix it? A deal killer for one party may not be a deal killer for another party. The old adage "where you stand often depends on where you sit" clearly applies here. For example, a lender that offers a higher lending rate than the buyer anticipated may significantly alter the attractiveness of the transaction from the buyer's perspective, but it may be a nonissue for the seller.

Understanding the Types of Deal Killers

Once the *source* of the deal killer has been analyzed, the respective quarterbacks should focus on the specific type of deal killer. Most deal killers can and should be resolved, either with creative restructuring, effective counseling, or precision document redrafting. Some deal killers cannot be resolved (they are just too big and hairy), and other deal killers should not be resolved (like trying to squeeze a square peg into a round hole).

Deal killers come in a wide variety of flavors, and include the following:

- Clashing egos
- Misalignment of objectives
- Inexperienced players
- Internal and external politics (board-level, executives, venture investors, etc.)
- Due diligence red flags/surprises
- Pricing and structural challenges (price vs. terms)
- Valuation problems
- Third-party approval delays
- Seller's, buyer's, or source of capital's remorse
- Employee and customer issues
- Overdependence on the founder, key employee, key customer, or relationship
- Loss of trust/integrity during the transactional process
- Nepotism
- Failure to develop a mutually agreeable post-closing integration plan
- Shareholder approvals
- Accounting or financial statement irregularities (post–Worldcom)
- Sarbanes-Oxley post-closing compliance concerns
- Breakdowns in leadership and coordination, resulting from too little or too many points of communication
- Too little or too much "principal to principal" communications
- Crowded auctions
- Impatience to get to closing, or, conversely, loss of momentum (flow and timing issues)

- Incompatibility of culture and/or business systems (e.g., IT infrastructure, costs and budgeting policies, compensation and reward programs, accounting policies, etc.)
- Force-feeding deals that don't meet M&A objectives (square peg/round hole)
- Who's driving the bus in this deal?
- Changes in seller performance during the transactional process (upside surprises *or* unexpected downside surprises)
- Loss of a key customer or strategic relationship during the transactional process
- Failure to agree on post-closing obligations, roles, and responsibilities
- Environmental problems (buyers less willing to rely on indemnification and insurance protections)
- Unexpected changes in the buyer's strategy or operations during the transactional process (including a change in management or strategic direction)

Fixing the Deal

Although a detailed discussion of the tools available to "kill a deal killer" is beyond the scope of the chapter—and they are probably as numerous as the tools available to the Orkin® man to kill the hundreds of different insects and rodents—some of the more common tools are listed below. The first step is for each quarterback to ensure that the transaction *can* and *should* be fixed. If so, these tools can be very valuable in mending a broken deal:

- Earn-outs and deferred and contingent post-closing consideration
- Representations, warranties, and indemnities (used to adjust allocation and assumption of risk)
- Adjusting the post-closing survival period of R&Ws (Representations and Warranties)
- Holdbacks and security interests
- Closing-date audits
- Third-party performance guaranties, performance bonds, escrows
- M&A insurance policies
- Restrictions on sale by seller of buyer's securities issued as part of the overall consideration

- Recasting of financial projections and retooling post-closing business plans

Conclusion

Bad deals deserve to die a peaceful death. Not all transactions are meant to be closed (1) at this time, (2) at this valuation, (3) between these parties, or (4) under these terms and conditions. But if a transaction *can* be saved, then it *should* be saved. The quarterback on each team must have the transactional experience, the business acumen, and the communication skills to diagnose the source and nature of the problem, and enough familiarity with all the tools available to get the transaction back on track toward closing.

PREPARING THE WORK SCHEDULE

Following the execution of the letter of intent, one of the first responsibilities of the buyer's legal counsel is to prepare a comprehensive schedule of activities ("work schedule") which serves as a task checklist and assignment of responsibilities. The primary purpose of the schedule is to outline all the events that must occur, and documents that must be prepared prior to the closing date and beyond. In this regard, the buyer's legal counsel acts as an orchestra leader assigning primary areas of responsibility to the various members of the acquisition team, as well as to the seller and its counsel. The buyer's counsel must also act as a "task master," to ensure that the timetable is met. Once all tasks have been identified and assigned, and a realistic timetable is established, then a firm closing time and date can be preliminarily determined.

Naturally, the exact list of legal documents which must be prepared and the specific tasks to be outlined in the work schedule will vary from transaction to transaction, usually depending on the specific facts and circumstances of each deal, such as: (1) whether the transaction is a stock or asset purchase; (2) the form and terms of the purchase price; (3) the nature of the business being acquired; (4) the nature and extent of the assets being purchased and/or liabilities being assumed; and (5) the sophistication of the parties and their respective legal counsel.

DUE DILIGENCE

After the buyer and seller's teams have made their preparations, narrowed the field, and executed the letter of intent, both sides must begin preparing for the due diligence process. This process involves a legal, financial, and strategic review of all the seller's documents, operating history, contractual relationships, and organizational structure. The seller and its team must organize the documents, and the buyer and its team must be prepared to ask all the right questions, and to conduct a detailed analysis of the documents provided. To the extent that the deal is structured as a merger, or when the seller will be taking the buyer's stock as all or part of its compensation, the process of due diligence is likely to be two-way, as the parties gather background information on each other.

Due diligence is usually divided into two working teams: (1) *financial and strategic,* to be conducted by the buyer's accountants and management team, and (2) *legal,* to be conducted by the buyer's counsel, with both teams comparing notes on open issues, and potential risks and problems, throughout the process. The legal due diligence will focus on the potential legal issues and problems that may serve as impediments to the transaction, as well as shed light on how the documents should be structured. The financial and strategic due diligence will focus on issues such as confirmation of the past financial performance of the seller, the integration of the human and financial resources of the two companies, confirmation of the operating, production, and distribution synergies and economies of scale to be achieved by the acquisition, and the gathering of information necessary for financing the transaction.

Overall, the due diligence process, when done properly, can be tedious, frustrating, time-consuming, and expensive. Yet it is a necessary prerequisite to a well-planned acquisition, and can reveal information about the target company and gauge the costs and risks associated with the transaction. Buyers should expect sellers to become defensive, evasive, and impatient during the due diligence phase of the transaction. This is usually because most business managers really don't enjoy having their business policies and decisions under the microscope, especially for an extended period of time, and by a party searching for skeletons in the closet. Eventually, the seller is likely to give an ultimatum to the prospective buyer: "finish the due diligence soon, or the deal is off." When negotiations have reached this point, it is best to end the examination process relatively soon. Buyers should resist the temptation to conduct a hasty "once over" (either to save costs or to appease the seller), yet at the same time should avoid "due diligence overkill," keeping in mind that due diligence is not a perfect process, and should not be a tedious fishing expedition for the seller. Some information will get missed, which is precisely why broad representations, warranties, liability holdbacks, and indemnification provisions should be structured into the final purchase agreement in order to protect the buyer. Meanwhile, the seller will negotiate for carve-outs (meaning the buyer must discover a "basket" of liabilities before it can seek reimbursement for undisclosed or unexpected liabilities), exceptions, and limitations to liability, to provide post-closing protection against surprises to the seller. The nature and scope of these provisions are likely to be hotly contested in the negotiations. Remember that the key objective of due diligence is not just to "confirm that the deal makes sense" (i.e., to confirm the factual assumptions and preliminary valuations underlying the terms under which the buyer will be negotiating the transaction), *but* rather to determine whether the transaction should proceed at all, recognizing at all times that there may be a need to "jump ship" if the risks or potential liabilities in the transaction greatly exceed what the buyer anticipated.

Effective due diligence is both an *art* and a *science*. The art is the style and experience to know which questions to ask, how and when to ask them, and the ability to create an atmosphere of both *trust* and *fear* in the seller and its team, which encourages full and complete disclosure. In this sense, the due diligence team is on a search and destroy mission, looking for potential problems and liabilities (the search), and finding ways to resolve these problems prior to closing, and/or to ensure that risks are allocated fairly and openly among the parties after closing (the destroy).

The science is in the preparation of comprehensive and customized checklists of the specific questions that will be presented to the seller and its advisors, maintaining a methodical system for organizing and analyzing the documents and data provided by the seller and its team, and being in a position to quantitatively assess the risks raised by the problems discovered in the process. One of the key areas is detecting the seller's obligations, particularly those that the buyer will be expected or required to assume after closing. The process is designed *first* to detect the existence of the obligation, and *second* to identify any defaults or problems in connection with these obligations that will affect the buyer on a post-closing basis.

The best way for the buyer and its team to ensure that virtually no stone remains unturned is through effective due diligence preparation and planning. The following two checklists should be helpful to buyers and their acquisition teams. The first is a legal checklist to guide the company's management team, while working closely with counsel to gather and review all legal documents that may be relevant to the structure and pricing of the transaction, the potential legal risks and liabilities to the buyer following the closing, and to identify all the consents and approvals, such as an existing contract that can't be assigned without consent from third parties and government agencies. The second checklist is designed to provide the acquisition team with a starting point for analysis of the seller from a management, marketing, and financial perspective, as well as "level the playing field" in the negotiations, since the seller will usually start with a greater level of expertise regarding its industry and its business than the buyer.

These checklists should be a guideline, not a crutch. The buyer's management team must take the lead in developing customized questions that pertain to the *nature* of the seller's business, and will set the pace regarding the level of detail and adequacy of the review. For example, at my law firm, we recently worked on a deal that involved the purchase of a hockey league in the Midwest. It was easy to apply the standard due diligence list and draw up questions regarding corporate structure and history, status of the stadium leases, team tax returns, and the protection of the team trademarks. The more difficult task was developing a customized list. In our role as legal counsel, I sat with my client to answer the question: "If you were buying a sports league, what would you need to review?" The key point here is that every different type of business has its own issues and problems, and that a standard set of questions will rarely be sufficient. The list included player and coaching contracts, stadium signage/promotional leases, league-wide and local team sponsorship contracts, the immigration status of each player, team and player performance statistics, the status of the contracts with each team's star players, scouting reports and drafting procedures, ticket sales (including walk up, advance, season, group, and coupons) for each team and game, promotional agreements with equipment suppliers and game-day merchandise, food and beverage concession contracts, the status of each team's franchise agreement, commitments made to cities for future teams, and unique per team advertising rates for dasher boards (the advertising spaces that surround the rink).

Common Mistakes Made by the Buyer During the Due Diligence Investigation

- Mismatch between the documents provided by the seller and the skills of the buyer's review team. It may be the case that the seller has particularly complex financial statements, or highly technical reports, which must be truly understood by the buyer's due diligence team. Make sure there is a capability fit.
- Poor communication and misunderstandings. The communications should be open and clear between the teams of the buyer and the seller. The process must be well orchestrated.
- Lack of planning and focus in the preparation of the due diligence questionnaires and in the interviews with the seller's team. The focus must be on asking the *right* questions, not just a lot of questions. Sellers will resent wasteful "fishing expeditions" when the buyer's team is unfocused.
- Inadequate time devoted to tax and financial matters. The buyer's (and seller's) CFO and CPA must play an integral part in the due diligence process, in order to gather data on past financial performance and tax reporting, unusual financial events, or disturbing trends or inefficiencies.

When done properly, due diligence is performed in multiple stages. First, a preliminary stage gathers all of the basic data and identifies specific topic areas where follow-up questions and data-gathering can be performed in subsequent rounds of due diligence.

Due diligence must be a cooperative and patient process between buyer and seller and their teams. Attempts at hiding or manipulating key data will only lead to problems for the seller down the road. Material misrepresentations or omissions can (and often do) lead to post-closing litigation, which is expensive and time-consuming for both parties. Another mistake often made by the seller is the human element of due diligence. Often the lawyers, accountants, and advisors are sent into a dark room in the corner of the seller's building without any support staff, computers, telephones, or even coffee. It is only human, as buyer's counsel, to be a little bit more cooperative in the negotiations when the seller makes it comfortable for you to do your job.

Common Due Diligence Problems and Exposure Areas

There is virtually an infinite number of potential problems and exposure areas for the buyer that may be uncovered in the review and analysis of the seller's documents and operations. The specific issues and problems will vary based on the size of the seller, the nature of its business, and the number of years that the seller (or its predecessors) has been in business.

- "Clouds" in the title to critical tangible (real estate, equipment, inventory) and intangible (patents, trademarks, etc.) assets. Be sure the seller has clear title to these assets, and that they are conveyed without claims, liens, and encumbrances.
- A wide variety of employment or labor law issues or liabilities may be lurking just below the surface that will not be uncovered unless the right questions are asked. Questions designed to uncover wage and hour law violations, discrimination claims, OSHA compliance, or even liability for unfunded persons under the Multi-Employer Pension Plan Act should be developed. If the seller has recently made a substantial workforce reduction (or if you, as the buyer, are planning post-closing layoffs), then the requirements of the Worker Adjustment and Refraining Notification Act (WARN) must have been met. The requirements of WARN include minimum notice requirements of 60 days prior to wide-scale terminations.
- The possibility of environmental liability under CERCLA or related environmental regulations
- Unresolved existing or potential litigation should be reviewed carefully by counsel
- A seller's attempt to "dress up" the financial statements prior to sale is often an attempt to hide inventory problems, research and development expenditures, excessive overhead and administrative costs, uncollected or uncollectible accounts receivable, unnecessary or inappropriate personal expenses, unrecorded liabilities, tax contingencies, and so on

11

INTELLECTUAL ASSET MANAGEMENT AND HARVESTING

CEOs and business leaders of small and growing companies are often guilty of committing a very serious strategic sin: the failure to properly protect, mine, and harvest the company's intellectual property. From 1997 to 2001, billions of dollars went into the venture capital and private equity markets. Entrepreneurs primarily used these proceeds to create intellectual property and other intangible assets. In many cases, five years later, however, emerging growth and middle market companies have failed to leverage this intellectual capital into new revenue streams, profit centers, and market opportunities because of a singular focus on the company's core business, or a lack of strategic vision or expertise to uncover, or identify, other applications or distribution channels.

Entrepreneurs and growing company ledgers may also lack the proper tools to understand and analyze the value of the company's intellectual assets. In a recent study by Professor Baruch Lev at NYU, only 15 percent of the "true value" of the S&P 500 was captured in their financial statements. Given the resources of an S&P 500 company, it is likely that smaller companies have their intangible assets even more deeply embedded, and the number for privately held companies may be as low as 5 percent. Imagine the consequences and opportunity cost if you were preparing to eventually sell your business (or even structure an investment with a venture capitalist or strategic investor) and 95 percent of your inherent value was left on the table! This gap in capturing and reflecting hidden value points out the critical need for a legal and strategic analysis of an emerging company's intellectual property portfolio.

INTELLECTUAL ASSET MANAGEMENT (IAM)

Intellectual Asset Management (IAM) is a system to create, organize, prioritize, and extract value from a set of intellectual property assets. The intellectual capital and technical know-how of a growing company are among its most valuable assets. They provide its greatest competitive advantages, and are the principal drivers of shareholder value, yet rarely do companies have adequate personnel, resources, and systems in place to properly manage and leverage these assets. IAM helps growing companies ensure that strategic growth opportunities are recognized, captured, and harvested into new revenue streams and markets. IAM also involves monitoring certain developments in the company's marketplace, such as:

- Gathering intelligence on direct, indirect, and potential competitors
- Monitoring developments abroad
- Keeping one step ahead of a constantly changing landscape (20,000 or more new patents issued per month in the United States alone)
- Maintaining license agreements and streams of royalty payments on both an inbound and outbound basis; that is, ensuring against under-reporting (outbound) and overpayments (inbound). Are you getting paid? Is there anyone you are paying, but shouldn't be? Are performance standards being met? Are you in relationships with the right parties? What could be done to strengthen existing relationships or distribution channels?

A review of your current IAM practices should include an analysis of the following:

- What IAM systems, procedures, and teams are in place now?
- How, and when, were these systems developed?

- Who is responsible for managing these systems within the company? To what degree are adequate systems for internal and external communication and collaboration currently in place?
- What are the ideas or technology harvesting, filters, and procedures for innovation decisional analysis (regarding moving forward, allocating funds, setting a timetable, and so on) currently in place?
- Is the strategy and the process for harvesting and leveraging intellectual assets reactive or proactive?
- What are the real or perceived hurdles—whether internal (politics, red tape, budgeting processes, organizational structure) and/or external (market conditions, state of the art, moving quickly, competitor's strategies, etc.)—that stand in the way of better IAM practices and procedures?
- What can be done to remove or reduce those barriers?

The first step in developing an effective IAM system is to conduct an intellectual property (IP) audit. The IP audit is a multidisciplinary process to gather data and take inventory on all of the growing company's intellectual property assets, so that they can then be managed and leveraged properly and profitably. An IP audit can also include a competitive assessment of the strength and depth of the company's inventory of intellectual assets relative to other companies with which they compete. This competitive assessment may be especially critical in anticipation of either a capital formation or merger/acquisition transaction. It can also be a useful tool to determine where future research and development dollars or branding budgets should be allocated, to the extent that the company is at a competitive disadvantage due to noticeable holes or dangerous weaknesses in its IP portfolio. As the company matures, its inventory of intellectual assets should be getting stronger and deeper, not more shallow, in order to protect its market position, as well as continue to deliver and maintain its value proposition to customers, employees, and channel partners.

The IP audit has seven primary phases, ranging from data-gathering to the development of policies and procedures (as demonstrated in Figure 11.1). There is a wide range of issues and action items that will need to be taken during each phase, depending on the results of the audit and overall IP objectives.

FIGURE 11.1 *Seven Primary Phases in the IP Audit for Growing Companies*

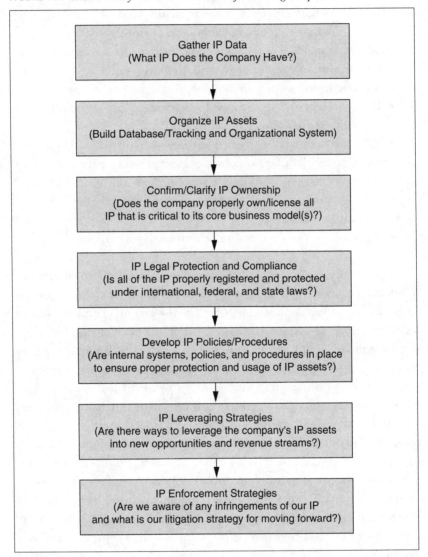

UNDERSTANDING STRATEGIC CATEGORIES OF INTELLECTUAL CAPITAL

Intellectual property is a subset of the broader category of intellectual capital. Intellectual capital is a difficult concept to grasp because it encompasses intangible items used to measure a company's success and wealth. Most fast-track growing companies are discovering that while intellectual capital may be hard to quantify, it is essential for survival. Intellectual capital typically falls into the following three categories:

1. **Human capital.** This category includes all the skills, experience, and ability of your employees. Creativity, innovation, and forward thinking drive a company and allow it to compete in an environment that is constantly becoming more complex and idea-dependent. Human capital is hard to measure, but is usually viewed in terms such as turnover and employee satisfaction.
2. **Organizational capital.** This category is limited to things owned by the company, such as patents, trademarks, copyrights, formulas, and databases. Converting human capital into organizational capital is difficult, and means collecting and retaining employee ability so it belongs to the company.
3. **Relationship capital.** This category places a premium on, and recognizes the value of, relationships as an intellectual asset. Vendors, customers, alliances, channel partners, and so on are all relationships that add intangible value to the company.

Intellectual capital has become the new inventory of the new economy, and it is critical that you understand how the intellectual property laws are used to protect these key assets. Without knowing your inventory levels of intellectual capital, you cannot accurately allocate the proper amount of resources to develop your business in the most profitable direction. Taking the time to study all of your growing company's assets may uncover attributes or strategies to use your capital in new ways that fully take advantage of your intangibles. Because these assets cannot be touched or felt, today's entrepreneur must rely on the tools, and sometimes weapons, offered by the various branches of intellectual property law. The key is to match the intangible asset you are trying to protect and/or leverage with the most effective legal and strategic tools available. This requires a basic understanding of the laws that protect intellectual property, as well as the strategies that are most effective to leverage intellectual property.

The role of the lawyer, as a legal and strategic advisor to companies who have grown through the leveraging of their intellectual property, in this critical process is to:

FIGURE 11.2 *Evolving Strategic Views toward Intellectual Capital (IC) Assets*

Traditional View	Enhance your competitive advantage and strengthen your ability to defend your competitive position in the marketplace (IC as a barrier to entry and as a shield to protect market share **(reactive and passive approach)**
Current View	Should not be used merely for defensive purposes but should also be viewed as an important asset and profit center which is capable of being monetized and generating value through licensing fees and other channels and strategies, *provided* that time and resources are devoted to uncovering these opportunities (especially dormant IC assets which do not currently serve at the heart of the company's core competencies or focus) **(proactive/systemic approach)**
Future View	*Premier* drivers of business strategy within the company and encompass human capital, structural/organizational capital, and customer/relationship capital. IAM systems need to be built and continuously improved to ensure that IC assets are used to protect and defend the company's strategic position in domestic and global markets and to create new markets, distribution channels, and revenue streams in a capital efficient manner to maximize shareholder value **(core focus/strategic approach)**

- Work with clients to find their intellectual property and hidden intangible assets (intellectual property protection and leveraging audits)
- Protect the intellectual property (through registration strategies and confidential agreements)
- Develop strategies to leverage the intellectual property (through joint ventures, alliances, and licensing)
- Look at these strategies in comparison to other growth strategies as alternatives

Our strategic analysis may include questions such as:

- What protectable competitive advantages has the company developed?
- What intellectual property law strategies can be used to protect ownership/use?
- How can this intellectual property be leveraged into revenue or profit streams?

- How can we use intellectual property to create substantial competitive advantages with durable revenue streams?

An entrepreneur's ability to grow a business and achieve success depends on how well he or she can invent and exploit new products and services; open up new distribution channels; foster new production and training techniques; implement new promotional and marketing campaigns; establish new pricing methods; and adapt to changes in competition, consumer preferences, or demographic trends. Your ability to identify, develop, and protect intellectual property rights is critical. Doing so can help your company:

- Improve the overall value and rate of growth by increasing intangible assets
- Create competitive advantages and barriers for competitors to enter the marketplace
- Understand the intellectual property rights of other firms
- Create licensing opportunities and additional revenue sources
- Build consumer goodwill and brand loyalty
- Provide maximum control over the development and ownership of the ideas and invention of employees

The development and protection of intellectual property plays a key role in building a foundation for growth.

Growing companies in today's service-driven and technology-dominant economy are focusing on the protection and leveraging of their intangible assets, in order to continue their development and succeed against their competition. This means that your team must devote greater amounts of time, attention, and resources to building and protecting brands, customer relationships, goodwill, proprietary formulae, strategic alliances, cross-licensing and co-branding alliances, and other intangible assets. The fast-track growing company's ability to develop, recognize, protect, and exploit these intangible assets is critical. To do so, however, you first need to understand the different categories of intellectual property and how each type is protected.

INTELLECTUAL PROPERTY DEVELOPMENT AS A DRIVER FOR INNOVATION AND NEW OPPORTUNITIES

The term "intellectual property" is typically used to refer to the following kinds of intangible assets:

- Patents
- Trademarks and brands
- Copyrights and creative works
- Customer databases and proprietary information
- Trade secrets and confidential information
- Trade dress
- Know-how and show-how
- Web site addresses and designs (encompassing trademark, copyright, and trade dress)

Intellectual property development, protection, and harvesting strategies are critical components of a company's ability to grow, yet many entrepreneurs do not devote the time and the resources to the process. Among the reasons commonly cited:

- Lack the time (too busy)
- Lack the desire (too lazy)
- Lack the skills/expertise (too ignorant)
- Lack the vision (too focused on their niche)
- Lack the resources (too capital constrained)
- Lack the leadership (too thin at the top)
- Lack the market (too focused on developing technology instead of markets for products)

Entrepreneurs must *first* develop a vision and set of values that puts innovation at, or near the top of, its priority list. Innovation drives business growth (as demonstrated in Figure 11.3).

The typical barriers to building a culture of innovation include:

- Leadership and governance
- Silos (lack of communication)

FIGURE 11.3 *Innovation Drives Business Growth*

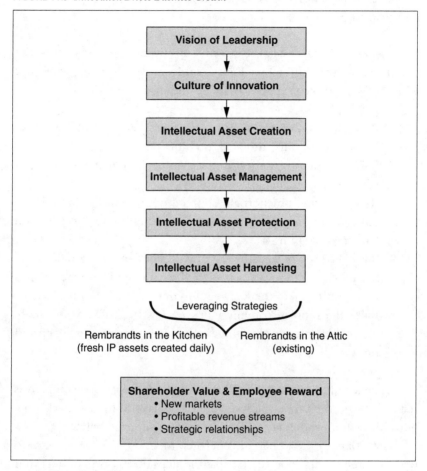

- Lack of systems: how and where to start
- Red tape
- Politics/turfmanship
- Lack of resources
- Time management constraints
- Demand is unclear
- Lack of rewards/compensation systems to motivate and encourage innovation
- Accountability
- Organizational chart: wrong people in the wrong jobs
- Lack of creative people and teams

Innovation Fuels Growth: Don't Be Penny-Wise and Pound-Foolish

It is very difficult to achieve growth objectives without a healthy dose of innovation. Innovation on a limited budget involves *making the most of what you have*. To accomplish this, follow these basic five rules:

1. Raise the ratio of innovators to total number of employees (may be as much about attitude as job function)
2. Raise the ratio of radical innovation to incremental innovation (pick something big to accomplish)
3. Raise the ratio of externally sourced innovation to that of internally sourced (may be cheaper to hire others to help you develop "the next big thing")
4. Raise the ratio of learning, over investment, in innovation (teaching people to innovate across the board may yield better results than putting all of the R&D eggs in one big basket or project)
5. Raise the ratio of commitment to a few high-quality and high-potential projects rather than to lots of smaller ones (go deep and not wide)

Once a culture of innovation is put in place, the growth company is ready to begin the process of leveraging its harvest into new market opportunities and profitable revenue streams, as depicted below.

The balance of this chapter is devoted to an overview of the various types of intellectual property, as well as the steps necessary to protect your key intangible assets under the various branches of federal and state intellectual property laws.

PATENTS

A patent grants the inventor the right to prevent others from making, using, selling, or offering to sell the invention throughout the United States, or from importing the invention into the United States for a limited period of time. To obtain a patent, the inventor submits an application with the U.S. Patent and Trademark Office (known as the "USPTO"). The application must be submitted within one year of public use or publication of the invention. There are three categories of patents available:

1. **Utility patents,** the most common, are issued to protect new, useful, nonobvious, and adequately specified articles of manufacture, machine processes, compositions of matter, or any improvements thereto, for a period of 20 years from the filing date of the application.
2. **Design patents** are issued to protect new, original, ornamental, and nonobvious designs for articles of manufacture for a period of 14 years from the date the patent is granted.
3. **Plant patents,** the least used, are issued to protect certain new varieties of plants that have been asexually reproduced for a term of 20 years from the filing date of the application.

The patent application and registration process can take from two to five years, and can be very costly. Because of this, before attempting to obtain a patent, you should conduct a cost-benefit analysis to determine if the benefits of being able to exclude others from making, using, or selling the invention outweigh the significant costs of prosecuting and protecting the patent. As part of this cost-benefit analysis, the leadership team of a growing company should consider:

1. Your company's stage of growth
2. Your company's position in the marketplace
3. The projected commercial value of the invention
4. The strength and scope of the claims that will ultimately be granted by the U.S. Patent and Trademark Office (USPTO)
5. Out-of-pocket expenses to obtain the patent, including legal fees, advertising, marketing, and retooling costs
6. The invention's proximity to existing patented and nonpatented technology (from an infringement and a commercial development perspective)
7. The company's ability to exploit the invention during the timeframe of exclusivity granted by a patent
8. The market value (and technological or commercial relevance and utility) of the invention two to five years down the road, after completion of the patent application process

9. The company's ability to enforce the patent following registration (given the high cost of patent litigation)
10. The availability of adequate alternatives for protecting the invention, such as state trade secret laws

If you decide to pursue a patent, before retaining a patent attorney, make sure that you *compile and maintain careful records* relating to the research and testing of the invention. The records should contain key dates, including the date the invention was conceived, and the date it was reduced to practice (in other words, the date the invention is well beyond the conceptual stage, and has either actually been developed and tested, or is so clearly described in the application that a third party skilled in the particular art could understand and actually develop the technology). The records should also demonstrate your diligence in developing and testing the invention. Make sure the records contain the corroboration of independent witnesses who are capable of understanding the nature and scope of the invention, and who will verify the dates mentioned above.

The next step is to conduct a search at the USPTO Public Search Room, located in northern Virginia, just outside of Washington, DC. An attorney experienced in this area usually conducts the search. The search will reveal those patents in your field that have already been issued, and how these patents may affect your application. The ramifications of any previously issued patents should be thoroughly discussed with your advisor, and may factor into your decision to apply for a patent.

The Application Process

The prosecution of a patent application is a complex process. First, the actual application must be compiled. The application consists of the following distinct parts:

- A clear and concise declaration that you are the original and sole inventor of the subject matter of the application
- Drawings of the invention (where applicable and necessary)
- One or more "claims of exclusivity" (These claims define the actual boundaries of the exclusive rights you hope to be granted. If it is drafted too narrowly, imitators and competitors may be able to

develop similar technologies and processes without fear of infringement. If it is drafted too broadly, you run the risk of rejection by the USPTO examiner, or face a subsequent challenge to the patent's validity by a competitor.)

- The appropriate filing fees

Once filed, a patent examiner at the USPTO will review the application to determine the patentability of the invention. As part of this review, the examiner will determine whether or not you have met the following statutory requirements:

- The invention consists of *patentable subject matter* (i.e., a process, machine, composition of matter, or article of manufacture, or a new and useful improvement to one of these)
- You are the *original inventor,* or discoverer, of the subject matter described in the patent application;
- The subject matter is *new* or *novel* (i.e., it is not already known to or used by others, has not been previously described in a printed publication, and is not merely a new use of an existing product)
- The subject matter is *useful,* and not merely of scientific or philosophical interest
- The subject matter is *nonobvious* to others in that particular trade or industry, as determined in the broad discretion of the USPTO examiner (i.e., the differences between the subject matter of the application and the current body of knowledge of those skilled in that area are more than marginal)

Protecting Your Patent

In order to preserve your rights, and continue to protect your interests, it is imperative that you institute an aggressive patent protection program once you obtain your patent. While the costs of such a program may be high, especially if you undertake any patent litigation, the rewards will be worthwhile. Should you successfully pursue an infringer, you may be entitled to an award of damages (that may be tripled by the court in extraordinary cases), as well as equitable relief, such as an injunction or accounting for profits.

Your patent protection program should include:

1. The use of proper notices of the existence of the patent on all labeling and marketing of the invention
2. Ongoing monitoring of new industry developments
3. Policing (and limiting) the activities of employees, licensees, and others who come into contact with the subject matter of the patent
4. Exploiting and saturating the market created by the patented product
5. Pursuing known or suspected infringers of the patent

Business Model Patents

The United States Circuit Court for the Ninth Circuit deemed novel methods of business patentable in the late 1990s. Ruling in the landmark case of *State Street Bank v. Signature Financial Group, Inc.,* the court found that Signature's patent for its "hub and spoke" mutual fund management process was valid. With the increased popularity of the Internet, many ways of doing business in cyberspace are being viewed as novel and patentable. Perhaps the best known Internet-related *business model patents* recently issued are for Priceline.com's reverse auction method and Amazon.com's "one-click" purchase feature. Both of these patent owners are aggressively trying to enforce their patents: Priceline.com by challenging a similar service offered by Microsoft, and Amazon.com by challenging Barnesandnoble.com's Express Lane online purchasing feature. With the onslaught of these business model patents, if your business model is dependent on e-commerce, you should consider the benefits of patent protection. However, the window may soon be closing on the number of business model patents that the USPTO is willing to grant, given the current backlog of filings.

International Patent Protection

As a general rule, protection provided by a given patent is limited to within the country in which it was granted. For example, a patent granted in the United States would not be infringed by a company manufacturing an identical product abroad, unless or until the foreign company starts manufacturing or selling the patented product in the United States. There are limited international intellectual property rights that may offer alternative protection to national rights. There are a number of international conventions governing IPRs, including:

- Paris Convention for the Protection of Industrial Property 1883
- Berne Convention for the Protection of Literary and Artistic Works 1886
- Patent Co-operation Treaty 1970 (PCT)
- WTO – Agreement on the Trade Related Aspects of Intellectual Property Rights 1994 (TRIPS)

None of these conventions establishes an international form of IPR valid in several countries. Rather, the conventions try to harmonize IPR protection, or simplify the application process.

The Paris Convention has two main principles: national treatment (i.e., foreigners from other signatory states are to be treated the same as domestic citizens, so far as patent protection for inventions is concerned); and right of priority (i.e., provided the correspondent application in Country B is filed within twelve months of filing in Country A, then it is backdated to the date of first filing).

The PCT's aim is to reduce unnecessary effort, work, and cost on the part of patent applicants. Once a single international patent application is filed at the patent office of a member country, it has the effect of it being filed in the first country and all other designated countries in which the applicant is interested. The local patent office transmits the international patent application to an international searching authority for a prior art search, which is then forwarded to all designated countries. The local patent office of each designated state then continues with the application in accordance with its own normal procedures.

TRIPS's aim is to narrow the gaps in the way IPR is protected around the world, and covers five broad issues:

1. How basic principles of the trading system and other intellectual property agreements should be applied
2. How to give adequate protection to IPRs

3. How countries should adequately enforce those rights
4. How to settle IPR disputes between members of the WTO
5. Special transitional arrangements in less developed countries

Within Europe, a similar system has existed under the European Patent Convention (EPC) since 1973. A single application is filed and examined by the European Patent Office (EPO). Once a patent is granted, it gives the same level of legal protection as a national patent in any of the contracting states that were designated in the application. There are currently 27 contracting countries, with another 4 expected to become members in due course.

TRADEMARKS AND SERVICE MARKS

Brands have become increasingly more important in the information-based and services economies. The best way for a growing company to protect its brands is under the federal trademark laws. These laws define a trademark or service mark as a word, name, symbol, or device used to indicate the origin and ownership of a product or service. Trademark status may also be granted to distinctive and unique packaging, color combinations, building designs, product styles, and overall presentations. Trademarks and service marks are afforded the same legal protections, but trademarks are used to identify and distinguish *products,* whereas service marks identify and distinguish *services.* These terms are used interchangeably throughout this chapter.

Trademark rights generally arise out of use of the mark in connection with specific products or services. Once used, the owner of a trademark has the right to use the mark in connection with the product it was intended to identify, to the exclusion of all subsequent users. In the United States, these rights may be protected by state statutory and/or common law, as well as by federal law (under the Lanham Act). Protection under federal law is enhanced by registering the mark with the United States Patent and Trademark Office (the USPTO).

A properly selected, registered, and protected mark can be of great importance to your business in establishing, maintaining, and expanding its market share. There is perhaps no better way to build and maintain a strong position in the marketplace than to build goodwill and consumer recognition in the identity (or "brand") of your products or services. The mark selected is the consumer's first impression of the nature and quality of the product or service you offer. As a result, many companies will select a mark that is easily understood by the public. While this allows the mark to serve as compressed advertising, it may be difficult to register and protect the mark because it is often too descriptive in nature. When selecting a mark, you should consider the following factors:

1. The nature of the product or service the mark will identify
2. The purchasing habits of the targeted consumer
3. The ease of recognition and pronunciation (keep it "short and sweet," when possible)
4. Marks used and/or registered by competitors and others in the industry
5. The availability of dollars to promote the mark
6. The adaptability of the mark to various applications and media

Types of Marks

When selecting a mark, you will want to ensure that you will be able to protect it. Not all words or phrases are entitled to trademark protection. As a preliminary matter, the mark must identify the product or service as coming from a particular source. The mark may not, however, be generic in nature, or merely describe the product or service it identifies. For example, a chain of auto body shops under the name "Auto Body Repair Shop" could not get a service mark because its name is too generic, yet MAACO is a nationally known name for the same services. Marks that are generally protectable include:

1. *Coined, fanciful, or arbitrary marks.* This is the strongest category of mark that can be protected. The trademark is either a coined word, like XEROX, or a word in common usage that has no meaning when applied to the goods or services in questions, such as Puffs (for facial tissues), Yoo-Hoo (for chocolate drinks), or Wonder (for bread). These marks are inherently distinctive for legal and

registration purposes; however, because of the obscurity of the mark, the burden is on the owner to establish goodwill.

2. *Suggestive marks.* Suggestive marks require the consumer to use some degree of imagination to determine the products or services identified by the marks. Examples of suggestive marks include Sun Maid (for raisins), Chips Ahoy (for cookies), and Champs (for retail sporting goods stores).

3. *Descriptive marks.* Trademarks that are merely descriptive of the products they identify cannot be protected unless the owner can establish distinctiveness, dubbed "secondary meaning." This means that the owner must demonstrate that the public associates the particular mark with the goods of the specific producer. This category includes names like Holiday Inn (for motels), Reddi wip (for whipped topping), and Quaker Oats (for oat cereal), all of which are descriptive, but registered because of their acquired distinctiveness.

There are several categories of marks that may not be protected under federal law, unless there is a demonstrable secondary meaning, similar to that required for descriptive marks. These include:

- Immoral, deceptive, or scandalous marks
- Marks that may disparage or falsely suggest a connection with persons, institutions, beliefs, or national symbols, or may bring them into contempt or disrepute
- Marks that contain the flag of the United States, or flag, coat of arms, or similar insignia of a state, municipality, or foreign nation
- Marks that are the name, portrait, or signature of a living individual, unless that person gives written consent
- Marks that are the name, portrait, or signature of a deceased president of the United States during the life of his widow, unless she gives her written consent
- Any mark that so resembles a mark already registered with the USPTO as to be likely, when applied to the applicant's goods, to cause confusion or mistake or to deceive
- Marks that are primarily geographically descriptive, or deceptively misdescriptive of the applicant's goods
- Marks that are primarily a surname

Federal Registration

One of the most important benefits to be gained from federal registration of your mark is that it serves as constructive notice to the rest of the United States that the trademark belongs to you. This is of utmost importance, since state common law and statutory protection usually only extend to the geographic area in which you are offering or selling your products or services. Without a federally registered mark, if a company in a remote geographic location subsequently decides to sell competing products under a similar mark, you may be barred from entering that local market if doing so would create consumer confusion. As long as your registration predates another's use of the mark, you will have the right to demand that the other company stop using the mark—even in markets you have yet to enter. Because common law rights are grounded in actual and prior use, however, even federal registration will not give you the right to stop others who used the same mark in their local market, prior to your registration. Consequently, it is important to apply for registration as early as is practicable.

Prior to the passage of the Trademark Law Revision Act of 1988 (TLRA), you could only apply for federal registration of a mark if you had actually used the mark in interstate commerce. This generally meant that a great deal of time and money may be invested in a new branding concept without having any assurance that the mark could ever be properly registered and protected. With the passage of the TLRA, however, you may now apply for registration of a mark based on *either* actual use or a "bona fide intention" to use the mark in interstate commerce. This allows the applicant to conduct some market research and further investigation, without the need to actually put the mark into commerce.

Whether the filing is made under the "actual use" or "intent to use" provisions, an application must be prepared and filed in the classification that is appropriate for the goods and services offered. A trademark examiner will then review the application to determine if it meets the statutory requirements, and whether similar trademarks have already been registered in the same or similar lines of business. You or your attorney must respond to all (if any) of the concerns of the examiner. This process continues until the application is either finally refused, or recommended by the examiner for publication in the *Official Gazette* (which serves as notice to the general public). Once published, anyone who believes that he or she would be injured by registration of the mark may file a Notice of Opposition within 30 days of the publication date. If no opposition is filed (or if an opposition is resolved in your favor), an application based on actual use will proceed to registration, and a Certificate of Registration will be issued in a few months.

If the application is based on an "intent to use" the mark, once it is published and successfully makes it through the publication process, a Notice of Allowance will be issued. You will then have *six months* to file a Statement of Use, with actual examples of use, such as marketing materials, receipts, invoices, newspaper clippings, etc. (commonly referred to as "specimens") attached. After satisfactory review of the Statement of Use and specimens, the mark will be registered. You may request extensions of time for filing of the Statement of Use for up to four successive six-month periods. Failure to file by the deadline will result in an abandonment and forfeiture of all fees paid.

If an Opposition is filed and the parties fail to resolve their differences, there will be a hearing before the Trademark Trial and Appeal Board (TTAB). TTAB only has the authority to determine who has the right to *register* the mark—not who has the right to *use* the mark. Objections regarding rights to use a mark in a given geographic area must be raised in a court of law. TTAB is also the appropriate body to appeal a final refusal of an application for registration.

Federal trademark registrations issued or renewed on or after November 16, 1989 will remain in force for ten years, and may be renewed for additional ten-year periods. Trademark registrations issued prior to November 16, 1989 remain in force for 20 years, and may be renewed for ten-year periods. Registrations may, however, be cancelled after six years, unless you file an affidavit of continued use with the USPTO, demonstrating that you are still using the mark in commerce, and have not abandoned it. A similar affidavit of use must accompany any application to renew the registration.

Although most marks are registered on the Principal Register of the USPTO, a mark that is actually in commercial use but that does not qualify for registration on the Principal Register may qualify for registration on the Supplemental Register. Marks typically registered on the Supplemental Register are those falling into one of the categories listed above that requires the establishment of secondary meaning (e.g., descriptive marks). Registration on the Supplemental Register does not provide the same level of protection afforded by registration on the Principal Register, but it does give you:

1. The right to bring suit in federal court and obtain certain statutory remedies for infringement
2. A possible right to apply for registration in those foreign jurisdictions requiring home country registrations
3. Protection against federal registration by another user of the same, or a confusingly similar, mark
4. The right to use the "TM" symbol to put the world on notice that you are claiming rights in the mark

Registration can be a complex and lengthy process (taking anywhere from 12 to 18 months for applications with minimal problems), but the commercial rewards may be substantial if the registered mark is properly used. These rewards include:

1. The right to protect against others using your mark in the future
2. The right to bring legal action in federal court for trademark infringement
3. The right to seek recovery of profits, damages, and costs in an infringement action, and, possibly, to seek triple damages and attorney fees in egregious cases
4. The right to deposit the registration with the United States Department of Customs in order to stop the importation of goods bearing an infringing mark
5. A basis for filing trademark applications in foreign countries

The Application for Registration

The application to register a mark on the Principal Register consists of:

- A written application
- A drawing of the mark that must be a black and white, or typed, rendition of the mark, used to print the mark in the *Official Gazette* and on the registration certificate)

- The required filing fee (which, effective January 10, 2000, is $325) for each class of goods or services covered in the application
- Three examples (called "specimens") showing actual use of the mark in connection with the goods or services, unless the application is based on an intent to use the mark. Specimens showing use of a trademark would include labels, product packaging, or pictures of the product showing the mark on the actual goods. Specimens showing use of a service mark would include advertising or marketing materials describing the services. Applicants of intent-to-use applications must submit examples of use with the Statement of Use filed after the Notice of Allowance issued (or they may amend their applications to include a statement of use prior to the publication of their marks)

Trademark Protection

When your mark is finally registered with the USPTO, a new battle against the rest of the world begins. You must develop an active trademark protection program designed to educate company staff, consultants, distributors, suppliers, and all others who may come in contact with the company's marks as to proper usage and protection of the marks. As with trade secret laws, the courts will usually only help those who have attempted to help themselves. A company that tolerates misuse of its marks by the public and/or fails to enforce quality control standards in any licensing of the mark may lose its trademark rights, and, therefore, one of its most valuable weapons in the war for market share.

A well-managed trademark protection program begins with a formal compliance manual drafted with the assistance of trademark counsel and the company's advertising agency. The compliance manual should contain detailed guidelines for proper trademark usage, grammar, and quality. For example, a trademark is correctly used only as a proper adjective; therefore, it should always be capitalized and modify a noun. An example of a commonly misused trademark in this context is XEROX®, which is often used improperly as a noun (to refer to the end product instead of the source of the process, or even as a verb to refer to the process itself). The trademark should always be used in conjunction with the generic name of the class of products to which it belongs; for example, Kleenex®

facial tissues or Sunkist® orange juice. Once a trademark has been registered, you should develop compliance guidelines that should address the following:

- Proper display of the marks (use of the ®, ™, or © symbol)
- All documents, correspondence, and other materials on which the trademark must be displayed
- All authorized uses of the marks and prohibited uses (i.e., may not be used as part of a licensee's corporate name)

In addition to a compliance manual, you must develop strategies to monitor competitors and other third parties from improper usage or potential infringement of the mark. A staff member should be designated to search the Internet, read trade publications, business press, marketing materials of competitors, and in-house production, labeling, and correspondence to ensure that the mark is properly used and not stolen by competitors. If an infringing use is discovered, you must be vigilant in protecting your marks. This will require working closely with trademark counsel to ensure that all potential infringers receive letters demanding that such practices be immediately discontinued and infringing materials destroyed. As much evidence as possible should be gathered on each potential infringer, and accurate files kept, in the event that trademark infringement litigation is necessary to settle the dispute. The costs of litigation, and the likely result of a suit, should be carefully weighed against the potential loss of goodwill and market share before pursuing any court action. It may be wiser to allocate those funds toward advertising rather than toward legal fees, especially if the likelihood of winning is remote.

Infringement and Dilution

The principal reason why a trademark monitoring program must be maintained is to guard against trademark infringement or dilution. Under the Lanham Act, infringement is a demonstration by the owner of a registered mark that some third party is using a reproduction or imitation of the registered mark in connection with the offer or sale of goods and services in such a way that it will likely cause confusion, mistake, or deception from the perspective of the ordinary purchaser.

The exact definition of the "likelihood of confusion" standard has been the source of much debate over the years. The focus has always been on whether the ordinary purchaser of the product in question is likely to be confused as to the source of origin or sponsorship. There is a wide variety of factors that the courts have listed as criteria for determining whether a likelihood of confusion exists, such as:

- The degree of similarity and resemblance of the infringer's marks to the registered marks (in terms of visual appearance, pronunciation, interpretation, etc.)
- The strength of the registered mark in the relevant industry or territory
- The actual or constructive intent of the infringer
- The similarity of the goods or services offered by the infringer and the owner of the registered mark
- The overlap (if any) in the distribution and marketing channels of the infringer and the owner of the registered mark
- The extent to which the owner of the registered mark can demonstrate that consumers were actually confused (usually demonstrated with consumer surveys and affidavits)

In addition to a federal cause of action for trademark infringement, the Federal Trademark Dilution Act of 1988 (which amended the Lanham Act of 1946) and many state trademark statutes provide owners of certain marks with an antidilution remedy. This remedy is available when a third party uses a mark in a way that dilutes the distinctive quality of a mark that has been registered under the state statute, or used under common law. The owner of the registered mark and the diluting party need not be in competition, nor must a likelihood of confusion be demonstrated. However, in order to make a claim for dilution, the trademark must have a "distinctive quality," meaning that it must enjoy very strong consumer loyalty, recognition, and goodwill. Under the federal law, this antidilution protection is only available to "famous marks."

Trademark rights are often the most valuable asset of an emerging growth company in today's competitive marketplace. The goodwill and consumer recognition that trademarks and service marks represent have tremendous economic value, and are therefore usually worth the effort and expense of properly registering and protecting them. This will also require a commitment by management to implement and support a strict trademark compliance program that will include usage guidelines for all departments inside the company, as well as for suppliers, licensees, service providers, and distributors. Online monitoring services, clipping services, semi-annual trademark searches, media awareness programs, designation of in-house compliance officers, warning letters to infringers and diluters, and even litigation are all part of an aggressive trademark protection program.

International Trademark Protection

As a general rule, trademark rights are based on actual use in each country. Entrepreneurs and leaders of growing companies doing business abroad can take advantage of an international system (the "Madrid System") that permits the simultaneous registration of trademarks in as many as fifty-six countries using a single standardized application.

The Madrid System is comprised of two treaties, the Madrid Agreement Concerning the International Registration of Marks (Madrid Agreement) and the Madrid Protocol for the International Registration of Trademarks (Madrid Protocol), both administered by the World Intellectual Property Organization (WIPO) located in Geneva, Switzerland. On November 2, 2002, President Bush signed the implementing legislation for the Madrid Protocol. For U.S. franchisors and other companies that maintain international trademark portfolios, access to the Madrid System presents an opportunity to streamline, and significantly reduce the cost of, global trademark acquisition and management.

For U.S. trademark owners in need of international trademark protection, the availability of the Madrid System, in many cases, may eliminate the need to file separate applications in each country where trademark protection is required. For example, the availability of the Madrid System will mean that a U.S. company in need of trademark protection in China, Japan, the United Kingdom, and Morocco (all members of the Madrid Protocol) will simply file one standardized application in the United States Patent and Trademark Office (USPTO), pay one fee, and obtain a single registration covering the series of underlying national applications in each of the named countries. The resulting registration will have one registration number and one renewal date.

However, the Madrid System is *not* a substantive trademark law, and an application filed under it does not result in a "Madrid Registration." That is, while the registration issued under the Madrid System is often referred to as an "international registration," it differs from registrations issued under the auspices of such collective organizations as the European Union because it is not a freestanding, supranational registration. Instead, the Madrid System provides a *centralized mechanism* for simultaneously obtaining, in effect, separate national registrations, based either on a pending application or existing registration on file in the national trademark office of the applicant's "home country."

In order to file an application under the Madrid System, the applicant must be a "qualified owner" of either a pending application or a registration on file in the national trademark office of the applicant's "home country."

UNDERSTANDING COPYRIGHTS

According to the 1976 Copyright Act, a copyright is a form of protection available to the author of original "literary, dramatic, musical, artistic, graphical, sculptural, architectural, and certain other intellectual works which are fixed in any tangible medium of expression." The owner of a copyright generally has the exclusive right to do, or authorize others to do, the following: *reproduce* the copyrighted work; *prepare derivative* works; *distribute and transmit* copies of the work; and *perform or display* the copyrighted work.

Congress has struggled to keep up with the many modes of authorship that were not contemplated when the original copyright laws were written in 1790. Computers, photography, television, phonograph records, motion pictures, videodiscs, the Internet, and advanced telecommunications have presented new challenges to legislators as to how to protect the rights of innovators and pioneers.

The latest major revision of the copyright laws was the 1976 Copyright Act. Under the revised laws, a copyright is recognized and can be protected as soon as a literary or artistic work is created in any tangible medium of expression. This gives the copyright owner control over access to, and publication of, the work right from the start. Copyright protection is typically only available to the person whose labor created the work;

however, it is also available for certain types of compilations (the assembly of pre-existing materials) and derivative (translations, re-creations, etc.) works. The Sonny Bono Term Extension Act of 1998 added 20 years to the copyright term. The term of protection is now 95 years from publication date, or 120 years from creation date, whichever expires first.

Work for Hire

Typically, the author of the work is the owner of the copyright. Under the doctrine of "work made for hire," works developed by an employee are considered to be works owned by the employer. The 1976 Copyright Act defines a "work for hire" as being either an employee preparing a work within the scope of his or her employment, or a work specially ordered or commissioned if the parties expressly agree in a signed written document that the work will be owned by a party other than the author as a work for hire.

Under a recent major Supreme Court case, it was determined that the presumption that the work of employees is owned by their employer does not necessarily apply to freelance workers or independent contractors, *unless* there is a written agreement stating that it is the clear intent of the parties that the copyright to the work will belong to the "commissioning party" and not the "creating party."

Notice of Copyright

The author of a work that is protected by copyright should, whenever possible, use a notice of copyright to put the world on notice that the author claims the work as a copyright. The prescribed notice consists of (1) "©" or the word "copyright," (2) the year of first publication of the work, and (3) the name of the copyright owner. However, as explained in Figure 11.5, the lack of a copyright notice does not necessarily mean that the author does not intend to protect his or her rights to the work.

Copyright Registration

Pursuant to the Act, copyright protection arises *as soon as the work is created and fixed in a tangible medium* of expression. The work need not be registered prior to its publication; however, registration is necessary if the author wants to take advantage of the many benefits and protections offered under the Copyright Act, which include the right to sue for infringement, the ability to obtain damages, and to prevent others from using the work. Materials are protected, therefore, *without registration,* provided they contain the required statutory notice of copyright. Any materials filed for copyright registration become public record. It is, therefore, advisable to examine whether registration would compromise the confidentiality of any trade secrets that may be contained in the work. For example, the content of a new marketing brochure is a natural candidate for copyright registration; however, the contents of a confidential operations manual should not be registered, due to its proprietary nature.

Infringement

In order to enforce rights in court for copyright infringement, the author must register and deposit copies of the work in the Library of Congress depository. The Copyright Office then examines the application for accuracy, and determines whether the work submitted is copyrightable subject matter. The Copyright Office, unlike the Patent and Trademark Office, will not compare the works to those already registered, and does not conduct interference or opposition proceedings. The copyright laws, however, do provide remedies for private civil actions. Remedies for copyright infringement include injunctions against unauthorized use, attorneys' fees, damages for lost profits, and certain statutory damages. These enforcement rights and remedies must be weighed against the fact that once a written work is registered, the public, including competitors, may view it. Thus, it may make more sense to protect proprietary materials as trade secrets, rather than expose them to the public through the Library of Congress.

A copyright generally is infringed by the unauthorized use or copying of the work. However, because it is usually difficult to prove copying and provide proof of "access" to the work and "substantial similarity" from the viewpoint of a reasonable person, the alleged infringer bears the burden of proving that his or her work has been independently created, and is not a copy of the copyrighted work. Before claiming copyright infringement, be aware that there are several limitations on the

Some Quick Tips to Remember about the Ever-Changing World of Copyright Law

---

1. Copyright protection can extend to computer programs, as a set of statements or instructions to be provided to a computer in order to achieve a specific result.

2. In order to qualify for protection, the work must be fixed in a tangible medium of expression. Copyright protects the *expression* of ideas, but *not* ideas, procedures, facts, or principles on a stand-alone basis.

3. Copyright law issues permeate the legal issues surrounding the Internet. Don't put on the World Wide Web what you don't intend others to use without adequate notice. Some courts have interpreted the ability of a "Web surfer" to view or browse your "work" as an "implied license" to use your work. Make sure you use the appropriate copyright notices.

4. The purchase of copyrighted work does not necessarily mean you own the underlying copyright. The object of the copyright can be separated under the law from the intangible copyright interest. The actual copyright interest can only be transferred by a signed agreement or by operation of law. For example, if you buy a sculpture, you have the right to display it in your home or office, but without the actual agreement of the copyright owner, you do not have the right to sell pictures of it, nor may you create a mold to reproduce the sculpture for distribution.

5. As explained in the section on "work for hire," independent contractors and freelance workers normally own the copyright for what they create, not the company who pays for it, unless a document specifies otherwise.

6. The absence of a formal copyright notice does not mean that the given work may be duplicated without the permission of the creator. The amendments to the Copyright Act of 1976 allow an author more flexibility. Keep in mind that it is not safe to assume that something is in the public domain merely because it lacks a formal copyright notice.

exclusive rights of a copyright owner. In addition, there are several acts that may be taken regarding the work without triggering an actionable remedy for infringement. These include use of the basic idea expressed in the work, the independent creation of an identical work without copying, and "fair use" of the work for purposes of criticism, comment, news reporting, teaching, scholarship, or research.

The federal copyright laws make willful copyright infringement for commercial profit a crime. The court is required to order a fine not to exceed $10,000, or imprisonment not to exceed one year, or both, as well as seizure, forfeiture, and destruction or other disposition of all infringing reproductions, and all equipment used in their manufacture. The following civil remedies are among those also available to the holder of any exclusive rights in the copyrighted work under federal law:

1. An injunction against future infringement
2. Actual damages suffered by the copyright owner
3. Any additional profits of the infringer
4. Full costs incurred to enforce the copyright, including reasonable attorneys' fees

TRADE SECRETS

A trade secret may consist of any type of information, including a formula, pattern, compilation, program, device, method, technique, or process that derives independent economic value from not being generally known to other persons who could obtain economic value from its disclosure or use. The information does not need to be unique or even invented by its owner to be protected, as long as the data is kept confidential and provides value to the company. A company uses its trade secrets to give it an advantage over competitors, and therefore must be treated by its owner as confidential and proprietary. The scope of protection available for trade secrets may be defined by a particular contract or fiduciary relationship, as well as by state statutes and court decisions. Unlike other forms of intellectual property protection, there are no federal civil statutes that provide for the registration of trade secrets because state law typically protects them.

Many emerging growth companies owe their success in part to the competitive advantage they enjoy by virtue of some confidential formula, method, design, or other type of proprietary know-how, and generally understand the importance of protecting trade secrets against unauthorized disclosure or use by a current or former employee, licensee, supplier, or competitor. Disclosure can cause severe and irreparable damage, especially to a smaller company where trade secrets may be the company's single most valuable asset.

Courts have generally set forth three requirements for information to qualify for trade secret protection: (1) the information must have some commercial value; (2) the information must not be generally known or readily ascertainable by others; and (3) the owner of the information must take all reasonable steps under the circumstances to maintain its confidentiality and secrecy. Examples of trade secrets include business and strategic plans, research and testing data, customer lists, manufacturing processes, pricing methods, and marketing and distribution techniques. In order to maintain the status as a trade secret, a company must follow a reasonable and consistent program for ensuring that the confidentiality of the information is maintained.

There are many factors, however, in addition to those discussed above, that courts have considered in deciding the extent to which protection should be afforded for trade secrets. Among those factors most often cited are:

1. The extent to which the information is known by others outside the company (including the efforts by the company to keep the information guarded from disclosure)
2. The value of the information, including the resources expended to develop the information, and whether the information truly provides a competitive advantage
3. The amount of effort that would be required by others to duplicate the effort or reverse engineer the technology
4. The nature of the relationship between an alleged infringer and the owner of the trade secret

Unlike many large corporations, smaller companies cannot generally afford a complicated security system to protect their trade secrets. With the mobile nature of today's work force, turnover caused by promotion within, and the chaotic nature of most growing businesses, it is practically impossible to prevent a determined employee from gaining relatively easy access to the company's proprietary information. Unfortunately, it is, therefore, easier to simply ignore the problem and do nothing at all about it. However, there are some fundamental, affordable, and practical measures that are discussed later in this chapter that the company can readily adopt to protect the data that is at the core of its competitive advantage.

Implementing a Protection Program

Even in an effort to protect trade secrets, there is such a thing as overkill. In fact, like the boy who cried wolf, if an emerging growth business tries to protect every aspect of its operation by classifying everything in sight as a "trade secret," it is likely that virtually nothing at all will be afforded protection when put to the test. Genuine trade secrets may be diluted if the owners (and their managers) try to protect too much.

The process of establishing a trade secret protection and compliance program should start with a "trade secret audit" to identify which information is *genuinely* confidential and proprietary. Each type of business will have its own priorities; however, all companies should consider financial, technical, structural, marketing, engineering, and distribution documents to be candidates for protection. The owner should next classify and develop security measures for protecting these documents. A separate office manual should be drafted for employees, written in basic terms, to inform them of trade secret protection procedures. The importance of following procedures in the manual could then be supported with timely interoffice memoranda, employee seminars, and incentive programs. Trade secret protection must be a part of the orientation program for newly hired employees, and departing employees should be fully briefed on their continuing duty and legal obligation to protect the secrets of their former employer. Periodic reviews of the technical and creative staffs are also recommended to identify new and existing trade secrets and reiterate the duty of nondisclosure. The central components of such a compliance program are as follows:

- Conduct appropriate background checks on employees with access to critical or confidential information.
- Ensure that adequate building security measures are taken, such as restricted access to highly sensitive areas, fences or gates to protect the premises, visitor control and log-in procedures, alarm systems, and locked desks, files, and vaults for proprietary documents. Post signs and notices in all appropriate places.
- Purchase stamps to be placed on documents that are trade secrets, in order to give notice to users of their proprietary status, and restrict the photocopying of these documents to limited circumstances.
- Designate a Trade Secret Compliance Officer who will be in charge of all aspects relating to the proper care and monitoring of trade secrets.
- Restrict employee access to trade secrets. Ask: Do they really "need to know" this information to do the job properly?
- Carefully review advertising and promotional materials and press releases to protect trade secrets. Restrict access for interviews by reporters and other members of the media. Everyone has one horror story about the "wandering reporter" who brought his camera along for the ride, or about the company that was so proud of its new product that it inadvertently disclosed the proprietary features of the discovery in its promotional materials.
- Ensure that *all* key employees, marketing representatives, service providers, licensees, prospective investors or joint venturers, customers, suppliers, or anyone else who has access to the company's trade secrets has signed a carefully prepared confidentiality and nondisclosure agreement.
- Police the activities of former employees, suppliers, and licensees. Include post-term obligations in agreements that impose a duty for the former employee to keep the company aware of his or her whereabouts.
- If trade secrets are contained on computers, use passwords and data encryption to restrict access to terminals and telephone access through modems.
- Establish controlled routing procedures for the distribution and circulation of certain documents.
- Purchase a paper shredder, and use when appropriate.

- Restrict photocopying of documents. Use legends and maintain log books on the whereabouts of originals.
- Monitor the trade press and business journals for any news indicating a possible compromise and/or exploitation of your trade secrets by others.
- Employees must be provided with guidelines on the care and use of confidential documents. This data should never be left unattended in the office, cars, airplanes, hotel rooms, trade shows, conventions, meetings, or conferences.
- Conduct exit interviews with all employees who have had access to the company's trade secrets. Remind them of their obligations not to use or disclose confidential and proprietary data owned by the company, and of the costs and penalties for doing so. Notify the future employer in writing of these obligations, especially if it is directly or indirectly competitive. Conversely, in order to avoid litigation as a defendant, remind new employees of the company's trade secret policies, and that they are being hired for their skills and expertise, *not* for their knowledge of a former employer's trade secrets.

Protecting against Misappropriation

Trade secret misappropriation—often referred to as "corporate espionage" or "trade secret piracy"—occurs when a trade secret is obtained by another party's breach of a confidential relationship, or through improper means. It has been estimated that corporate espionage costs U.S. businesses up to $100 billion annually.

All states have long upheld the protection of trade secrets as a matter of common law. At least 43 states have also adopted some version of the Uniform Trade Secrets Act, which affords civil remedies for trade secret piracy. Many states also have penal codes making trade secret theft a crime. Congress enacted the Economic Espionage Act in 1996, creating broad federal criminal remedies to deter misappropriation, and a number of international treaties and agreements also now address trade secret piracy.

In order to be able to bring an action for misappropriation, you must either establish a legal duty owed by those who come in contact with the information not to disclose or use the information, or prove that the information came into the hands of the misappropriator through a wrongful act.

The simplest way to create this duty is by agreement. The owner of a small or growing business should have a written employment agreement with each employee who may have access to the employer's trade secrets. The employment agreement should contain provisions regarding the nondisclosure of proprietary information as well as covenants of nonexploitation and noncompetition, applicable both during and after the term of employment. These covenants will be upheld and enforced by a court if they are reasonable, consistent with industry norms, and are not overly restrictive. Such an agreement will go a long way toward proving to a court that the owner intended to and, in fact, took reasonable steps to protect the trade secrets in the event of any subsequent litigation. The agreement should only be the beginning, however, of an ongoing program to make employees mindful of their continuing duty to protect the trade secrets of the employer. In some states, the unauthorized removal or use of trade secrets may also be a felony under criminal statutes.

Employment is not the only context in which this duty of nondisclosure might arise. An entrepreneur submitting proposals or business plans to prospective investors, lenders, licensees, franchisees, joint venturers, lawyers, accountants, or other consultants should take steps to ensure confidentiality at the commencement of any such relationship in which trade secrets may be disclosed in presentations, meetings, and documents.

Protecting trade secrets. In order to bring a lawsuit against another party for trade secret misappropriation, the plaintiff must demonstrate:

1. Existence of a trade secret
2. Communication to the defendant
3. Defendant was in a position of trust or confidence (some duty not to disclose)
4. Information constituting the trade secrets was used by defendant to the injury of the plaintiff

In analyzing whether these essential elements are present, the court will consider the following factors:

1. Was there any relationship of trust and confidence, either by express agreement or implied, which was breached?
2. How much time, value, money, or labor has been expended in developing the trade secret?
3. Had the trade secret reached the public domain? If so, through what channels?
4. Has the company maintained a conscious and continuing effort to maintain secrecy (agreements of nondisclosure, security measures, etc.)?
5. What were the mitigating circumstances surrounding the alleged breach or misappropriation?
6. What is the value of the secret to the company?

Remedies for misappropriation. The most important, and most immediate, remedy available in any trade secret misappropriation case is the temporary restraining order and preliminary injunction. This remedy immediately restrains the unauthorized user from continuing to use or practice the trade secret, pending a hearing on the owner's charge of misappropriation. Prompt action is necessary to protect the trade secret from further unauthorized disclosure. If the case ever makes it to trial, the court's decision will address the terms of the injunction, and may award damages and profits resulting from the wrongful misappropriation of the trade secret. However, you should be aware that there are certain risks to evaluate before instituting a trade secret suit. The company may face the risk that the trade secret at issue, or collateral trade secrets, may be disclosed during the course of the litigation. Certain federal and state rules of civil procedure and laws of evidence will protect against this risk to a limited extent. The prospective plaintiff should also consider that trade secret law is very unsettled, and often turns on the facts of each case. Establishing the "paper trail" needed to prove all of the elements of misappropriation may be virtually impossible in some cases. Such lengthy litigation is likely to be cost-prohibitive for the average small business owner. This is all the more reason why preventive and protective measures are a far more attractive alternative than litigation.

Protective Measures for Departing Employees

Growing companies must be aware of their rights and obligations when attempting to protect intellectual property in connection with a departing employee. For example, if an employee had threatened to leave the company if certain plans were not implemented, could the employee leave and take the intellectual property with him? No employer can prevent an enterprising employee from using his or her personal skills and experience in the launch of a new venture or in a new job. The law does not mandate, nor will it enforce, an agreement requiring an employee to "clean their mental slate" upon departure. There is a fine line between what knowledge belongs to the employee and what belongs to the former employer. Courts have attempted, relatively unsuccessfully, to develop some objective standard for what an employee in a particular position would have learned, regardless of where he or she might have been employed. Growing companies should note, however, that a few states, such as Pennsylvania, have determined that an employee *may use* trade secrets that were created by the employee while still in the employ of the former employer. Another 12 or so states, including California, severely limit, or even prohibit, the nature and scope of noncompetition agreements.

In analyzing a claim against a departed employee, the company should consider the following factors: (1) to what information was the employee exposed that truly constituted a trade secret; (2) the terms of any employment or noncompetition agreements to which the employee was a party; (3) steps taken by the company to protect the secret; (4) the extent to which this secret could have been discovered through "reverse engineering"; (5) the extent to which the employee used any company assets or resources to form his own business; (6) the extent to which the employee acquired this knowledge independent of his work at the company; (7) the extent to which the employee contracted current vendors or customers of the company during, or after, his employment with the company; (8) the similarity of the product or service to be offered to the company's product; and (9) the proximity of the new business to the former employer. Overall, the courts will be hesitant to stifle competition and the entrepreneurial spirit of the employee, absent some express agreement or foul play. However, a clear breach of an agreement or a noncompetition clause or the misappropriation of a customer list or proprietary data should be pursued.

Protecting Trade Secrets and Company Data against *Netspionage*

In the Internet age, it is difficult to secure trade secrets and other intangibles using traditional physical security methods like burglar alarms. Even newfangled information technology (IT) related security, like passwords and firewalls, might not be enough to protect these assets. This is especially true for companies with a significant Internet presence, who tend to be targets of so-called corporate "netspionage." More than 59 percent of companies with a significant Internet presence suffered break-ins during 1998.

Emerging growth companies should take the following measures to mitigate against the risk of netspionage:

1. Periodically test firewalls and other security systems
2. Monitor the intranet, extranet, and Internet for indications of theft
3. Deploy strategic cryptographic systems
4. Implement intrusion-detection technology
5. Establish electronic evidence-recovery capability
6. Respond to incidents and investigate anomalies

TRADE DRESS

Trade dress is a combination or arrangement of elements that make up the interior and/or exterior design of a business, usually in the context of a retail establishment or restaurant business. For example, trade dress can be symbols, designs, product packaging, labels and wrappers, exterior building features, interior designs, greeting cards, uniforms, etc. used to build brand awareness and loyalty with consumers. Trade dress is protected by federal and state trademark laws if it distinguishes the goods or services of one company from those of its competitors. Protectable trade dress consists of three elements: (1) a combination of features (used in the presentation, packaging, or "dress" of goods or services); (2) that which is nonfunctional; and (3) whose distinctiveness reveals to consumers the source of goods or services. For example, in *Taco Cabana International, Inc. v. Two Pesos,* the jury found the following combination of restaurant décor features to be protectable:

- Interior and patio dining areas decorated with artifacts, bright colors, paintings, and murals
- Overhead garage doors sealing off the interior from the patio areas
- Festive exterior paintings having a color scheme using top border paint and neon stripes
- Bright awnings and umbrellas
- Food-ordering counter set at an oblique angle to the exterior wall and electronic communication with the food preparation and pickup areas
- Exposed food preparation area accented by cooking and preparation equipment visible to the consumer
- Condiment stand in the interior dining area proximate to the food pickup stand

Suggestions for Enhancing the Strength of Trade Dress

- Adopt a combination of several features
- Ensure that several of the features are unique
- Avoid using features which are arguably functional
- Use the features consistently and continuously
- Include as many of the features as possible in advertising
- Refer to trade dress features in advertising and promotional literature
- Advertise as extensively as possible
- Carry the "theme" of the trade dress throughout the entire business
- Keep competitors from adopting similar combinations of features, and from using features that are unique to your trade dress
- Where possible, federally register the trade dress or its components
- Do not advertise utilitarian advantages of any trade dress you wish to protect
- Keep detailed records of instances of possible consumer confusion between your trade dress and a competitor's subsequently adopted trade dress

The best way to avoid trade dress infringement claims is *prevention*. To prevent such claims, avoid copying competitors' trade dress, investigate competitors' potential trade dress rights, and consult a skilled trademark attorney. Also, it may also be advisable to use disclaimers, and to be cautious when you have a potentially aggressive opponent.

SHOW-HOW AND KNOW-HOW

Certain types of intellectual property are treated as such primarily because some third party is willing to buy or license it from a company or individual that possesses a particular expertise. In such cases, *show-how* consists of training, technical support, and related educational services, whereas *know-how* usually takes the form of information that has been reduced to written, rather than spoken, form. Know-how and show-how usually arise in the context of a licensing agreement, where the licensee is requesting support services in addition to the tangible technology or patent central to the subject matter of the agreement. To the extent that the know-how or show-how is confidential and proprietary, the law of trade secrets will generally govern it, unless otherwise covered by a patent. To the extent that the know-how or show-how is nonproprietary and constitutes common knowledge, it will be governed by the term and conditions of the agreement between the parties.

IDEAS AND CONCEPTS

As a general rule, a mere idea or concept does not qualify for patent, copyright, trade secret, or trademark protection. The right to the exclusive use of an idea is lost by voluntary disclosure, unless the following three elements are present: (1) the idea is in a concrete form; (2) the idea is original and useful; and (3) the idea is disclosed in a situation where compensation is contemplated. If this test is satisfied, the idea may qualify as a "property right," and may be protected under theories of implied contract, unjust enrichment, misappropriation, breach of a fiduciary relationship, or passing off. Recovery under these circumstances usually will depend on the relationship between the idea submitter and the idea receiver, as well as the facts surrounding the disclosure.

As a general rule, the law of intellectual property seeks to protect and reward the creative firm, innovator, or entrepreneur for their efforts by prohibiting misappropriation or infringement by competitors. It is therefore crucial that the legal considerations to protect these "crown jewels" are incorporated into the strategic marketing plan of any emerging business. If proper steps are not taken to protect these new products, services, and operational techniques, then it will be extremely difficult to maintain and expand the company's share of the market because others will be free to copy these ideas as if they were their own.

The proper protection and, where possible, registration of intellectual property is essential to building and sustaining a company's growth. The procedures and expenses necessary to protect these valuable *intangible assets* are crucial to the continued well-being of the company and its ability to continue to survive in a competitive marketplace.

12

LICENSING AND FRANCHISING

Licensing is a contractual method of developing and exploiting intellectual property by transferring rights of use to third parties *without* transferring ownership. Virtually any proprietary product or service may be the subject of a license agreement, ranging from the licensing of the Mickey Mouse character by Walt Disney Studios in the 1930s to modern-day licensing of computer software and high technology. From a legal perspective, licensing involves complex issues of contract, tax, antitrust, international, tort, and intellectual property law. From a business perspective, licensing involves weighing the advantages of licensing against the disadvantages compared to alternative types of vertical distribution systems. From a strategic perspective, licensing is a means to uncover hidden or underutilized value in your portfolio of intellectual assets, creating new income streams and market opportunities in order to maximize shareholder value.

Many of the economic and strategic benefits of licensing a growing company can enjoy closely parallel the advantages of franchising, namely:

- Spreading the risk and cost of development and distribution
- Achieving more rapid market penetration
- Earning initial license fees and ongoing royalty income

- Enhancing consumer loyalty and goodwill
- Preserving the capital that would otherwise be used for internal growth and expansion
- Testing new applications for existing and proven technology
- Avoiding or settling litigation regarding a dispute over ownership of the technology

The disadvantages of licensing are also similar to the risks inherent in franchising, such as:

- A somewhat diminished ability to enforce quality control standards and specifications
- A greater risk of another party infringing upon the licensor's intellectual property
- A dependence on the skills, abilities, and resources of the licensee as a source of revenue
- Difficulty in recruiting, motivating, and retaining qualified and competent licensees
- The risk that the licensor's entire reputation and goodwill may be damaged or destroyed by the act or omission of a single licensee
- The administrative burden of monitoring and supporting the operations of the network of licensees

The usage and application of intellectual assets inside large as well as medium and small companies range from being actively exploited to benignly neglected, to everything in between. Research and development efforts may yield new product and service opportunities that are not critical to the company's core business lines, technologies that become "orphans" (e.g., lacking internal support or resources) due to political reasons or changes in leadership, or products or services that the company simply lacks the expertise or the resources to bring the to the marketplace. In other cases, the underlying technology may have multiple applications and usages, but the company does not have the time or resources to develop the technology beyond its core business. Well-managed intellectual capital-driven companies will recognize these assets as still having significant value, and develop licensing programs. For example, IBM reported well over $2 billion in licensing revenues in its 2005 Annual Report;

much of this revenue represented high margin cash flow streams which also helped offset its research and development costs. Other industry leaders such as GE, Texas Instruments, Dow Chemical, and DuPont are building organizational infrastructure, strategies, and systems to do a better job of managing and licensing their intellectual capital assets. Value extraction and harvesting through licensing is a key theme running throughout the boardrooms of corporate America, and is not limited to Fortune 500 companies. Businesses of all sizes and with relatively small intellectual property portfolios can still apply these same strategic principles and approaches to the management of their intellectual capital.

Companies of all sizes are realizing that invention for the sake of the inventor, *or* innovation without revenue streams, can be very harmful to shareholder value. In a post-Enron world in which boards of directors are governed by Sarbanes-Oxley, and an unforgiving capital market, no company can afford to ignore valuable assets and let them go to waste. If there is no desire or resources available to *directly* transform an innovation into new products and services, then licensing (as well as joint ventures, which are discussed in the next chapter) offers an excellent way to *indirectly* bring these innovations to the marketplace, particularly in rapidly moving industries in which the windows of opportunity may be limited.

It is also critical to develop an overall set of intellectual capital licensing policies, strategies, and objectives. The goals of the licensing program should be aligned with the overall strategic goals and business plans of the company. The licensing process should help determine those technologies or brands that will be made available for licensing, those that will not be, and why. The process should also define how licensees will be selected, how their performance will be monitored and measured, and under what circumstances licensees will be terminated.

Failure to consider all the costs and benefits of licensing could easily result in a regrettable strategic decision or an unprofitable license agreement due to either an underestimation of the licensee's need for technical assistance and support, or an overestimation of the market demand for the licensor's products and services. In order to avoid such problems, a certain amount of due diligence should be conducted by the licensor prior to any serious negotiations with a prospective licensee. This preliminary investigation generally includes market research, legal steps to fully protect intellectual property, and an internal financial analysis of the technology with respect to pricing, profit margins, and costs of production and distribution. It will also include a more specific analysis of the prospective licensee with respect to its financial strength, research and manufacturing capabilities, and reputation in the industry.

UNDERSTANDING LICENSING 101

Licensing promotes rapid market penetration by shifting the capital costs of expansion, and shares many of the same risks inherent in franchising, such as the possible loss of quality control and a dependence on the skills and resources of the licensee. In addition, there has been a recent emphasis on brand-extension licensing, which is discussed later in this chapter.

The two principal types of licensing occur at two different levels in the marketplace: (1) technology licensing, a strategy that involves finding a licensee in order to exploit industrial and technological developments; and (2) merchandise and character licensing, a strategy that involves licensing a recognized trademark or copyright to a manufacturer of consumer goods in markets not currently served by the licensor.

TECHNOLOGY TRANSFER AND LICENSING AGREEMENTS

A technology transfer and licensing agreement is a marriage often made between an entrepreneur with the technology but without the resources to adequately penetrate the marketplace as licensor, and a larger company that has sufficient research and development, production, human resources, and marketing capability to make the best use of the technology. The industrial and technological revolution has witnessed a long line of very successful entrepreneurs who have relied on the resources of larger organizations to bring their products to market, such as Chester Carlson (xerography), Edwin Land (Polaroid cameras), Robert Goddard (rockets), and Willis Carrier (air-conditioning). As the base for technological development becomes broader, large companies look not only to entrepreneurs and small businesses for new ideas and technologies, but also to each other, foreign countries, universities, and federal and state governments to serve as licensors of technology.

In the typical licensing arrangement, the proprietor of intellectual property rights (patents, trade secrets, trademarks, and know-how) permits a third party to make use of these rights, according to a set of specified conditions and circumstances set forth in a licensing agreement.

Why Growing Companies Develop Technology Licensing Programs

1. To match promising technology with the resources necessary to bring it to the marketplace
2. To raise capital and earn royalty income (e.g., there are many entrepreneurs who have had doors slammed in their face by commercial banks and venture capitalists who ultimately obtained growth capital and cash flow from licensees)
3. As a defensive strategy; this can occur from one of two perspectives: (1) The licensor may want to have its competitors as licensees instead of watching as they eventually develop their own technology, or (2) the licensee may want to preempt a competitor, or gain access to its confidential information by approaching the competitor to obtain a license. (*Warning:* Some competitors will acquire an exclusive license to technology merely to "sit on it" so that it never enters the marketplace. Be prepared to negotiate into the agreement certain performance standards or limits to exclusivity in order to avoid such a trap.)
4. To shift (or share) the product liability risk inherent in the production or marketing of hazardous or dangerous products with the licensee
5. To reach new geographic markets unfamiliar to the technology proprietor, such as overseas, where the technology may need to be adapted or otherwise modified to meet local market conditions
6. To make the widest possible use of the technology by licensing other applications or by-products of the technology that may be outside the licensor's expertise or targeted markets
7. To avoid or settle actual or pending litigation (many litigants in intellectual property infringement or misappropriation cases wind up settling the case using some form of a cross-license in lieu of costly attorney's fees and litigation expenses).

Licensing agreements can be limited to a very narrow component of the proprietor's intellectual property rights, such as one specific application of a single patent, or they can be much broader, such as in a classic "technology transfer" agreement, through which an entire bundle of intellectual property rights are transferred to the licensee, typically in exchange for initial fees and royalties. The classic technology transfer arrangement is actually more akin to a "sale" of the intellectual property rights, with a right by the licensor to get the intellectual property back if the licensee fails to meet its obligations under the agreement.

Key Elements of a Technology Licensing Agreement

Once the decision to enter into formal negotiations has been made, the terms and conditions of the license agreement should be discussed. Naturally, these provisions vary, depending on whether the license is for merchandising an entertainment property, exploiting a given technology, or distributing a particular product to an original equipment manufacturer (OEM) or value-added reseller (VAR). As a general rule, any well-drafted license agreement should address the following topics:

Scope of the grant. The exact scope, extent of exclusivity, and subject matter of the license must be initially addressed in the license agreement. Any restrictions on the geographic scope, rights and fields of use, permissible channels of trade, restrictions on sublicensing (including the formula for sharing sublicensing fees if provided), limitations on assignability, or exclusion of enhancements or improvements to the technology (or expansion of the product line) covered by the agreement should be clearly set forth in this section.

Term and renewal. The commencement date, duration, renewals and extensions, conditions to renewal, procedures for providing notice of intent to renew, grounds for termination, obligations upon termination, and licensor's reversionary rights in the technology should all be included in this section.

Performance standards and quotas. To the extent that the licensor's consideration will depend on royalty income that will be calculated from the licensee's gross or net revenues, the licensor may want to impose certain minimum levels of performance in terms of sales, advertising, promotional expenditures, and human resources to be devoted to the exploitation of the technology. There might also be milestone payments tied to the achievement of certain key events, such as regulatory approvals of the core technology. Naturally, the licensee will argue for a "best efforts" provision that frees it from performance standards and quotas. In such cases, the licensor may want to insist on a minimum royalty level that will be paid regardless of the licensee's actual performance.

Payments to the licensor. Virtually every type of license agreement includes some form of initial payment and ongoing royalties to the licensor. Royalty formulas vary widely, however, and may be based upon gross sales, net sales, net profits, fixed sum per product sold, or a minimum payment to be made to the licensor over a given period of time, or may include a sliding scale in order to provide some incentive to the licensee as a reward for performance. Royalty rates may vary from industry to industry, and in some cases will vary depending on the licensed product's stage of development. For example, in a typical merchandise licensing agreement, royalty rates range from 7 to 12 percent of net sales, depending on the strength of the licensor's brands, whereas manufacturing royalty rates may be lower when the licensee needs to make significant capital expenditures in order to bring the product to the marketplace. In the biotechnology and medical device industries, the royalty rates may vary based on the stage of development of the product and its progression through the FDA approval process. A biotech or pharmaceutical treatment or compound that has already cleared Phase III approval (the final approval phase of the FDA process) may command royalties as high as 20 percent of sales, whereas a pre-clinical trial product or compound may only command a royalty rate of 2 percent, depending on the likelihood of ultimate commercialization.

Quality control assurance and protection. Quality control standards and specifications for the production, marketing, and distribution of the products and services covered by the license must be set forth by the licensor. In addition, procedures should be included in the agreement that allow the licensor an opportunity to *enforce* these standards and specifications, such as a right to inspect the licensee's premises; a right to review, approve, or reject samples produced by the licensee; and a right to review and approve any packaging, labeling, or advertising materials to be used in connection with the exploitation of the products and services that are within the scope of the license. Certain types of licensors may also want to consider the placing of a ceiling on the allowances for returned merchandise, perhaps in the 3 to 5 percent range of total goods sold. This helps prevent the licensee from producing a significant amount of substandard product that could dilute the brand, damage the technology, or otherwise expose the licensor to harm or potential liability.

Insurance and indemnification. The licensor should take all necessary and reasonable steps to ensure that the licensee has an obligation to protect and indemnify the licensor against any claims or liabilities resulting from the licensee's exploitation of the products and services covered by the license. These provisions should address any minimum insurance coverages (naming the licensor as an additional insured), as well as discuss an exclusion from liability or ceilings on the responsibilities of the licensee.

Accounting, reports, and audits. The licensor must impose certain reporting and record-keeping procedures on the licensee in order to ensure an accurate accounting for periodic royalty payments. Further, the licensor should reserve the right to audit the records of the licensee in the event of a dispute or discrepancy, as well as determine provisions as to whom will be responsible for the cost of the audit in the event of an understatement.

Duties to preserve and protect intellectual property. The obligations of the licensee, its agents, and its employees to preserve and protect the confidential nature and acknowledge the ownership of the intellectual property being disclosed in connection with the licensing agreement must be carefully defined. Any required notices or legends that must be included on products or materials distributed in connection with the license agreement (such as the status of the relationship between licensee and licensor, or identification of actual owner of the intellectual property) are also described in this section. The agreement should also be clear as to which party will handle, and at whose expense and control, any disputes regarding the ownership of the intellectual property.

Technical assistance, training, and support. Any obligation of the licensor to assist the licensee in developing or exploiting the subject matter being licensed is included in this section of the agreement. The assistance may take the form of personal services, or documents and records. Either way, any fees due to the licensor for such support services that are over and above the initial license and ongoing royalty fee must also be addressed.

Warranties of the licensor. A prospective licensee may demand that the licensor provide certain representations and warranties in the license agreement. These may include warranties regarding the ownership of the intellectual property, such as absence of any known infringements of the intellectual property, restrictions on the ability to license the intellectual property, or warranties pledging that the technology has the features, capabilities, and characteristics previously represented in the negotiations.

Infringements. The license agreement should contain procedures under which the licensee must notify the licensor of any known or suspected direct or indirect infringements on the subject matter being licensed. The responsibilities for the cost of protecting and defending the technology should also be specified in this section.

Termination. The license agreement should provide some guidance regarding the licensor's ability to terminate the rights granted in the event of material breach (such as nonpayment of royalties), change in control, insolvency, or other default of the licensee. The notice and procedures for termination should be discussed, as well as the "wind-down" or "phase-out" periods following termination.

Tips for the Prospective Licensor

Finding the right dance partner. The quest for the appropriate licensee should be approached with the same zeal and diligence as the search for a marriage partner. No stone should remain unturned, either in narrowing the field of prospective licensees or in the due diligence process applied to a particular proposed licensee. The goals and objectives of each party, the financial strength of the licensee, the licensee's past licensing practices, the qualifications of the licensee's jurisdiction (other states, other countries), and the skills of the licensee's sales and marketing team should all be examined prior to the commencement of the negotiation of the license agreement. Access to the licensor's intellectual property should be severely restricted unless, and until, these criteria have been examined and met to the satisfaction of the licensor.

Avoiding the inferiority complex. Although a small company or entrepreneur looking to license its technology to a larger business often faces an uphill battle, this is not sufficient reason to merely "roll over" in the licensing negotiations. There are too many horror stories of entrepreneurs who were impressed and intimidated by the larger company's resources and lawyers, and as a result "sold their soul" at far below the current or eventual market value of the technology.

Don't go in naked; don't be a motormouth. Many prospective licensors make the mistake of telling too little or saying way too much in the initial meetings and negotiations with the prospective licensee. Finding the right balance of disclosure to pique the interest of the licensee without "giving away the farm" is never easy. Fortunately, there is a commonly accepted solution: the licensing memorandum. The licensing memorandum, when used in tandem with confidentiality agreements, can provide the prospective licensee with the information it needs to conduct the preliminary analysis without jeopardizing the rights of the licensor. The memorandum should contain a discussion of the technology and the portfolio of intellectual property rights that protect the technology, the background of the proprietor, the projected markets and applications of the technology, the proposed terms and financial issues between licensor and licensee, and a discussion of existing competitive technology and technological trends that could affect the future value of the license.

Things can and will change—be prepared. Like marriages, most licensing agreements are intended to continue over a long period of time. As a result, it is difficult to predict technological, social, economic, and political trends that will affect the rights and obligations of the licensor and licensee during the term of the agreement. Licensing agreements, like all legal documents, require a certain degree of precision to be enforceable and workable for the parties; however, the inevitability of change should result in a framework of trust and flexibility. Not every detail will be addressed, nor every change in the external environment anticipated. Technologies become obsolete, governments get overthrown, rock stars lose popularity, movie sequels flop, and a corporation's personnel may be restructured, but the licensing agreement must be flexible enough to handle unforeseen changes.

FIGURE 12.1 *Technology Licensing to Create Multiple Revenue Streams*

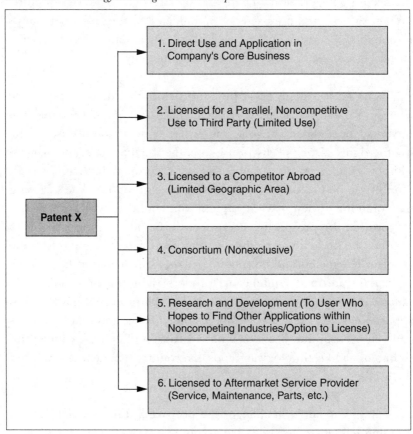

Special Issues in Negotiating and Drafting Technology Licensing Agreements

There are a wide variety of special contractual issues that must be addressed in the preparation of a technology license agreement. These include:

Defined terms. Although many entrepreneurs may initially view this first section of the license agreement as "legal boilerplate," it is often the most hotly contested component. It is intended to do much more than make the document easier to read, but rather defines some of the key aspects of the relationship with respect to the specific field of the technology licensed, the territory to be covered, the milestones and objectives that must be met, the specific patents or trademarks that will be included within the scope of the license, and the nature of the compensation to be paid to the licensor.

Reports to the licensor, record keeping by the licensee. In all licensing agreements, adequate reporting and record keeping by the licensee is critical to ensure that the licensor receives all royalty payments when due. In a technology licensing agreement, additional reports should be prepared monthly or quarterly that disclose the licensee's actual use of the technology; research studies or market tests that have directly or indirectly used the technology; the marketing, advertising, or public relations strategies planned or implemented that involve the technology; progress reports regarding the meeting of established performance objectives and timetables; reports of any threatened or actual infringement or misappropriation of the licensor's technology; and any requests for sublicenses or cross-licenses that have been made by third parties to the licensee.

Exclusivity of the license granted. The term *exclusive*, in the context of a licensing agreement negotiation, is often misunderstood. Exclusivity could apply to a territory, an application of the technology, or a method of production of the products that result from the technology. Exclusivity may or may not include the licensor itself, and may or may not permit the granting of sublicenses or cross-licenses to future third parties who are not bound by the original license agreement. Exclusivity may or may not be conditioned on the licensee meeting certain predetermined performance standards. Exclusivity may be conditional on the continued employment, for a limited period of time, of certain key technical staff of the licensee. All these issues, surrounding what seems to be a "simple" term, must be discussed in the negotiations and ultimately addressed in the license agreement.

Technical support and assistance; dependence on key personnel. The proper development and exploitation of the technology often depends on the availability of the proprietor and the licensor's technical team to provide support and assistance to the licensee. The conditions under which this team will be available to the licensee should be included in the technology license agreement. Provisions should be drafted to deal with scheduling conflicts, the payment of travel expenses, the impact of disability or death of the inventor, the availability of written or videotaped data in lieu of the inventor's physical attendance, the regularity and length of periodic technical support meetings, and the protection of confidential information.

MERCHANDISE AND CHARACTER LICENSING AGREEMENTS

The use of commonly recognized trademarks, brand names, sports teams, athletes, universities, television and film characters, musicians, and designers to foster the sale of specific products and services is at the heart of today's merchandise and character licensing environment. Manufacturers and distributors of products and services license these words, images, and symbols for products that range from clothing and housewares to toys and posters. Certain brand names and characters have withstood the test of time, while others fall prey to fads, consumer shifts, and stiff competition.

The trademark and copyright owners of these properties and character images are motivated to license for a variety of reasons. Aside from the obvious desire to earn royalty fees and profits, many manufacturers view this licensing strategy as a form of merchandising to promote the underlying product or service. The licensing of a trademark for application on a line of clothing helps to establish and reinforce brand awareness at the consumer level. For example, when R.J. Reynolds Tobacco Company licenses a leisure apparel manufacturer to produce a line of Camel wear, the hope is to sell more cigarettes, appeal to the lifestyle of its targeted consumers, maintain consumer awareness, *and* enjoy the royalty income from the sale of the clothing line. Similar strategies have been adopted by manufacturers in order to revive a mature brand or failing product. In certain instances, the spin-off product that has been licensed was almost as financially successful as the underlying product it was intended to promote.

Brand name owners, celebrities, and academic institutions must be very careful not to grant too many licenses too quickly. The financial rewards of a flow of royalty income from hundreds of different manufacturers can be quite seductive, but must be weighed against the possible loss of quality control and dilution of the name, logo, or character. The loyalty of the licensee network is also threatened when too many licenses are granted in closely competing products. Retailers also become cautious when purchasing licensed goods from a licensee if there is a fear that quality control has suffered, or that the popularity of the licensed character, celebrity, or image will be short-lived. This may result in smaller orders and an overall unwillingness to carry inventory, especially in the toy industry, in which purchasing decisions are being made by (or at least influenced by) the whims of a five-year-old child, who may strongly identify with a character image one week, and then turn away to a totally different character image the next week. It is incumbent on the manufacturers and licensees to develop advertising and media campaigns to hold the consumer's attention for an extended period of time. Only then will the retailer be convinced of the potential longevity of the product line. This requires a balancing of the risks and rewards between licensor and licensee in the character licensing agreement in the areas of compensation to the licensor, advertising expenditures by the licensee, scope of the exclusivity, and quality control standards and specifications.

In the merchandise licensing community, the name, logo, symbol, or character is typically referred to as the Property, and the specific product or product line (e.g., the T-shirts, mugs, posters, etc.) is referred to as the Licensed Product. This area of licensing offers opportunities and benefits to both the owners of the properties and the manufacturers of the licensed products. For the owner of the property, brand recognition, goodwill, and royalty income are strengthened and expanded. For the manufacturer of the licensed products, there is an opportunity to leverage the goodwill of the property to improve sales of the licensed products. The manufacturer has an opportunity to "hit the ground running" in the sale of merchandise by gaining access to, and use of, an already established brand name or character image.

Naturally, each party should conduct due diligence on the other. From the perspective of the owner of the property, the manufacturer of the licensed product should demonstrate an ability to meet and maintain quality control standards, possess financial stability, and offer an aggressive and well-planned marketing and promotional strategy. From the perspective of the manufacturer of the licensed property, the owner of the property should display a certain level of integrity and commitment to quality, disclose its future plans for the promotion of the property, and be willing to participate and assist in the overall marketing of the licensed products. For example, if a star basketball player was unwilling to appear for promotional events designed to sell his own specially licensed line of basketball shoes, this would present a major problem, and it would likely lead to a premature termination of the licensing relationship.

Tips for Successful Brand Licensing

Choose your partners wisely. Brand licensing typically requires a closer working relationship between licensor and licensee than does technology or software licensing, to make sure that consistent brand image is maintained in all relevant market segments. Be clear in your articulation and enforcement of brand promise, positioning, and brand values. The core of the brand must have values that transcend, and add value to, products and services in new categories and segments; it must also mean something to the consumer, and have enough loyalty to carry over into other industries and applications.

Build in checks and balances, both operationally and contractually. All brand licensing, co-branding, and brand-extension licensing should add to the value of the core brand of the owner/licensor, not dilute or harm that value. Build in quality control provisions, inspection and performance standards, and marketing and usage guidelines to protect the integrity of your brands.

Be proactive in developing new potential applications, market segments, and licensed categories into which your brands could be licensed. Do not rely solely on your licensees for new ideas or new product development. Licensing is a proactive, not reactive, way to build shareholder value when it is implemented properly. Keep pushing your licensees to produce goods and services bearing your name that will be innovative and product leaders in the segments, not "more of the same under a different name."

Get involved in product design, packaging, product features (materials, shapes, etc.), and promotional plans of your licensees. Do not let brand licensing be a part-time commitment of the marketing department of the company. Make sure that proper resources are committed to building a brand licensing department that will review quarterly and annual business plans of licensees, enforce performance milestones and quality control guidelines, and coordinate joint marketing efforts, such as trade shows, promotional campaigns, and sales meetings.

Special Issues in Negotiating and Preparing Merchandise and Character Licensing Agreements

There are several key areas that must be addressed in the preparation and negotiation of a merchandise licensing agreement. These include:

- Scope of the territorial and product exclusivity
- Assignability and sublicensing rights
- The definition of the property and the licensed products
- Quality control and approval
- Ownership of artwork and designs
- Term renewal rights and termination of the relationship
- Initial license and ongoing royalty fees
- Performance criteria for the licensee
- Liability insurance
- Indemnification
- Duty to pursue trademark and copyright infringement
- Minimum advertising and promotional requirements
- Accounting and record keeping of the licensee

- Inspection and audit rights of the licensor
- Rights of first refusal for expanded or revised characters and images
- Limitations on licensee's distribution to related or affiliated entities
- Representations and warranties of the licensor with respect to its rights to the property
- The availability of the licensor for technical and promotional assistance
- Miscellaneous provisions, such as law to govern, inurement of goodwill, nature of the relationship, notice, and force majeure

The definition of the scope of permitted use is usually accomplished with the assistance of schedules, illustrations, and exhibits. For example, suppose a manufacturer of children's sportswear wanted to license the likeness of basketball star Michael Jordan for a new line of clothing. Will the property consist of unlimited use of the name and likeness of Mr. Jordan, or will it be only for a specific drawing or caricature of his face? Similarly, will the licensed products be defined as virtually any style or size of children's sportswear, or will they be limited to "children's short-sleeved T-shirts up to size 20 and matching children's short pants?" Naturally, there is room for much variation and negotiation in these defined terms. In order to avoid claims and litigation over unauthorized use of the property, the licensor and licensee should clearly communicate their intent to counsel before preparation of the merchandise licensing agreement.

The key economic issue in the agreement is the section dealing with royalty payments that must be paid to the licensor by the licensee, in exchange for the use of the property over a period of time. The royalty obligation is usually stated as a fixed percentage of the licensee's sales of the licensed products, or as a lump sum per unit of the licensed product. Royalty rates are based purely on market forces and the negotiation skills of the parties and their counsel. This section must also address the basis for the calculation of the royalty payment (e.g., gross revenues, net sales, etc.), any minimum royalty payments that must be paid quarterly or annually by the licensee to the licensor, any adjustments to the royalty rate (which is tied to performance, inflation, a change in market conditions, etc.), royalties on noncash sales, and the licensee's obligation to prepare reports and statements to support the calculation of the royalty payment.

BRAND-EXTENSION LICENSING

In the past few years, one specific form of merchandise licensing known as brand-extension licensing has rapidly grown in importance. This type of licensing is designed to widen the depth and the breadth of the market for the products or services identified with the owner's brand, but with the development and distribution costs borne by the licensed third party. Some of these transactions have proven to be natural extensions of the brand and some are not. For example, the licensing of the Sunkist name for orange soda or Hershey's for chocolate milk were brand extension licensing projects. Brand-extension licensing has been a valuable and profitable strategy for companies to penetrate new markets with minimal capital investment or market research, generate new income streams, build the value of the company's brand name, and increase overall brand awareness. For example, Gerber successfully entered the nursery monitor business through brand-extension licensing. It seems unlikely that a company like Gerber would have launched into the electronics industry without the strategic benefits of a brand-extension licensee.

It is estimated that in the United States alone, retail sales of *licensed* branded products surpassed $80 billion in the year 2005, and will exceed $100 billion in the near future. Products borne of brand-extension licensing have become staples for consumers who regularly seek quality and value through brand names. Subject to strict quality control guidelines, companies with registered trademarks can penetrate new markets, build new profit centers, increase brand awareness and recognition, facilitate international expansion, and even modernize a brand's image with the appropriate brand-extension licensing strategic partners. Of course, there is a limit to what the consumer will accept. Naturally, it would do little to enhance the image or brand recognition of Ben & Jerry's if they licensed their name to an automobile parts manufacturer in order to produce a new line of tires. Nor will their "implied endorsement" be likely to enhance the sale of the tires. Yet the move by Starbucks to license its name for a limited line of ice cream seems to be a big hit with quality conscious consumers who know the Starbucks name as a symbol of quality, and readily accept the jump from gourmet coffee to upscale coffee-flavored ice cream.

The temptation to extend the equity and value of your brand into other areas is not without its risks. There are issues of quality control, the risk of over-branding or misbranding from a consumer perspective, and product liability. The key to successful brand extension is that the brand itself must stand for something greater than the original product, *and* that the consumer's perception of the extended brand is a natural one. The brand on a stand-alone basis must represent an attitude or a feeling, or have a cachet that holds water when it is applied to another product. It worked well when the Gap brand-extended a license for perfume and when Calvin Klein brand-extended a license for eyewear, but backfired for Harley-Davidson when it extended its brand by awarding a license for a line of cigarettes. Although the extension seemed natural, consumers were not convinced that the motorcycle manufacturers had a brand that would lend quality and value to a pack of smokes. Even nonlicensed brand extensions that would have seemed a home run have failed due to inadequate market research. For example, when Americans started eating more chicken than beef, A-1 steak sauce launched a poultry sauce that did very poorly, notwithstanding a multi-million-dollar advertising budget. Researchers missed the fact that the A-1 brand had been associated in their minds with *steak*, and not necessarily with *sauce* in general. Yet other brand-extension licensing deals have succeeded in spite of a lack of basic logic. One might think that the last thing anyone would want to smell like is a sweaty basketball player, yet Michael Jordan's line of men's cologne has sold reasonably well. This superstar's cachet has transcended his athletic accomplishments, and even at the peak of his athletic career, his salary from playing basketball was as little as ten percent of his overall income from endorsements, licensing, business deals, and investments.

Developing Effective Brand Licensing Programs

Developing an effective brand-extension licensing program involves the following components:

- **Discipline.** Avoid the temptation to overbrand. A key part of brand management is determining your "zone of appropriateness," and figuring out what your brand *does not* represent. This can be even more important than understanding what it *does* represent.
- **Market research.** It is critical to really understand your customers and their reasons for being loyal to your brand. An understanding

of the source of that loyalty will lead to natural zones of expansion into other products and services, if you listen carefully.

- **Due diligence.** The selection of the right brand-extension licensees who have strong reputations in their industries and the resources to execute well-written market development plans is critical.
- **Quality control.** The brand owner must take a proactive role in maintaining and enforcing quality control standards in the manufacturing and distribution of the branded products or services. This includes not only direct quality issues, but also indirect issues, such as the distribution channels selected, the nature of the advertising and marketing campaigns, and so on.

An effectively managed brand-extension licensing program can build brand awareness and brand equity if the company understands why consumers have an affinity with the brand, and this trust is not violated or misinterpreted. To the extent that brands can influence consumer behavior and gain consumer confidence, they can be a very powerful marketing tool and an intangible income-producing asset.

ACHIEVING GROWTH THROUGH BUSINESS FORMAT FRANCHISING

Over the last three decades, franchising has emerged as a popular expansion strategy for a variety of product and service companies. Recent International Franchise Association (IFA) statistics demonstrate that retail sales from franchised outlets comprise nearly 50 percent of all retail sales in the United States, estimated at more than $900 billion, and employing some ten million people in 2005. These impressive figures notwithstanding, franchising as a method of marketing and distributing products and services is really only appropriate for certain kinds of companies. There are a host of legal and business prerequisites that must be satisfied before any company can seriously consider franchising as an alternative for rapid expansion.

What has made franchising so popular in the United States? From the perspective of the franchisor, franchising represents an efficient method of rapid market penetration and product distribution, without the typical capital costs associated with internal expansion. From the perspective of the franchisee, franchising offers a method of owning a business, but with a mitigated chance of failure due to the initial and ongoing training and support services offered by the franchisor. From the perspective of the consumer, franchised outlets offer a wide range of products and services at a consistent level of quality, and at affordable prices.

In an era of tight financial markets, companies of all sizes are focused on Capital-Efficient Growth Strategies. Many companies view franchising as a way to leverage their brands, systems, proprietary products, and expertise in a manner that creates new revenue streams and opens new markets without significant capital expenditures.

A commitment to quality, fairness, and effective communication among franchisors and franchisees should go a long way in reducing disputes. Current and prospective franchisors must be committed to supporting and servicing the franchises they sell. Franchisors that develop strategic plans that focus on the *quantity* of franchisees, rather than the *quality* of franchisees and training, are surely headed for disaster.

Many companies prematurely select franchising as a growth alternative, and then haphazardly assemble and launch the program. Other companies are urged to franchise by unqualified consultants or advisors who may be more interested in professional fees than in the long-term success of the franchising program. This has caused financial distress and failure at both the franchisor and franchisee level, and usually results in litigation. Current and future members of the franchising community must be urged to take a responsible view toward the creation and development of their franchising programs.

Responsible franchising starts with an understanding of the strategic essence of the business structure. There are three critical components of the franchise system: the brand, the operating system, and the ongoing support provided by the franchisor to the franchisee. The brand creates the demand, allowing the franchisee to initially *obtain* customers. The brand includes the franchisor's trademarks and service marks, its trade dress and décor, and all the intangible factors that create customer loyalty and build brand equity. The operating system essentially "delivers the promise," thereby allowing the franchisee to *maintain* customer relationships and build loyalty. The ongoing support and training provide the impetus for growth, providing the franchisee with the tools and tips to *expand* its customer base and build its market share. The responsibly built franchise system is one that provides value to its franchisees by teaching them how to get, and keep, as many customers as possible, that consume as many products and services as possible, and as often as possible. In fact, most litigation in franchising revolves around the gap between the actual needs of the franchisees to remain competitive in the marketplace, and the reality of what support the franchisor is capable of providing. The genesis of the disappointment begins during the recruitment phase of the relationship and continues beyond the start-up as the franchisee struggles to remain competitive, unless the franchisor delivers on its promises and is committed to providing excellent initial and ongoing training and support.

Reasons for Franchising

There are a wide variety of reasons cited by successful franchisors as to why franchising has been selected as a method of growth and distribution. Through franchising, they are able to:

- Obtain operating efficiencies and economies of scale
- Increase market share and build brand equity
- Use the power of franchising to get and keep more and more customers (building customer loyalty)
- Achieve rapid market penetration at a low capital cost
- Reach the targeted consumer effectively through cooperative advertising and promotion
- Sell products and services to a dedicated distributor network
- Replace the need for internal personnel with motivated owner/operators
- Shift the primary responsibility for site selection, employee training and personnel management, local advertising, and other administrative concerns to the franchisee, licensee, or joint venture partner with the guidance or assistance of the franchisor

In the typical franchising relationship, the franchisee shares the risk of expanding the market share of the franchisor by committing its capital and resources to the development of satellite locations modeled after the proprietary business format of the franchisor. The risk of business failure of the franchisor is further reduced by the improved competitive position, the reduced vulnerability to cyclical fluctuations, the existence of a captive market for the franchisor's proprietary products and services (due to the network of franchisees), and the lowered administrative and overhead costs enjoyed by a franchisor.

The Foundation of Franchising

Responsible franchising is the *only* way that franchisors and franchisees will be able to harmoniously co-exist in the twenty-first century. Responsible franchising requires a secure foundation from which the franchising program is launched. Any company considering franchising as a method of growth and distribution, or any individual considering franchising as a method of getting into business, must understand the key components of this foundation:

- **Proven prototype** location (or chain of stores) that will serve as a basis for the franchising program. The store, or stores, must have been tested, refined, and operated successfully and be consistently profitable. The success of the prototype should not be too dependent on the physical presence or specific expertise of the system's founders.
- **Strong management team** made up of internal officers and directors (as well as qualified consultants) who understand both the particular industry in which the company operates and the legal and business aspects of franchising as a method of expansion
- **Sufficient capitalization** to launch and sustain the franchising program to ensure that capital is available for the franchisor to provide both initial, as well as ongoing, support and assistance to franchisees (a lack of a well-written business plan and adequate capital structure is often the principal cause of demise of many franchisors)
- **Distinctive and protected trade identity** that includes federal and state registered trademarks, as well as a uniform trade dress—appearance, signage, slogans, and overall image
- **Proprietary and proven methods of operation and management** that can be reduced to writing in a comprehensive operations manual, are not easy for competitors to duplicate, maintain their value to

the franchisees over an extended period of time, and can be enforced through clearly drafted and objective quality control standards

- **Comprehensive training programs for franchisees** that integrate all the latest education and training technologies, and that take place both at the company's headquarters and on-site at the franchisee's proposed location at the outset of the relationship, and on an ongoing basis

- **Field support staff** who are skilled trainers and communicators must be available to visit and periodically assist franchisees, as well as monitor quality control standards

- **Set of comprehensive legal documents** that reflect the company's business strategies and operating policies. Offering documents must be prepared in accordance with applicable federal and state disclosure laws, and franchise agreements should strike a delicate balance between the rights and obligations of franchisor and franchisee.

- **Demonstrated market demand** for the products and services developed by the franchisor that will be distributed through the franchisees. The franchisor's products and services should meet certain minimum quality standards, not be subject to rapid shifts in consumer preferences (e.g., fads), and be proprietary in nature. Market research and analysis should be sensitive to trends in the economy and specific industry, the plans of direct and indirect competitors, and shifts in consumer preferences. It is also important to understand what business you are *really* in. For example, many of the major oil company franchisors thought that they were in the *gasoline* business until they realized that they were in the *convenience* business, and quickly jumped into mini-marts, fast food, and quick-service restaurants, either directly or via co-branding.

- **Set of carefully developed uniform site selection criteria and architectural standards** that can be readily and affordably secured in today's competitive real estate market

- **Genuine understanding of the competition** (both direct and indirect) that the franchisor will face in marketing and selling franchises to prospective franchisees, as well as the competition the franchisee will face when marketing the franchisor's products and services

- **Relationships** with suppliers, lenders, real estate developers, and related key resources as part of the operations manual and system

- **Franchisee profile and screening system** in order to identify the minimum financial qualifications, business acumen, and understanding of the industry that will be required by a successful franchisee
- **Effective system of reporting and record keeping** to maintain the performance of the franchisees and ensure that royalties are reported accurately and paid promptly
- **Research and development capabilities** by the franchisor for the introduction of new products and services on an ongoing basis to consumers through the franchised network
- **Communication system** that facilitates a continuing and open dialogue with the franchisees, and as a result, reduces the chances for conflict and litigation within the franchise network
- **National, regional, and local advertising, marketing, and public relations programs** designed to recruit prospective franchisees, as well as consumers to the sites operated by franchisees

Strategic Prerequisites to Launching a Franchising Program

The most important strategic prerequisite for the success of any business format franchise system is the operation and management of a successful prototype. This prototype location is where virtually all operating problems are to be resolved, recipes and new products tested, equipment and design decisions made, management and marketing techniques tested, a trade identity and goodwill established, and financial viability proven. The franchisor is selling a tried and tested package to a franchisee, and the contents of that package must be clearly identified prior to sale. It is irresponsible and potentially illegal to ask someone to part with their life savings to invest in a system that is not ready for replication.

The concept of a system or prescribed business format that is operated according to a uniform and consistent trade identity and image is at the heart of a successful franchising program. Therefore, a prospective franchisor must be able to reduce all aspects of running the business to be franchised into an operations and training manual to be used by franchisees in the day-to-day operation of their business. These systems must be adequately and clearly communicated in the initial and ongoing training program. If a company offers services that are highly personalized or a product that is difficult to reproduce, then franchising may not be the most viable alternative for growth because of the difficulty of replicating these systems or products in the operator's manual, or in the training program. Similarly, if all the "kinks" in the system have not yet been worked out, it is probably premature to consider franchising.

There are a number of other important business and strategic factors that must be considered before franchising. First, franchising should not be viewed as a solution to undercapitalization, or as a "get rich quick" scheme. While it is true that franchising is less capital-intensive than constructing additional company-owned sites, the initial start-up costs for legal, accounting, and consulting fees can be extensive. Second, franchisors must view franchising as the establishment of a series of long-term relationships. The ongoing success of the company as a franchisor will depend on the harmony of these relationships. A field support staff must be built to provide ongoing services to the existing franchisees, as well as to maintain quality control and uniformity throughout the system. New products and services must be developed so that the franchisee can continue to compete with others in its local market. Innovative sales and marketing strategies must be continually established to attract new customers and retain existing patrons of the franchised outlet. If the franchisor expects the franchisee to continue to make its royalty payment on gross sales each week, then an array of valuable support services must be provided on an ongoing basis to meet the franchisee's changing needs.

Prospective and current franchisors must always bear in mind that first and foremost, franchising is about *relationships*. The franchisor and franchisee knowingly and voluntarily enter into a long-term interdependent relationship, each depending on the other for its success. The exact nature of the franchisor-franchisee relationship has been compared to many others. There are parallels to the relationship between parent and child, between a football coach and his team, between a conductor and his orchestra, and between a landlord and his tenants. The franchise license has been compared to a driver's license. You may use and renew the privilege of driving, but you are subject to the rules of the road and the payment of ongoing fees. Like the relationship between franchisor and franchisee, you have the freedom to drive, but not necessarily however, or wherever, you want. The focus must be on how can *we* (franchisor and franchisee) work together for each other's benefit.

Yes, franchising is about *relationships*. And like the most sacred of relationships, marriage, if the parties are to stay committed to each other for the long term, then both franchisor and franchisee must respect one another, stay loyal to one another, and search for ways to strengthen their bond every day.

A recent survey indicates that this focus on the strategic aspects of the franchisor-franchisee relationship seems to work. While more than one-half of our nation's marriages wind up in divorce, nearly 92 percent of the nation's franchises stay married and say they would get married again. In a recent survey conducted by the Gallup Organization and published by the International Franchise Association (IFA) Educational Foundation, more than nine out of ten of the franchise owners surveyed said they were either very or somewhat successful. Of those who had been in business 11 years or more, 96 percent indicated they were very or somewhat successful. Gallup surveyed 1,001 U.S. franchisees, of which nearly eight out of ten own only one franchised small business. Women accounted for 28 percent of the franchisees, and nearly half of those who responded had a professional or managerial position before purchasing a franchise, while nearly two in ten were involved in either services, labor, or retail sales. Given the high satisfaction ratings, it is not surprising that 65 percent of the franchise owners said they would purchase the same franchise again if given the opportunity. Of those who wouldn't buy the same franchise again, 43 percent said they would consider buying a different one. Nearly two-thirds said they would be less successful if they had tried to open the same type of business on their own and not as part of a franchise system.

The franchisor who wishes to meet or exceed the levels of success indicated in the survey must build a culture of honesty, trust, passion, and genuine commitment to long-term success. This often begins in the recruitment process by carefully screening and educating qualified candidates to ensure that your long-term objectives are truly shared and best interests truly aligned. This type of strategy will lead to mutually beneficial relationships, and significantly decrease the chances of litigation. Some degree of franchisee failure will be inevitable. There are typically two types of factors at play: ones that you can control, and ones that you often can't. You *can* control the quality of your systems, training and support tools, and the innovation of your marketing to help increase the chances of success. Other than through careful screening and continuous monitoring, you *cannot* typically control local market conditions, or changes in the franchisee's personal life that may also affect his or her performance.

Today's franchisor must have an initial and ongoing commitment to being creative and competitive. Market conditions and technology that affect franchising are changing constantly, and the 21st-century franchisee expects you to change at the same pace. For example, the ability to adapt your franchising system to allow for growth and market penetration into alternative and nontraditional venues is critical. Creative and aggressive franchisors in the retail and hospitality industries are always searching for new locations where captive markets may be present, such as airports, hotels, hospitals, highway roadside travel plazas, universities, sports arenas, or military bases. In these locations the trends toward outsourcing, the demand for branded products and services, and the desire to enhance the captive customer's experience have all opened up new doors and opportunities for franchising. In other cases, franchisors have pursued co-branding strategies to penetrate these new markets, taking advantage of the desire of convenience stores, grocery store chains, and gas stations to provide their patrons with an enhanced customer experience and offer a comprehensive and integrated solution to their consumers' needs. A trend toward branding and the ability to share costs, positioning toward differentiation, and penetrate new market segments at a relative low cost has opened up many doors for the creative and aggressive franchisor who is committed to capturing more market share and serving more and more customers.

Legal and Regulatory Issues in the Offer and Sale of Franchises

The offer and sale of a franchise is regulated at both the federal and state level. At the federal level, the Federal Trade Commission (FTC) in 1979 adopted its trade regulation Rule 436 (the "FTC Rule") that specifies the minimum amount of disclosure that must be made to a prospective franchisee in any of the 50 states. In addition to the FTC Rule, more than a dozen states have adopted their own rules and regulations for the offer and sale of franchises within their borders. Known as the registration states, they include most of the nation's largest commercial marketplaces such as California, New York, and Illinois. These states generally follow a more detailed disclosure format known as the Uniform Franchise Offering Circular (the UFOC).

The states that require full registration of a franchise offering prior to the selling of a franchise are California, Illinois, Indiana, Maryland, Minnesota, New York, North Dakota, Rhode Island, South Dakota, Virginia, and Washington. Other states that regulate franchise offers include Hawaii, which requires filing of an offering circular with the state authorities, and delivery of an offering circular to prospective franchisees; Michigan and Wisconsin, which require filing of a "Notice of Intent to Offer and Sell Franchises"; Oregon, which requires only that presale disclosure be delivered to prospective investors; and Texas, which requires the filing of a notice of exemption with the appropriate state authorities under the "Texas Business Opportunity Act."

The FTC Rule regulates two types of offerings: (1) package and product franchises, and (2) business opportunity ventures. The first type involves three characteristics: (1) the franchisee sells goods or services that meet the franchisor's quality standards (in cases where the franchisee operates under the franchisor's trademark, service mark, trade name, advertising, or other commercial symbol or "mark" designating the franchisor) and that are identified by the franchisor's mark, (2) the franchisor exercises significant assistance in the franchisee's method of operation, and (3) the franchisee is required to make payment of $500 or more to the franchisor, or a person affiliated with the franchisor, at any time before to within six months after the business opens.

Business Opportunity Ventures also involve three characteristics: (1) the franchisee sells goods or services that are supplied by the franchisor, or a person affiliated with the franchisor; (2) the franchisor assists the franchisee in any way with respect to securing accounts for the franchisee, securing locations or sites for vending machines and rack displays, or providing the services of a person able to do either; and (3) the franchisee is required to make payment of $500 or more to the franchisor, or a person affiliated with the franchisor, at any time before to within six months after the business opens.

Relationships covered by the FTC Rule include those within the definition of a "franchise," and those *represented* as being within the definition when the relationship is entered into, whether or not they, in fact, are within the definition. The FTC Rule exempts (1) fractional franchises, (2) leased department arrangements, and (3) purely verbal agreements. The FTC Rule excludes (1) relationships between employer and employees and among general business partners, (2) membership in retailer-owned cooperatives, (3) certification and testing services, and (4) single trademark licenses.

Among other things, the FTC Rule requires that every franchisor offering franchises in the United States deliver an offering circular (containing certain specified disclosure items) to all prospective franchisees (within certain specified time requirements). The FTC has adopted and enforced its rule pursuant to its power and authority to regulate unfair and deceptive trade practices. The FTC Rule sets forth the *minimum* level of protection that shall be afforded to prospective franchisees. There is no private right of action—that is, a franchisee cannot sue—under the FTC Rule; however, the FTC itself may bring an enforcement action against a franchisor that does not meet its requirements. Penalties for noncompliance have included asset impoundments, cease and desist orders, injunctions, consent orders, mandated rescission or restitution for injured franchisees, and civil fines of up to $10,000 per violation.

The information in the offering circular must be current as of the completion of the franchisor's most recent fiscal year. In addition, a revision to the document must be promptly prepared whenever there has been a material change in the information contained in the document. The FTC Rule requires that the disclosure document must be given to a prospective franchisee at the earliest of either (1) the prospective franchisee's first personal meeting with the franchisor; (2) ten business days prior to the execution of a contract; or (3) ten business days before the payment of money relating to the franchise relationship. In addition to the disclosure document, the franchisee must receive a copy of all agreements that it will be asked to sign at least five business days prior to the execution of the agreements.

Developing and Enforcing System Standards

The glue holding the typical franchise system together consists of the uniform policies, procedures, and specifications that must be followed by all franchisees. These rules and regulations, typically found in the operations manual, must be (1) *carefully planned* and developed by the franchisor; (2) *clearly articulated* by the franchisor to the franchisees, both initially and on an ongoing basis; (3) *accepted* by the network of franchisees as being understood and reasonable; (4) *consistently applied;* and (5) *rigidly enforced* by the franchisor, typically through its field support staff. Obviously, the development of uniform standards is of little utility unless there are systems in place for monitoring and enforcing these standards, as well as penalties for noncompliance with the standards, which are typically found in the franchise agreement.

Compliance with quality control standards requires mutual respect by, and among, the franchisor and all of its franchisees. The franchisor must be reasonable and resist the temptation to "go hog wild" in the development and enforcement of system standards. The franchisee must understand that reasonable standards are in the best interests of all franchisees in the network. Franchisees typically have a "love-hate" relationship with system standards. On the one hand, they appreciate reasonable standards that result in happy consumers, and "weed out" noncomplying franchisees. On the other hand, they detest standards that are unattainable, vaguely communicated, and arbitrarily or too rigidly enforced (especially against *them*).

System standards, which are prescribed in the operations manual and other written and electronic communications from the franchisor, are deemed to be part of the franchise agreement under the contract law doctrine of incorporation by reference. System standards dictate, among other things:

- Required and authorized products and services to be offered and sold
- Manner in which the franchisee may offer and sell these products and services (including product preparation, storage, and handling and packaging procedures)
- Required image and appearance of facilities, vehicles, and employees
- Designated and approved suppliers and supplier approval procedures and criteria
- Types, models and brands of required operating assets (including equipment, signs, furnishings, furniture, and vehicles) and supplies (including food ingredients, packaging, and the like)

- Use and display of the trade and service marks
- Sales, marketing, advertising, and promotional programs, and the materials and media used in these programs
- Terms and conditions of the sale and delivery of items that the franchisee acquires from the franchisor and its affiliates
- Staffing levels and training
- Days and hours of operation
- Participating in market research, testing of the product, and service development programs
- Payment, point-of-sale, and computer systems
- Reporting requirements
- Insurance requirements
- Other operational rules

These standards that a franchisor implements at the beginning, and during the course of the franchisee relationship, and the franchisor's willingness and ability to enforce those standards uniformly, usually will determine the success of the franchise system. It is essential that system standards be communicated to franchisees in well-organized and understandable formats.

The obvious dilemma is that many of the system standards listed above are moving targets. They can and will change as technology and market conditions change, and franchisors must be able to modify the system standards without seeking an addendum to the franchise agreement every time a modification to the system is necessary. The franchisor must build a culture in which change is inevitable, expected, and warmly embraced by the franchisee right at the start of the relationship. Changes to the system must be viewed as a positive evolution of the business format, not a burden. To accomplish this, however, there must be a culture of trust. The franchisee wants to be assured that these changes are reasonable and necessary. If the change involves new products and services, the franchisee wants to be assured that adequate market research went into the development of these new concepts, and that they are not the whimsical or hare-brained idea of the franchisor's founder. Most franchisors build in a certain degree of flexibility into their franchise agreements to allow for the peaceful implementation of system changes.

As a general rule, the franchisor has an obligation to develop system standards and procedures that are reasonable and attainable. Once developed, the standards and procedures should be clearly communicated and uniformly enforced. The enforcement must be neither too loose nor too rigid. If the penalties for noncompliance are too loose, the franchisor will be viewed as a toothless lion that neither intends nor has the power to insist on compliance. If the enforcement is too rigid, the standards will be resented and disregarded, resulting in litigation and poor franchisee morale throughout the network.

Many times, the enforcement strategy adopted depends on the franchisor's own stage of growth. For example, a gentle rap on the knuckles (in lieu of an actual termination) may be more prudent early on in the franchisor's own development because of the potential impact of a dispute at this stage. The costs of litigation, the perception of actual and prospective franchisees, and the nature of the infraction should all be considered. If a "quasi-acquiescence" policy of enforcement is adopted by the younger franchisor, then issues of a potential waiver of your claims should be discussed with legal counsel. As the franchisor grows and matures, it becomes easier to enforce system standards rigidly, and to apply significant penalties for noncompliance because the threat of termination becomes a more powerful deterrent.

Subfranchising, Area Development Agreements, and Related Documents

Most franchises are sold to individual owner/operators, who will be responsible for managing a single site in accordance with the franchisor's business format and quality control standards. A recent trend in franchising, however, has been the sale of "multiple-unit franchises" to aggressive entrepreneurs, who will be responsible for the development of an entire geographic region.

The two primary types of multiple-unit franchises are: (1) *subfranchisors*, who act as independent selling organizations that are responsible for the recruitment and ongoing support of franchisees within their given region; and (2) *area developers*, who have no resale rights, but are themselves responsible for meeting a mandatory development schedule for their given region. There are a wide variety of variations on these two principal types of multiple-unit franchises. For example, some franchise relationships that are at the inception single units, wind up as multiple-unit owners through the use of option agreements, or rights of first refusal. Other franchisors have experimented with co-development rights among adjacent franchisees, franchises coupled with management agreements (under those circumstances when the franchisee deserves to be more passive), equity participation by franchisors in franchisees (and vice versa), employee ownership of franchisor-operated units, and co-development rights between the franchisor and franchisee.

As a general rule, the inclusion of multiple-unit franchises in a franchisor's development strategy allows for even more rapid market penetration, and less administrative burdens. Often, however, the franchisee demands the right to develop and operate multiple units. In this particular situation, there is a wide range of legal and strategic issues that must be addressed when multiple-unit franchises are included in the overall franchising program.

Structuring Area Development Agreements

The key issues in structuring an area development agreement usually revolve around the size of the territory, fees, the mandatory timetable for development, and ownership of the units. The franchisor will usually want to reserve certain rights and remedies in the event that the franchisee defaults on its development obligations. The area developer must usually pay an umbrella development fee for the region, over and above the individual initial fee that is to be due, and payable as each unit becomes operational within the territory. The amount of the fee will vary, depending on factors, such as the strength of the franchisor's trademarks and market share, the size of the territory, and the term (and renewal) of the agreement. This development fee is essentially a payment to the franchisor that prevents the franchisor from offering any other franchises within that region (unless there is a default).

Structuring Subfranchising Agreements

Subfranchise agreements present a myriad of issues that are not raised in the sale of a single-unit franchise, or an area development agreement. This is primarily because the rewards and responsibilities for the subfranchisor are much different than for the area developer, or single-unit operator. In most subfranchising relationships, the franchisor will share a portion of the initial franchise fee and ongoing royalty with the subfranchisor, in exchange for the subfranchisor assuming responsibilities within the given region. The proportions in which fees are shared usually have a direct relationship to the exact responsibilities of the subfranchisor. In addition, the subfranchisor will receive a comprehensive regional operations manual that covers sales and promotions, training and field support that is over and above the information contained in the operations manuals provided to individual franchisees. Some of the key issues that must be addressed in the subfranchise relationship include:

- How will the initial and ongoing franchise fees be divided among franchisor and subfranchisor? Who will be responsible for the collection and processing of franchise fees?
- Will the subfranchisor be a party of the individual franchise agreements? Or will direct access be limited to franchisor and individual franchisee?
- What is the exact nature of the subfranchisor's recruitment, site selection, franchising, training, and ongoing support to the individual franchisees within its region?
- Who will be responsible for the preparation and filing of franchise offering documents in those states where the subfranchisor must file separately?
- What mandatory development schedules and related performance quotas will be imposed on the subfranchisor?
- Will the subfranchisor be granted the rights to operate individual units within the territory? If yes, how will these units be priced?
- What will the subfranchisor be obligated to pay the franchisor initially for the exclusive rights to develop the territory?
- What rights of approval will the franchisor retain, with respect to the sale of individual franchises (e.g., background of the candidate, any negotiated changes in the agreement, decision to terminate, etc.)?
- What rights does the franchisor reserve to modify the size of the territory, or repurchase it from the subfranchisor?

A subfranchisor enters into what is typically referred to as a Regional Development Agreement with the franchisor, pursuant to which the subfranchisor is granted certain rights to develop a particular region. The Regional Development Agreement is *not* in itself a franchise agreement to operate any individual franchise units; rather it grants the subfranchisor the right to sell franchises to individuals using the franchisor's system and proprietary marks solely for the purpose of recruitment, management, supervision, and support of individual franchisees. To the extent that the subfranchisor itself develops units, then an individual franchise agreement for each such unit must be executed.

The relationship between franchisor and subfranchisor is unique and somewhat complicated. If the appropriate individual is chosen, the relationship can be mutually beneficial. The advantages of such a relationship to the franchisor include rapid market penetration, the delegation of obligations it would otherwise be required to fulfill to each franchisee in its network, and the ability to collect a percentage of the initial franchise fee and royalty fees from each franchisee, generally without the same level of effort that would be required in a single-unit relationship.

13

JOINT VENTURES AND STRATEGIC ALLIANCES

Another key strategy for leveraging intellectual property is to establish partnering relationships, whereby two or more companies work together to achieve a specific purpose, or toward the attainment of common business objectives. Joint Ventures, Strategic Partnering, Cross-Licensing, Co-Branding and Technology Transfer Agreements are all strategies designed to obtain one or more of the following: (1) direct capital infusion in exchange for equity and/or intellectual property or distribution rights; (2) a "capital substitute" where resources that would otherwise be obtained with capital are obtained through joint venturing; or (3) a shift of the burden and cost of development (through licensing), in exchange for a potentially more limited upside.

These various types of partnering arrangements have been used for a wide variety of business purposes, including: joint research and co-promotion; distribution and commercialization (particularly between defense and government contractors looking for new applications, and markets for products initially developed for the military and governmental sectors); and cross-licensing and sub-licensing of new technologies. The participants to these agreements can be at various points in the value chain or distribution channel—from potential competitors (e.g., cooperate, rather than compete, as a precursor to a merger and/or to join forces to fend off an even larger competitor), to parallel producers (e.g., to widen or integrate product lines), to parties linked at different points in the vertical distribution channel (e.g., to achieve distribution efficiencies).

One of the key factors to analyze when structuring these relationships is the respective *positions* of each party that will influence structure, economies, and key objectives (see Figure 13.1).

In **Goliath/Goliath** partnering transactions, two very large companies get together to co-market or cross-promote each other's brands, either to capture more customers, or to achieve certain efficiencies. Two easy-to-understand examples are two major airlines that serve different primary geographic hubs honoring each other's frequent flyer programs, or McDonald's promoting a new Disney film by offering licensed toys when a consumer buys a kid's meal.

In **David/David** partnering relationships, two smaller companies, both with limited resources, come together to leverage off each other's strengths on a peer-to-peer basis, in order to achieve a defined business purpose, or set of objectives. An example might be two small government contractors with complementary skills entering into a teaming agreement in order to jointly bid on a new Request for Proposal (RFP) that neither could qualify for alone. Many of the principles discussed in this chapter should be carefully reviewed to make sure each partner gets the benefit of their end of the bargain. The key to peer-to-peer partnering relationships is avoiding greed. To work well, *each* party's objectives must be met, and the sharing of the rewards must be parallel with the level of effort and sharing of the risks.

In **David/Goliath** partnering relationships, a smaller company joins with a much larger strategic ally that may be a large domestic corporation, a foreign conglomerate, or even a university or government agency looking to commercialize a given technology. In these transactions, David and its counsel must work hard to negotiate and protect the benefits and

FIGURE 13.1 *Partnering Relationships*

Goliath/Goliath	David/David
David/Goliath	Networks of Davids and Goliaths

objectives of the relationship, since it will be subject to the red tape, bureaucracy, and potential shifts in strategic focus that are typical at many Goliaths.

In **Networks of Davids and Goliaths,** there are multiple participants in the joint venture, strategic alliance, cooperative, or consortium, each maintaining their operational and ownership autonomy, but coming together to share resources, distribution channels, or costs in some way to increase revenues or reduce expenses. The alignment of shared interests may be very broad or may be more limited—such as cooperative advertising, or a shared Web site or toll-free phone number, to generate new business. In emerging technology industries, value webs may be created by five or six companies who are each bringing a technical component or solution to the table to meet a customer's (or series of customers) real or perceived needs.

As technology develops rapidly, competition becomes more intense, business operations become more global in nature, and industry convergence takes place on a number of different fronts. The number and the pace of deal-making in the joint venture and strategic alliances areas is very likely to quicken and increase over the next few years. The need to combine and share core competencies and resource capabilities, but in a manner and within a structure in which autonomy can be preserved, must be a key component in any fast-growing company's business strategy.

UNDERSTANDING THE DIFFERENCES BETWEEN JOINT VENTURES AND STRATEGIC ALLIANCES

A *joint venture* is typically structured as a partnership, or as a newly formed and co-owned corporation (or limited liability company), in which two or more parties are brought together to achieve a series of strategic and financial objectives on a short-term or a long-term basis. Companies considering a joint venture as a growth strategy should give careful thought to the type of partner they are looking for, and what resources each party will contribute to the newly formed entity. Like raising a child, each parent will make his or her respective contribution of skills, abilities, and resources.

A *strategic alliance* refers to any number of collaborative working relationships where no formal joint venture entity is formed, but where two independent companies become interdependent by entering into a formal or informal agreement, built on a platform of: (1) mutual objectives; (2) mutual strategy; (3) mutual risk; and (4) mutual reward. The relationships are commonly referred to as: (1) teaming; (2) strategic partnering; (3) alliances; (4) cross-licensing; and (5) co-branding.

Regardless of the specific structure, the underlying industry, or even the actual purpose of the strategic relationship, *all* successful joint venture and strategic alliance relationships share a common set of essential success factors including:

- Complementary unified force or purpose that bonds the two or more companies together
- Management team committed to the success of the venture, free from politics, or personal agendas
- Genuine strategy synergy where the "sum of the whole truly exceeds its individual parts" (e.g., $2 + 2 + 2 = 7$)
- Cooperative culture and spirit among the strategic partners that leads to trust, resource-sharing, and a friendly chemistry among the parties
- Degree of flexibility in the objectives of the joint venture, to allow for changes in the marketplace and an evolution of technology
- Actual alignment of management styles and operational methods, at least to the extent that it affects the underlying project (as in the case of a strategic alliance), or the management of the new company created (as in the case of a formal joint venture)
- Level of focus and leadership among all key parties that is necessary to the success of *any* new venture or business enterprise

The strategic benefits of these relationships include:

- Developing a new market (domestic/international)
- Developing a new product (research and development)
- Developing/sharing technology
- Combining complementary technology
- Pooling resources to develop a production/distribution facility
- Acquiring capital
- Executing a government contract
- Gaining access to a new distribution channel, network, or sales/ marketing capability

FIGURE 13.2 *Understanding the Differences between Joint Ventures and Alliances*

	Joint Ventures	Strategic Alliance
Term	Usually Medium to Long-Term	Short-Term
Strategic Objective	Often serves as Precursor to a Merger	More Flexible and Noncommital
Legal Agreements and Structure	Actual legal entity formed	Contract-Driven
Extent of Commitment	Shared Equity	Shared Objectives
Capital Resources	Each party makes a capital contribution of cash or intangible assets	No specific capital contributions (may be shared budgeting or even cross-investment)
Tax Ramifications	Be on the lookout for double taxation unless pass-through entities utilized	No direct tax ramifications

DUE DILIGENCE BEFORE SELECTING JOINT VENTURE OR STRATEGIC ALLIANCE PARTNERS

Care should be taken to conduct a thorough review of prospective candidates, and extensive due diligence should be done on the final candidates that are being considered for a joint venture or strategic alliance. Develop a list of key objectives and goals to be achieved by the joint venture or alliance, and compare this list with those of your final candidates. Take the time to understand the strategic fit (or potential tension) to the corporate culture and decision-making process within each company. Consider some of the following issues: (1) How do their decision-making methods fit with your own processes? (2) What about each prospective partner's previous experiences and track record with other joint venture relationships? (3) Why did these previous relationships succeed or fail?

In many cases, small companies looking for joint venture partners select a Goliath that offers a wide range of financial and nonfinancial resources that will allow the smaller company to achieve its growth plans. The motivating factor under these circumstances for the larger company is to get access and distribution rights to new technologies, products, and services. In turn, the larger company offers access to pools of capital, research and development, personnel, distribution channels, and general contacts that the small company desperately needs.

But proceed carefully. Be sensitive to the politics, red tape, and different management practices that may be in place at a larger company that will be foreign to many small firms. Try to distinguish between that which is being promised, and that which will actually be delivered. If the primary motivating force for the small firm is really only capital, then consider whether alternative (and perhaps less costly) sources of money have been thoroughly explored. Ideally, the larger joint venture partner will offer a lot more than just money. If the primary motivating force is access to technical personnel, then consider whether it might be a better decision to recruit these resources separately, rather than entering into a partnership in which you give up a certain measure of control. Also, consider whether strategic relationships or extended payments terms with vendors and consultants can be arranged in lieu of the joint venture.

DRAFTING A MEMORANDUM OF UNDERSTANDING PRIOR TO STRUCTURING THE AGREEMENTS

Prior to drafting the definitive joint venture or alliance agreements, whether by and among peers or in a David-and-Goliath transaction, it is critical to hammer out a Memorandum of Understanding on all critical points of the relationship, and for the lawyers to use a starting point in the preparation of the formal agreements. The Memorandum of Understanding should address the following topics:

Spirit and purpose of the agreement. Outline why the partnering arrangement is being considered; what are its perceived mission and objectives? Describe "operating principles" that will foster communication and trust. What are the strategic and financial desires of the participants?

Scope of activity. Address what products, services, buildings, or other specific projects will be included, and excluded, from the venture. Identify target markets (i.e., regions, user groups, etc.) for the venture, and any markets excluded from the venture that will remain the domain of the partners. If the venture has purchase and supply provisions, state that the newly formed entity or arrangement will purchase, or supply, specific products, services, or resources from or to the owners.

Key objectives and responsibilities. Clarify and specify objectives and targets to be achieved by the relationship, when you expect these objectives to be achieved, any major obstacles anticipated, and the point at which the alliance will be self-supporting, be bought out, or be terminated. Participants should designate a Project Manager, who will be responsible for their company's day-to-day involvement in the alliance. If a separate detached organization will be created, the key persons assigned to the venture should be designated, if practical. Responsibilities should be outlined to make it clear to other partners who will be doing what.

Method for decision making. Each partnering relationship will have its own unique decision-making process. Describe who is expected to have the authority to make what types of decisions in what circumstances, who reports to whom, and so on. It should be designated at this point if one company will have operating control.

Resource commitments. Most partnering relationships involve the commitment of specific financial resources, such as cash, equity, staged payments, loan guarantees, and so on to achieve the ultimate goals. Other "soft" resources may be in the form of licenses, knowledge, R&D, a sales force, contracts, production, facilities, inventory, raw materials, engineering drawings, management staff, access to capital, the devotion of specific personnel for a certain percentage of their time, and so on. If possible, these "soft" resources should be quantified with a financial figure so that they can be affixed a monetary value along with the cash commitments. In some circumstances, the purchase of buildings, materials, consultants, advertising, and other resources will require capital. These external costs should be itemized and allocated between the partners in whatever formula is agreed upon. If any borrowing, entry into equity markets (public offerings, private placements, etc.), or purchase of stock in one of the partners is anticipated, these should be noted. In anticipation of additional equity infusions, the partners should agree about their own ability to fund the overruns, or enable the venture to seek outside sources. The manner of handling cost overruns should be addressed. Pricing and costing procedures should be mentioned if applicable.

Assumption of risks and division of rewards. What are the perceived risks? How will they be handled, and who will be responsible for problem-solving and risk assumption? What are the expected rewards (new product, new market, cash flow, technology, etc.)? How will the profits be divided?

Rights and exclusions. Who has rights to products and inventions? Who has rights to distribute the products, services, technologies, etc.? Who gets the licensing rights? If the Confidentiality and Non-Competition Agreements have not yet been drafted in final form at this point, they should be addressed in basic form here. Otherwise, if more definitive documents have been signed, simply make reference to these other agreements.

Anticipated structure. This section of the Memorandum of Understanding should describe the intended structure (written contract, corporation, partnership, or equity investment). Regardless of the legal form, the terms, percentages, and formulas for exchange of stock, if possible at this stage, should be spelled out. Default provisions and procedures should be addressed at least at the preliminary level.

STRUCTURING THE JOINT VENTURE OR STRATEGIC ALLIANCE

Unlike franchising, distributorships, and licensing, which are almost always vertical in nature, joint ventures, alliances, and even consortiums are structured at *either* horizontal or vertical levels of distribution. At the horizontal level, the joint venture is often a precursor to an actual merger, in which two or more companies operating at the same level in the distribution channel join together (either by means of a partnership-type agreement, or by joint ownership of a specially created corporation) to achieve certain synergies or operating efficiencies. Fast growth companies should consider the following key strategic issues before and during joint venture or strategic alliance negotiations:

- Exactly what types of tangible and intangible assets will be contributed to the joint venture by each party? Who will have ownership rights to the property contributed during the term of the joint venture and thereafter? Who will own property developed as a result of joint efforts?
- What covenants of nondisclosure or noncompetition will be expected of each joint venturer during the term of the agreement and thereafter?
- What timetables or performance quotas for completion of the projects contemplated by the joint venture will be included in the agreement? What are the rights and remedies of each party if these performance standards are not met?
- How will issues of management and control be addressed in the agreement? What will be the respective voting rights of each party? What are the procedures in the event of a major disagreement or deadlock? What is the fallback plan?

Once the joint venturer has discussed all the preliminary issues, a formal joint venture agreement or corporate shareholders' agreement should be prepared with the assistance of counsel. The precise terms of the agreement between the parties depend upon the nature and the structure of the arrangement. At a minimum, however, the following topics should be addressed in as much detail as possible:

Nature, purpose, and trade name for the joint venture. The parties should set forth the legal nature of their relationship, along with a clear statement of purpose, to prevent future disputes as to the scope of the arrangement. If a new trade name is established for the venture, provisions should be made as to the use of the name, and any other trade or service marks registered by the venture upon termination of the entity or project.

Status of the respective joint venturers. The agreement should clearly indicate whether each party is a partner, shareholder, agent, independent contractor, or any combination thereof. Agent status, whether actual or imputed, can greatly affect liability between the venturers, and with regard to third parties.

Representations and warranties of each joint venturer. Standard representations and warranties will include ability and authority to enter into the joint venture arrangement, ownership of key IP assets that will be used by the joint venture, and so on.

Capital and property contributions of each joint venturer. A clear schedule should be established of all contributions, whether in the form of cash, shares, real estate, or intellectual property. Detailed descriptions will be particularly important if the distribution of profits and losses is to be based upon overall contribution. The specifics of allocation and distribution of profits and losses among the venturers should also be clearly defined.

Scope of the joint venture commitment. The agreement should carefully define the scope and degree of exclusivity of the commitment to one another. Any restrictions on one or more of the joint venturers' abilities to enter into other transactions that could be viewed as directly or indirectly competitive to the core business of the joint venture should be clearly defined. Any noncompete covenants, confidentiality provisions, noncircumvention privileges, rights of first refusal, and other agreements should all be included in this section, including a mechanism for dealing with potential conflicts of interest, and usurpation of corporate opportunity issues.

Management, governance, control, and voting rights of each joint venturer. If the proposed partners envision joint management of the venture, it will be necessary to specifically address the appointment and control of officers and directors, as well as the keeping of books, records, and bank accounts; the nature and frequency of inspections and audits; insurance and cross-indemnification obligations; annual budgeting and business planning processes; and pension and employee benefits matters, as well as responsibility for administrative and overhead expenses.

Rights in joint venture property. Joint venture partners should be especially mindful of intellectual property rights, and should clearly address the issues of ownership use and licensing entitlements, not only for the venturers' presently existing property rights, but also for future use of rights (or products or services) developed in the name of the venture itself.

Restrictions on transferability of ownership interest in the joint venture. Stringent conditions should be placed on the ability of the venturers to transfer or grant liens or encumbrances on their ownership interests in the joint venture entity to third parties. This section should probably vest a right of first refusal to purchase the equity interests, either in the entity or the other joint venture partners.

Default, dissolution, and termination of the joint venture. The events that constitute a default, the opportunity to cure, the obligations of the venturers, and the distribution of assets should be clearly defined; procedures in the event of bankruptcy and/or insolvency of either the joint venture entity or one of its partners should also be addressed in this section.

Dispute resolution procedures. The parties may wish to consider arbitration or mediation as an alternative dispute resolution mechanism. The mechanics, venue, and prescribed processes to be followed in the event of a dispute should also be included in this section.

Miscellaneous. Provisions should also be made indicating (1) the governing law, (2) remedies under force majeure situations, (3) procedures for notice and consent, and (4) the ability to modify or waive certain provisions.

In addition to the core joint venture documents, there may be a wide variety of ancillary agreements that may be necessary to reflect all the terms of the business arrangements between the two parties. It may also be necessary to obtain "third party" consents from lenders, landlords, venture investors, and others who may have the authority to block the proposed arrangement, or when the proposed transaction would be deemed to have triggered a "change in control" clause in a set of loan or investment documents. The ancillary documents will vary based on the objectives, complexity, and nature of the transaction and may include:

- **Asset purchase agreements:** when the newly formed JV entity may be purchasing assets from one or more of the partners beyond the capital contributions
- **Equipment and real property leases/subleases:** when the newly formed JV entity may be leasing or subleasing office space or equipment from one or more of its owners
- **License agreements:** when technology and/or brands will be licensed by the JV partners (and not assigned) to the newly formed entity
- **Technical assistance and services agreements:** when one or more of the JV partners will be providing support or assistance to the newly formed JV entity, either on a monthly-fee or pay-as-you-go hourly basis
- **Management and support agreements:** when one of the joint venture partners provides certain management or administrative support services to the newly formed JV entity
- **Distribution and marketing agreements:** when one or more of the joint venture partners have certain distribution and marketing rights, or obligations that relate to the new products or services that the JV entity will produce or offer
- **Employment agreements:** providing the rights and responsibilities of the leadership team of the JV
- **Supply agreements:** setting the price, conditions, and terms of any supplies or services that will be sold by one of the JV owners to the JV entity

CO-BRANDING AS A TYPE OF STRATEGIC ALLIANCE

Co-branding is a type of partnership relationship whereby two established brand names combine in order to bring added value, economies of scale, and customer recognition to each product. Businesses of all sizes, including many fast-track growth companies, are realizing the significant cost of establishing brand awareness and the economies of scale that can be achieved when the expense of this important task is shared. Campaigns and strategies to build brand recognition, brand loyalty, and brand equity have been launched by thousands of companies that recognize that a well-established brand can be the single most valuable asset on the balance sheet. This new focus on *brand equity* has set the stage for a wide variety of co-branding and brand-extension licensing transactions. Companies with strong quality-oriented brands (as well as professional sports teams, athletes, and celebrities) have sought to create new sources of revenues and leverage their largest intangible asset—their reputation—to add to the strength of their income statements. To build brand awareness, companies are spending more money on media advertising and promotional campaigns, and less on store displays and coupons.

Co-branding has recently emerged as a very popular type of strategic alliance. At the heart of the relationship, two or more established brands are paired and positioned in the marketplace to bring added value, economies of scale, and synergistic customer recognition and loyalty to increase sales and create a point of differentiation. Co-branding has appeared in many different forms, including:

Financial services co-branding. In the early 1990s, credit card companies pioneered co-branding with credit cards paired with airlines or telecommunications companies for mutual branding and shared rewards.

FIGURE 13.3 *Tips for Structuring Strategic Relationships and Avoiding Classic Pitfalls and Mistakes*

- Negotiating Ostrich Deals—The senior level executives cannot have their heads in the sand when defining key objectives. You must include middle-level management and technical personnel—who will ultimately be responsible for the success or failure of the relationship—in the goal-making process.

- Disregarding the impact on other potential alliance partners or the foreclosure of other opportunities. Think through how a deal with this *particular* alliance partner will impact your ability to do other deals.

- Overlooking details or taking shortcuts toward alliance objectives. The planning process *before* signing the definitive documents is critical and when it gets skipped the relationship is much more likely to fail.

- Understanding the impact of the deal on customers and vendors. How will customers and vendors perceive and interact with this alliance or joint venture? Will they be forced to shift relationships? Will they be willing to do so? What is in it for them?

- Mutual trust, respect, and balanced sharing of risks and rewards must be key themes of the relationship, particularly in David/Goliath scenarios in which the parties cannot rely on peer-to-peer dynamics to create balance. Being sensitive to the needs and attitudes of your partner is the key to all types of relationships.

- Overly aggressive timetable for meeting objectives—which only puts unrealistic pressures on the parties to perform, leading to frustration and disappointment.

- The responsibilities and contributions of each party should be clearly addressed with systems and procedures to create accountability and consequences for failure to meet responsibilities.

- The agreement must include provisions for resolving conflicts when they occur. Ignoring the problem or letting conflicts fester will not solve anything, nor will dragging the relationship beyond the term of its useful or practical life achieve anything. If the relationship is no longer working, don't be afraid to bring it to a prompt end. The agreement should also include enough flexibility to allow the relationship to evolve and adapt to new challenges and shifts in market conditions.

- A clear focus is very important. An ambiguous charter, scope, or purpose results in uncoordinated activities and confusion among the employees who are on the front line trying to make the venture succeed.

- Management, leadership, good chemistry, and an ability to communicate on tough issues are all hallmarks of an effective partnering arrangement. The senior executives of both companies must be committed to making the relationship work and take visible steps in that direction. The management and operational styles and methods must be compatible, or adjusted to be so, at least with respect to this venture.

- Form must follow function; there should be a clear fit between the legal structure selected and the operational objectives of the partnering arrangement. Being overly rigid would be a poor choice for a preliminary "dip our toes in the water" first type of partnering relationship and vice versa.

- Do them often. Do them right. The more experience that a fast-track growing company can gather by seeking out partnering relationships, the greater the chances of success. These alliances and partnering relationships need to be a core part of the business growth strategy, not just an ad hoc event.

- Make sure each alliance partner avoids a "Not Invented Here" mentality. If each alliance partner assumes that their ideas and work product are superior to those of their partner(s), then they are blocking themselves from an ability to learn and truly profit from the working relationship.

Consumer product ingredient co-branding. A strong brand appears as an ingredient in another product in order to enhance sales and cross-consumer loyalty (e.g., Post Raisin Bran using Sun-Maid raisins in its cereal, Archway's use of Kellogg's All-Bran in its cookies, Ben & Jerry's Heath Bar Crunch ice cream, PopTarts with Smuckers fruit fillings, etc.).

Implied endorsement co-branding. The co-branded name or logo is used to build consumer recognition even if there is no *actual* ingredient used in the product (e.g., John Deere's logo on the back of a Florsheim boot, the Doritos Pizza Craver tortilla chips that feature Pizza Hut's logo on the packaging, or its Taco Supreme chips that feature Taco Bell's logo.

Actual composite co-branding. The co-branded product actually uses a branded pairing of popular manufacturing techniques or processes (e.g., Timberland boots with Gore-Tex fabric, furniture with Scotchguard protectants, Dell or Gateway computers with Intel inside, etc.).

Designer-driver co-branded products. Certain manufacturers have co-branded with well-known designers to increase consumer loyalty and brand awareness. For example, the Eddie Bauer edition of the Ford Explorer has been a very strong seller and means of product differentiation.

Retail business format co-branding. This type of co-branding is growing rapidly within the retailing, hospitality, and franchising communities where retail co-branding is being used to attract additional customers, create complementary product lines to offset different consumer tastes (such as Baskin-Robbins and Dunkin' Donuts), or consuming patterns (e.g., combining a traditional breakfast-only consumer traffic pattern with a lunch-only traffic pattern), or to sell additional products or services to a "captured customer."

Companies considering co-branding initially focus on the viability of the strategic fit between the brands. For example, a hypothetical Godiva/Slim•Fast line of chocolate snack bars would benefit the Slim•Fast brand by its association with Godiva's superior chocolates. However, this pairing would detract from Godiva's upscale brand image. In this scenario, there is not likely to be a fit between the brands. It is also important to understand consumer perceptions of each product, and its attributes, in order

Advantages and Disadvantages of Using Co-branding as a Growth Strategy

Advantages of Co-branding
- Share costs
- Share marketing and packaging costs
- Share rent, utilities, and other overhead if in same location
- Expand into international markets
- Easier to get brand recognition for your brand if tied to a well-known domestic brand (in foreign market); many foreign markets enjoy "American" products, so the co-branding works to their advantage
- Creates conveniences for customers, which can increase business for both companies, and additional traffic creates impulse buys

Disadvantages of Co-branding
- It can be difficult to build consensus between co-branding partners
- Marketing has to be agreed upon by both parties; loss of time of bringing to market, and loss of flexibility
- Bad publicity for one company can affect the other
- If one brand fails to live up to its promises made to its partner, co-branding relationships can dissolve
- If co-branding flops, both companies feel the pain. And consumers may become confused about new products, diminishing the value of both

to better determine whether the two brands have a common set of attributes. It may be helpful to rate the favorableness of each brand separately, then as a co-branded product, and then explore the relative contribution each brand makes to the effectiveness of the co-branded product.

The ability to penetrate new markets, generate new income streams, build the value of the company's brand name, and increase overall brand awareness has made co-branding a very viable and profitable strategy for companies. However, the temptation to extend the equity and value of your brand into other areas poses certain risks. There are quality control issues, the risk of over-branding or misbranding from a consumer perspective, and product-liability issues. The key to successful co-branding is that the brand itself must stand for something greater than the original product, and that the consumers' perception of the extended brand is a natural one.

14

BUILDING EFFECTIVE CHANNEL PARTNER RELATIONSHIPS

Today's growing companies face a number of strategic and relationship management issues regarding the development of their channels, ranging from their initial establishment, to the selection of appropriate channel partners, to the growth of the channel as a whole and the individual growth of their partnered organizations. There are also many challenges to be addressed regarding the development and maintenance of multiple channels and the various types of channel partners contained therein.

Channel partner relationships can make or break a company. If the relationships that you rely upon to effectively reach the "end customer," whether via dealers, distributors, systems integrators, value-added resellers, agents, and franchisees, among others, are broken, stale, underperforming, unfocused, unappreciative, unimaginative, lazy, bored, or unfaithful, it will have a direct and harmful impact on your brand, your shareholder value, and your bottom line. If time, attention, and resources are focused on nurturing and supporting these relationships, then the company is very likely to meet and exceed its growth objectives. The role and importance of a strong channel partner program as a critical growth priority cannot be underestimated.

Companies of all sizes and in all industries face many challenges when they attempt to build a healthy and profitable set of channel relationships. Today's domestic and international marketplaces are fast-moving and highly competitive, making it difficult to maintain and grow loyalty with channel partners. In this environment, growing companies must work to prevent flat channel performance in terms of sales, new product rollout and adoption, and market penetration, all of which can be caused by lack of support, burnout, and complacency. Even while companies endeavor to maintain loyalty and increase efficiency, they must also decrease the costs of maintaining these partnerships. There are several means of accomplishing this. First, companies should avoid focusing on top-down growth objectives at the expense of building and strengthening channel partner relationships and profitability from the bottom up. Second, corporate headquarters and its individual channel partners must align and communicate on goals, objectives, and the "performance metrics dashboard." And third, the company must make a commitment to basic business management, ongoing growth training, and overall channel health.

A company that allocates corporate resources in an effective manner to support, train, and enhance the financial performance of channel partners will be well positioned to meet the challenges of today's marketplace. A successful growth company analyzes channel performance and terminates unproductive channel relationships in order to focus channel management's time, effort, and financial resources on building profitable relationships and encouraging new, high potential partnerships.

When building an effective set of channel relationships, the following strategic issues must be considered. First, it is important to consider the status of your current channel partner relationships. How much time, energy, and monetary resources have you invested in analyzing the success of your current channel relationships? Analyzing the functionality of current channels and how you bring your products and services to the marketplace will help you determine if you are getting the most out of your channel partners. Determine what defines a successful channel relationship for your company, and how you approach an underperforming relationship.

Next, you will need to look at how you manage your channel partners. What steps are you taking to support, motivate, educate, and com-

FIGURE 14.1 *Channel Builders versus Channel Killers*

Channel Builders	Channel Killers
• Communication on a regular and meaningful basis	• Politics and turfmanship
• Partners are selected on their ability to bring new capabilities and open up new markets (e.g., federal government sales) on behalf of the mothership	• Allowing partners to become "fat and lazy" • Failure to "pull the trigger" and terminate the deadwood from the channel
• R&D/Innovation leading to real and desired new product lines and enhancements	• Designated territories that are too big *or* too small
• Value-added field support and education	• Talking to each other only when there is a problem (instead of proactively and regularly brainstorming opportunities)
• Innovative solutions come from primarily the channel partners not just the mothership	• Failure to understand, recognize, and support "micro-market" differences in channel partner territories
• Regular channel partner effectiveness audits and market-by-market analysis	• Allowing annual golf and steak dinner conferences to serve as a substitute for service value-added support
• Constant focus on the *real* needs of the end customer and competitive forces	

municate with your current channel partners? It is important to develop a systematic approach to collaboration on both a horizontal and vertical level. You must also reach clarity and agreement with each of your channel partners as to each party's objectives, strategy, commitment, and capabilities, and establish performance metrics. These goals and performance metrics must be reviewed and re-evaluated periodically, on a partner-by-partner basis. Minimum standards must be in place and enforced, and there should be clear consequences for not meeting these standards.

Finally, you need to evaluate your channel relationships from the point of view of your partners. What competitive choices do your channel partners have as alternatives to your products or services, and how are you identifying, maintaining, and improving your competitive advantage? If you are dissatisfied with your channel partner relationships, some issues to consider include: a struggling or broken business model underlying the channel partner relationship; horizontal or vertical conflicts within the channel; how these conflicts arise, and at what cost; the degree to which your channel partner is insulated from the end customer; and, if so, whether this communication barrier has hurt product development.

STRUCTURING CHANNEL PARTNER RELATIONSHIPS

When structuring a channel partner relationship, the following key variables and metrics should be considered:

- Focus/scope/product lines
- Performance standards and objectives
- Territory
- Degree of exclusivity
- Roles and responsibilities
- Control over channel
- Long-term commitment vs. flexibility
- Assumption of risk
- Ownership of inventory conduit

Additional factors affecting channel partner selection and economic terms include:

- Complexity of the product
- Degrees of specialization
- Logistics and transportation
- Needs of end customer
- Availability of trade credit
- Financial support by manufacturer
- Market trends
- Product liability risk
- Degrees of aftermarket support
- Best practices
- Industry norms
- Storage and warehousing capabilities

- Ease of termination of relationship
- Role of the Internet/e-commerce

CHANNEL PARTNER MANAGEMENT STRATEGIC PLANNING

To effectively manage your channel partners, you must understand the underlying value of your company's products and services, and the end customer's buying habits and preferences—as well as the value proposition and decisional factors for your distribution channel partners. Establish channel objectives that are aligned with your end customers' buying behaviors. You must design and establish channel systems, and evaluate the performance of these systems. Consider the benefits of joining existing channels versus starting new channels, versus buying existing channels (M&A). Another strategic planning element involves modifying existing channels due to changes in management, key objectives, new marketplace conditions, new product lines, brand strength or weakness, product life cycles, and so on. Each *cause* for the need for change in a channel may require a different result, or employ a different strategy.

An important aspect of strategic planning is managing channel conflict. Again, the cause, whether it is conflicting goals or perceptions of role, territorial disputes caused by overlap, cannibalization or encroachment, or politics, will dictate the cure. Some methods of managing conflict include: evaluating channel members and direct/indirect channels of distribution; training and rehabilitating channel members, and terminating problematic channel members.

UNDERSTANDING TYPES OF CHANNEL PARTNER RELATIONSHIPS

There are many different type of channel partner relationships, including:

- Distributors
- Sales representatives

FIGURE 14.2 *Improving Channel Partner Performance*

At the core, channel partner training programs should focus on: (a) supporting your strongest partners ("A Players"); (b) improving your average partners ("B Players"); and (c) turning around your weakest channel partners ("C Players").

Characteristics of Partner	Focus of Training	Goals
Strongest of the "A Players"	Strategic Planning Expansion Strategies	Keep them Strong, Loyal, Motivated, and Focused Gather and Analyze "Best Practices"
"A Players" who have lost focus or who suffer from relationship staleness, laziness, or boredom	Succession Planning Business Planning Realignment of Goals	Reinvigorate their Commitment Bring New Initiatives and Fresh Ideas to the Table
"B Players" with "A Player" potential	Business Planning and Capital Formation Building Effective Teams Coaching and Mentoring to get to the next level	Provide them with the Tools for Growth Mentor them into "A Players"
Underperforming "B Players"	Motivation and Analysis of Underperformance	Analysis of Growth Hurdles and Challenges Goal setting and Organizational Analysis
"C Players" who with focused rehabilitation can become "B Players"	Business Planning Fundamentals Strategic Performance Audit Leadership and Management Coaching	Deep Analysis to Get them to "B Level" Intense Focus on Business Plans and Sales Training
Weakest of the "C Players"	Transition and Phase-out	Terminate the Relationship

- Value-added resellers
- Wholesalers
- Jobbers
- Cooperatives
- Consortiums
- Direct-to-retailers
- Internet

The key questions to consider when choosing channel partners are the likely sales, costs, profits, and risks inherent in each channel alternative.

Distributorships, Dealerships, and Sales Representatives

Many industries have different names for their channel partners and view them strategically in different ways. Many growing product-oriented companies choose to bring their wares to the marketplace through independent third-party distributors and dealerships. These dealers are generally more difficult to control than licensees or franchisees, and as a result, the agreement between the manufacturer and the distributor is much more informal than a franchise or license agreement. Manufacturers of electronic and stereo equipment, computer hardware and software, sporting goods, medical equipment, and automobile parts and accessories commonly use this type of arrangement.

In developing distributor and dealership agreements, growing companies must be careful to avoid being included within the broad definition of a franchise under FTC Rule 436, which would require the preparation of a disclosure document. To avoid such a classification, the agreement should impose minimal controls over the dealer, and the sale of products must be at bona fide wholesale prices. In addition, the manufacturer must offer no more than minimal assistance in the marketing or management of the dealer's business. A well-drafted distributorship agreement should address the key issues outlined in the sidebar below.

Distributors are often confused with sales representatives, but there are many critical differences. Typically, a distributor buys the product from the manufacturer, at wholesale prices, with title passing to the distributor when payment is received. There is usually no actual fee paid by the distributor for the grant of the distributorship, and the distributor is typically

Elements of Distributorship Agreement

1. What is the scope of the appointment? Which products is the dealer authorized to distribute, and under what conditions? What is the scope, if any, of the exclusive territory to be granted to the distributor? To what extent will product, vendor, customer, or geographic restrictions be applicable?
2. What activities will the distributor be expected to perform in terms of manufacturing, sales, marketing, display, billing, market research, maintenance of books and records, storage, training, installation, support, and servicing?
3. What obligations will the distributor have to preserve and protect the intellectual property of the manufacturer?
4. What right, if any, will the distributor have to modify or enhance the manufacturer's warranties, terms of sale, credit policies, or refund procedures?
5. What advertising literature, technical and marketing support, training seminars, or special promotions will be provided by the manufacturer to enhance the performance of the distributor?
6. What sales or performance quotas will be imposed on the dealer as a condition to its right to continue to distribute the manufacturer's products or services? What are the rights and remedies of the manufacturer if the dealer fails to meet these performance standards?
7. What is the term of the agreement and under what conditions can it be terminated? How will post-termination transactions be handled?

permitted to carry competitive products. The distributor is expected to maintain some retail location or showroom where the manufacturer's products are displayed. The distributor must maintain its own inventory storage and warehousing capabilities. The distributor looks to the manufacturer for technical support; advertising contributions; supportive repair, maintenance, and service policies; new product training; volume discounts; favorable payment and return policies; and brand name recognition. The manufacturer looks to the distributor for in-store and local promotion, adequate inventory controls, financial stability, preferred display and stocking, prompt payment, and qualified sales personnel. Managing and controlling distributors can be even more difficult than franchisees (especially because the benefits of a comprehensive franchise agreement are lacking) and many state antitermination statutes regulate the termination of these relationships.

The sales representative or sales agent is an independent marketing resource for the manufacturer. The sales representative, unlike the distributor, does not typically take title to the merchandise, maintain inventories or retail locations, or engage in any special price promotions unless these are instigated by the manufacturer.

CUSTOMER AND VENDOR RELATIONSHIPS

In many ways, the relationship that a growing company has with its customers and vendors must be managed and nurtured (and analyzed from time to time) in the same fashion as channel partners.

Managing Customer Relationships

In order to manage and nurture your customer relationships, you must consider if you are customer-centric in your organizational structure and mission. Why or why not? If you have been customer-centric, you need to determine if this focus has been effective, and if you are getting results. Customer relationships are key assets of a growth company, and you must take steps to expand either the volume or the diversity of products and services being offered to existing customers.

You also need a strategy for obtaining new customers that keeps a handle on your *actual* customer acquisition costs, per lead, presale, and so on. And to the contrary, what is the cost of losing a customer? You must have systems in place for measuring and monitoring the effectiveness of customer relationship strengthening initiatives. Be sure that marketing is not a black hole within your organization.

Evaluating Customer Relationships

The goal of any growth company must be to get and keep more and more customers, who buy more and more products and services, and tell others about these products and services. An important method of achieving this goal is understanding your customers—your best customers, and your worst. As much can be learned from what you are doing wrong as can be from what you are doing right:

1. Who are your ten strongest customers?
   - How did you get them?
   - Why have they remained loyal?
   - Has the relationship strengthened? Expanded? Is it shrinking?
   - Have they referred any new customers to you? Why or why not?
2. Who are your ten weakest customers?
   - Why are they weak?
   - Were they weak when you first obtained them? (Customer's intake issues)
   - If not, how and why did they become weak?
   - What risks do they pose to your company? Direct or indirect? Financial? Reputation risk? Morale?
   - Can they be strengthened? Or put back on the right track?
   - How much time is devoted to managing these relationships?
3. Do you *really* understand why customers continue to buy from you?

Becoming Your Customers' Ally

A hidden weapon for growth is aligning your business strategy with the interests of your customers. To accomplish this you must regularly engage in meaningful conversation, and get real feedback from customers. If you can understand what problems your customers face that you solve better than anyone else, you are one step closer to seeing yourself as your customers' ally. It is also important to understand what aspects of your business are *not* important to your customers. From this feedback and understanding, you can develop strategies to convert suspects into prospects into customers into referral sources into lifers. By aligning your company with your customers, you can properly leverage your customer relationships into new and recurring revenue streams without violating their trust or diluting their loyalty.

Marketing to the Biggest Customer on the Planet— The Federal Government

One customer that no growing business should overlook is the federal government. What portion of your sales are made to the federal government? If you have not pursued this strategy, what are the reasons that have prevented you? Related customers who should be part of your strategy are state and local governments. First, you must have a product or service that the government wants to buy. Then, you need to develop a plan to get started; are RFPs or sole-source contracts the best method? How do you reach the key decision makers, third-party access and influence, proactive or reactive?

A competitive analysis of government contracts as a growth strategy should include:

- Who else is already selling to the government within my industry(ies)?
- Which of my products or services are best suited for government sales?
- How can I monitor where the "hot areas" of demand exist within the government, specific sections, or agencies?
- Will any of our product or service lines need to be modified or adapted to meet the requirements of a federal buyer or government agency?
- Should we use a third party agent to generate sales? Or a strategic partner?

The federal government may be the biggest customer on the planet, but such a big prize comes with special considerations. You cannot treat the federal government as just another new commercial vertical market; it is an entirely new market, with different players, motivations, and its own language. When dealing with the federal government, patience, resources, expertise, and capabilities are all key, as are reputation and quality references. You should have a government Rolodex. If you don't have one, hire one. You must be able to meet government needs. A desire and ability to handle and manage large projects is critical. You have to be ready to modify your existing product or service lines to meet federal requirements, or to position your alternatives as attractive to federal agencies.

EVALUATING VENDOR RELATIONSHIPS

Just as you must evaluate your channel partner and customer relationships, you need to understand your relationships with your vendors. Who are your key vendors, and what value do they add to your company? Perhaps a good test of the quality of your vendor relationships is to consider when was the last time you were "pleasantly surprised" by them. If you need to rack your brain, then you may be being taken for granted. In this case, it might be time to consider and evaluate alternative sources for these products and services.

You should be getting MFN treatment regarding price, terms, service, support, warranty, and so on. If you are not getting this treatment, why not? Some vendors offer financing for their products and services. Your vendors should play a role facilitating and supporting your growth. If they are not, you should consider if there are better, or more supportive, alternatives available. Before you make a switch, you must be aware of the *real* and *perceived* costs of making a switch.

BUSINESS GROWTH RESOURCES DIRECTORY

ORGANIZATIONS DEDICATED TO BUSINESS GROWTH

There are literally thousands of trade associations, networking groups, venture clubs, and other organizations which directly or indirectly focus on the needs of small business owners, entrepreneurs, growing companies, women-owned businesses, minority-owned businesses, importers and exporters, and virtually every other group that shares common interests. Some of the more established groups with a genuine nationwide presence and solid track record include:

Alliance of Independent Store Owners and Professionals (AISOP)
P.O. Box 2014 Loop Station
Minneapolis, MN 55402
612-340-1568

AISOP was organized to protect and promote fair postal and legislative policies for small business advertisers. Most of its 4,000+ members are independent small businesses that rely on reasonable third-class mail rates to promote their businesses and contact customers in their trade areas.

American Electronics Association
601 Pennsylvania Avenue, NW
Suite 600, North Building
Washington, DC 20004
202-682-9110

The American Electronics Association offers human resources services, management development programs, executive networking, public policy leadership, and other services.

American Entrepreneurs Association
655 15th Street, NW, Suite 460
Washington, DC 20005
202-659-2979

The American Entrepreneurs Association was established to provide small business owners with benefits and discounts that are generally reserved for big businesses, such as express shipping, health insurance, and long-distance telephone rates.

American Farm Bureau Federation
600 Maryland Ave., SW, Suite 800
Washington, DC 20024
202-406-3600

As the nation's largest farm organization, the American Farm Bureau Federation promotes policies and provides programs that improve the financial well-being and quality of life for farmers and ranchers.

American Financial Services Association
919 18th Street, NW, Third Floor
Washington, DC 20006
202-296-5544

The American Financial Services Association acts as the national trade association for market funded providers of financial services to consumers and small businesses.

American Intellectual Property Law Association
2001 Jefferson Davis Highway, Suite 203
Arlington, VA 22202
703-415-0780

The American Intellectual Property Law Association is a national bar association composed mainly of lawyers that strives to improve the nation's intellectual property laws and their interpretation by the courts, and provides legal education to the public and to organization members on matters involving intellectual property.

American Small Business Association (ASBA)
206 E College Street, Suite 201
Grapevine, TX 76051
800-942-2722

ASBA's membership base consists of small business owners with 20 or fewer employees. ASBA members have access to the same advantages that larger corporations enjoy through member benefits and services.

American Society of Association Executives (ASAE)
1575 I Street, NW
Washington, DC 20005
888-950-2723

The American Society of Association Executives serves as an advocate for the nonprofit sector of the economy.

Association of American Publishers
50 F Street, NW, Suite 400
Washington, DC 20001
202-347-3375

Assists publishers by expanding the market for American books both nationally and abroad, promotes intellectual freedom and opposes censorship, and offers practical advice and information to assist members in the management and administration of their companies.

Association for Corporate Growth
International Headquarters
1926 Waukegan Road, Suite 1
Glenview, IL 60025
800-699-1331

The Association for Corporate Growth provides programs, education, and networking in the areas of middle-market corporate growth, corporate development, and mergers and acquisitions. The Association has about 5,500 members representing 2,500 companies in 36 chapters throughout North America and the United Kingdom.

Business Software Alliance
1150 18th Street, NW, Suite 700
Washington, DC 20036
202-872-5500

The Business Software Alliance is an international organization representing software and e-commerce ventures in 65 countries around the world. The Alliance educates consumers and governments about the positive impact software has on our lives, fights software piracy and Internet theft, and promotes greater trade opportunities.

Entrepreneurs Organization
500 Montgomery Street, Suite 500
Alexandria, VA 22314
703-519-6700

The Entrepreneurs' Organization is made up of young business professionals who have founded, co-founded, own, or control businesses with annual sales of one million dollars or more. The organization provides support, education, and networking opportunities to its members.

Ewing Marion Kauffman Foundation
4801 Rockhill Road
Kansas City, MO 64110
816-932-1000

The Kauffman Center sponsors the *entreworld.org* Web site, which serves as a critical resource for those entrepreneurs starting and growing businesses, and provides links to other resources on the Web.

International Franchise Association (IFA)
1501 K Street, NW, Suite 350
Washington, DC 20005
202-628-8000

The IFA serves as a resource center for current and prospective franchisees and franchisors, the media, and the government. The IFA has promoted programs that expand opportunities for women and minorities in franchising.

International Trademark Association
655 Third Avenue, 10th Floor
New York, NY 10017-5617 USA
212-642-1700

The International Trademark Association is a worldwide membership organization of trademark owners and advisors, and seeks to shape public policy, advance practitioners' knowledge, and educate the public and the media about the significance of trademarks in today's commercial environment.

Let's Talk Business Network
58 Harwood Drive East
Glen Cove, NY 11542
917-408-6175

Let's Talk Business Network acts as an entrepreneurial support community, providing products, a radio network, and a support network of more than 5,000 contacts for entrepreneurs who wish to discuss common business experiences and challenges.

Morino Institute
11600 Sunrise Valley Drive, Suite 300
Reston, VA 20191
703-620-8971

The Morino Institute attempts to explore and understand the opportunities and risks of the Internet and the New Economy to expand social progress, and seeks to create a dialogue on such issues among entrepreneurs and others.

National Association of Convenience Stores
1600 Duke Street
Alexandria, VA 22314
703-684-3600

The National Association of Convenience Stores is an international trade association representing 2,300 retail and 1,700 supplier company members, assisting these entities to increase their current effectiveness and profitability.

National Association of Development Companies (NADCO)
6764 Old McLean Village Drive
McLean, VA 22101
703-748-2575

NADCO is the trade group of community-based, nonprofit organizations that promote small business expansion and job creation through the SBA's 504 loan program, known as Certified Development Companies (CDC).

National Association for Female Executives (NAFE)
30 Irving Place, 5th Floor
New York, NY 10003
800-927-NAFE

Through education and networking programs, NAFE helps women share the resources and techniques needed to succeed in the competitive business world.

National Association of Investment Companies (NAIC)
1300 Pennsylvania Avenue, NW, Suite 700
Washington, DC 20004
202-204-3001

NAIC is the industry association for venture capital firms which dedicate their financial resources to investment in minority businesses.

National Association of Manufacturers (NAM)
1331 Pennsylvania Avenue, NW
Washington, DC 20004
202-637-3000

NAM serves as the voice of the manufacturing community and is active on all issues concerning manufacturing, including legal system reform, regulatory restraint, and tax reform.

National Association of Professional Employer Organizations (NAPEO)
901 N. Pitt Street, Suite 150
Alexandria, VA 22314
703-836-0466

NAPEO is the recognized voice of the PEO industry and is dedicated to working towards the goals of PEOs, their clients, and the regulatory and legislative bodies that monitor the industry.

National Association for the Self-Employed (NASE)
2121 Precinct Line Road
Hurst, TX 76054
703-683-1601

NASE helps its members become more competitive by providing over 100 benefits that save money on services and equipment. NASE's membership consists primarily of small business owners with few or no employees.

National Association of Small Business Investment Companies (NASBIC)
666 11th Street, NW, Suite 750
Washington, DC 20001
202-628-5055

The National Association of Small Business Investment Companies is dedicated to promoting a strong Small Business Investment Company industry. NASBIC provides professional programs and representation in Washington to promote the growth and vitality of this sector of the business community.

National Association of Wholesaler-Distributors
1725 K Street, NW, Suite 300
Washington, DC 20006
202-872-0885

The National Association of Wholesaler-Distributors is a trade association that represents the wholesale distribution industry, and is active in the areas of government relations and political action, research and education, and group purchasing.

National Association of Women Business Owners (NAWBO)
8405 Greensboro Drive, Suite 800
McLean, VA 22102
800-55-NAWBO

NAWBO uses its collective influence to broaden opportunities for women in business, and is the only dues-based national organization representing the interests of all women entrepreneurs in all types of business.

National Business League (NBL)
1511 K Street, NW, Suite 432
Washington, DC 20005
202-737-4430

NBL is primarily involved in business development among African Americans and serves as a voice for black business on Capitol Hill and in the federal government.

National Commission on Entrepreneurship
444 North Capital Street, Suite 399
Washington, DC 20001
202-434-8060

The National Commission on Entrepreneurship provides governmental and private-sector leaders with information and resources regarding the entrepreneurial sector of the economy, and seeks to recommend new public policies to protect and stimulate the creation and growth of an entrepreneurial economy and culture.

National Federation of Independent Business (NFIB)
53 Century Boulevard, Suite 300
Nashville, TN 37214
600 Maryland Avenue, SW, Suite 700
Washington, DC 20024
800-634-2669
800-552-6342

NFIB disseminates educational information about free enterprise, entrepreneurship, and small business. NFIB represents more than 60,000 small and independent businesses before legislatures and government agencies at the federal and state level.

National Foundation for Teaching Entrepreneurship, Inc. (NFTE)
120 Wall Street, 29th Floor
New York, NY 10005
212-232-3333

NFTE is an international nonprofit organization that introduces poor and at-risk young people to the world of entrepreneurship by showing them how to operate their own small business enterprises.

National Restaurant Association
1200 17th Street, NW
Washington, DC 20036
202-331-5900

Represents, promotes, and educates the restaurant industry. The National Restaurant Association is comprised of 43,000 member companies and 220,000 restaurant establishments.

National Retail Federation
325 Seventh Street, NW, Suite 1000
Washington, DC 20004
202-783-7971

The National Retail Federation is the world's largest retail trade association, providing programs and services in education, training, information technology, and government affairs to advance its members' interests.

National Small Business United (NSBU)
1156 15th Street, N.W.
Suite 1100
Washington, DC 20005
202-293-8830

The NSBU is a membership-based association of business owners which presents small business' point of view to all levels of government and the Congress.

National Venture Capital Association
1655 Fort Myer Drive
Suite 850
Arlington, VA 22209
703-524-2549

The National Venture Capital Association's mission is to define, serve, and promote the interests of the venture capital industry, to increase the understanding of the importance of venture capital to the U.S. economy and to stimulate the flow of equity capital to emerging growth and developing companies.

Opportunity International
2122 York Road
Oak Brook, Illinois 60523
800-793-9455

With partner organizations, Opportunity International provides loans and basic training in business practices to the poor, thereby breaking the cycle of poverty.

Small Business & Entrepreneurship Council (SBE Council)
1920 L Street, NW, Suite 200
Washington, DC 20036
202-785-0238
www.sbecouncil.org

SBE Council is a nationwide organization that works to protect small business and promote entrepreneurship through advocacy, research, training, education, and member networking. The group publishes the popular *Small Business Index,* which ranks the states according to their policy environments for business. SBE Council produces a highly acclaimed *Weekly Brief* e-newsletter that keeps its members up-to-date on policy, emerging business trends, and SBE Council activities and events.

U.S. Chamber of Commerce
1615 H Street, NW
Washington, DC 20062
202-659-6000

The U.S. Chamber of Commerce represents 3,000,000 businesses, 3,000 state and local chambers of commerce, 830 business associations, and 87 American Chambers of Commerce abroad. It works with these groups to support national business interests and includes a Small Business Center (202-463-5503).

U.S. Hispanic Chamber of Commerce
2175 K Street NW, Suite 100
Washington, DC 20037
800-USH-CC86

The U.S. Hispanic Chamber of Commerce advocates the business interests of Hispanics and develops minority business opportunities with major corporations and at all levels of government.

Turnaround Management Association
100 South Wacker Drive, Suite 850
Chicago, Illinois 60606
312-578-6900

The TMA publishes the *Journal of Corporate Renewal* six times per year.

Women Entrepreneurs, Inc. (WE Inc.)
P.O. Box 367
Oakton, VA 22124
703-627-8283
www.we-inc.org

WE Inc. is a nonprofit business association dedicated to helping women entrepreneurs succeed through advocacy, training, and networking. WE Inc.'s volunteer advisors produce key tips on business growth, going global, taxes, and human resource issues. In conjunction with the Department of Labor Women's Bureau, WE Inc. hosts *Flex Options,* a project dedicated to helping employers implement and enhance workplace flexibility programs. WE Inc. also helps women business owners and leaders in developing countries through entrepreneurial training and capacity building in the areas of advocacy, communications, and network and coalition organization.

FEDERAL AGENCIES

Bankers Association for Finance and Trade
1120 Connecticut Avenue, N.W., 5th Floor
Washington, DC 20036
202-663-7575
www.baft.org

A financial trade association whose membership represents a broad range of internationally active financial institutions and companies that provide important services to the global financial community. BAFT serves as a forum for analysis, discussion, and action among international financial professionals on a wide range of topics affecting international trade and finance, including legislative/regulatory issues.

Bureau of Export Administration
202-582-4811
www.bxa.fedworld.gov

The export control provisions of the EAR are intended to serve the national security, foreign policy, nonproliferation, and short supply interests of the United States and, in some cases, to carry out its international obligations. The EAR also include some export controls to protect the United States from the adverse impact of the unrestricted export of commodities in short supply.

Export-Import Bank (Eximbank)
811 Vermont Avenue, NW
Washington, DC 20571
800-565-3946
www.exim.gov

Offers financing assistance for potential exporters and companies of all sizes interested in doing business abroad.

Federal Trade Commission
600 Pennsylvania Avenue, NW
Washington, DC 20580

Provides guidance to businesses that may need to comply with a variety of federal rules and regulations.

International Business Exchange Network

Contact your local Chamber of Commerce.

National Trade Data Bank on the Internet
800-STAT-USA
202-482-1986 to subscribe
www.stat-usa.gov
stat-usa@doc.gov

STAT-USA/Internet, a service of the U.S. Department of Commerce, is a single point of access to authoritative business, trade, and economic information from across the federal government.

Trade Information Center
International Trade Administration
U.S. Department of Commerce
Washington, DC 20230
800-USA-TRADE
202-482-4473
www.trade.gov/td/tic

Provides comprehensive resources for information on all U.S. federal government export assistance programs.

U.S. Department of Commerce (DOC)
Herbert C. Hoover Building
14th Street & Constitution Ave., NW
Washington, DC 20230
202-482-2000

Offers a wide variety of programs and services relating to economic development, international trade, and minority business. The U.S. Patent and Trademark Office (800-786-9199) is a division of the DOC which processes federal patent and trademark applications and publishes various resources on the protection of intellectual property.

U.S. Small Business Administration (SBA)
409 Third Street, SW
Washington, DC 20416
800-827-5722
www.sba.gov

Offers a wide variety of financing programs, workshops and seminars, management and technical assistance, etc.—typically through its many district offices.

In addition to the agencies above, all major federal departments and agencies have an Office of Small and Disadvantaged Business Utilization (OSDBU) that is responsible for ensuring that an equitable share of government contracts are awarded to small and minority businesses. Some sample OSDBU office phone numbers within selected agencies include:

Department of Agriculture
202-720-7117

Department of Defense
703-614-1151

Department of Justice
202-616-0521

Agency for International Development
703-875-1551

Office of Personnel Management
202-606-2180

DIRECTORY OF INTERNATIONAL FRANCHISE ORGANIZATIONS

Argentine Franchise Association
Santa Fe 995, Piso 4
Buenos Aires 1059, Argentina
Attn: Richard Rivera, President
54-1-393-5263 (Tel)
54-1-393-9260 (Fax)

Associacao Portuguesa Da
    Franchise
Rua Castilho, n 14
Lisbon 1000, Portugal
Attn: Ms. Pascale Lagneaux,
    Directora General
351-1-315-1845 (Tel)
351-1-315-1845 (Fax)

Association Colombiana De
    Franquicias
Apartado Aereo 25200
Cali, Colombia
Attn: Francisco J. Patino, President
57-2-331-1086 (Tel)
57-2-331-7138 (Fax)

Association de Franchising de
    Chile (AFICH)
Hernando de Aguirre 128, of. 704
Providencia, Santiago, Chile
Attn: Carlos Fabia, President-Elect
56-2-234-4189 (Tel)
56-2-232-7759 (Fax)

Austrian Franchise Association
Nonntaler Hauptstrasse 48
Salzburg 5020, Austria
Attn: Mrs. Waltraud Frauenhuber
43-662-83-21-64 (Tel)
43-662-83-21-64 (Fax)

Belgische Franchise Federatie
Groot Molenveldlaan 52
1850 Grimbergen, Belgium
Attn: President
32-2-253-27-12 (Tel)
32-2-253-40-37 (Fax)

Brazil Franchise Association
Rua Professor Ascendino Reis,
    1548
Sao Paulo 04027-000, Brazil
Attn: Bernard Jeger, President
55-11-5711303 (Tel)
55-11-5755590 (Fax)

British Franchise Association
Thames View, Newton Rd.,
    Henley-on-Thames
Oxon RG9 1HG, United Kingdom
Attn: Brian Smart, Director
44-1491-578-049 (Tel)
44-1491-573-517 (Fax)

Bulgarian Franchise Association
25 A Ochrid Street
9000-Varna, Bulgaria
Attn: Ms. Lubka Kolarova, President
359-52-256-891 (Tel)
359-52-256-891 (Fax)

Canadian Franchise Association
5045 Orbitor Drive, Suite 201,
  Bldg. 12
Mississauga, Ont. L4W 4Y4, Canada
Attn: Richard B. Cunningham,
  President
905-625-2896 (Tel)
905-625-9076 (Fax)

Ceska Asociace Franchisingu
Rytirska 31, P.O. Box 706
11000 Praha 1, Czechoslovakia
Attn: President
42-2-242-30-566 (Tel)
42-2-242-30-566 (Fax)

Danish Franchise Association
Amaliegade 37
Copenhagen K 1256, Denmark
Attn: Peter Arendorff, President
45-33-156011 (Tel)
45-33-910346 (Fax)

European Franchise Federation
60, rue La Boetie
Paris 75008, France
Attn: Mr. Michel Micmacher,
  Chairman
33-1-5375-2225 (Tel)
33-1-5375-2220 (Fax)

Finnish Franchising Association
PI 39
Helsinki, SF 08501, Finland
Attn: Mr. Antti Wathen, Executive
  Officer
358-12-334-584 (Tel)
358-12-334-542 (Fax)

**Franchise Association of
  Southern Africa**
Kenlaw House, 27 De Beer St.,
  P.O. Box 31708
Braamfontein, 2017 South Africa
Attn: Jack Barber, Executive
  Director
27-11-4033468 (Tel)
27-11-4031279 (Fax)

**Franchisors Assn. of Australia &
  New Zealand**
Unit 9, 2-6 Hunter Street
Parramatta, NSW 2150, Australia
Attn: Berridge Hume-Phillips,
  Executive Director
61-2-891-4933 (Tel)
61-2-891-4474 (Fax)

French Franchise Federation
60, rue La Boetie
Paris 75008, France
Attn: Ms. Chantal Zimmer,
  Executive Director
33-1-5375-2225 (Tel)
33-1-5375-2220 (Fax)

German Franchise Association
Paul Heyse Str. 33-35
Munchen 80336, Germany
Attn: Mr. Felix Peckart
49-89-53-50-27 (Tel)
49-89-53-13-23 (Fax)

Handelen Hovedorganisasjon
Postboks 2483, Solli
Oslo 2 0202, Norway
Attn: Mr. Per Reidarson, President
47-22-558220 (Tel)
47-22-558225 (Fax)

Hong Kong Franchise Association
22/F Unit A United Centre,
  95 Queensway
Hong Kong
Attn: Charlotte Chow, Senior
  Manager
852-2529-9229 (Tel)
852-2527-9843 (Fax)

Hungarian Franchise Association
Secretariat: c/o DASY
P.O. Box 446
Budapest H-1537, Hungary
Attn: Dr. Istvan Kiss, Secretary
  General
361-212-4124 (Tel)
361-212-5712 (Fax)

Indonesia Franchise Association
  (AFI)
Jl. Pembangunan I/7
Jakarta 1030, Indonesia
Attn: Mr. Anang Sukandar

62-21-3802449 (Tel)
62-21-3802448 (Fax)

Irish Franchise Association
13 Frankfield Terrace, Summerhill
South Cork, Ireland
Attn: John Neenan, Director
353-21-316080 (Tel)
353-21-316080 (Fax)

Israel Franchise & Distribution
  Association
P.O. Box 3093
Herzeliya 46590, Israel
Attn: Michael Emery, Chairman of
  the Board
972-9-576-631 (Tel)
972-9-576-631 (Fax)

Italian Franchise Association
Corso di Porta Nuova, 3
Milano 20121, Italy
Attn: Michele Scardi, General
  Secretary
39-2-29003779 (Tel)
39-2-6555919 (Fax)

Japan Franchise Association
Elsa Bldg. 602, Roppongi, 3-13-12,
  Minato-ku
Tokyo 106, Japan
Attn: Mr. Sigeyuki Ochiai, Exe.
  Managing Director
81-3-34010421 (Tel)
81-3-34232019 (Fax)

Malaysian Franchise Association
Lot 8 Plaza Putra dataran,
  Merdeka, Jalan Raja
Kuala Lumpur 50050, Malaysia
Attn: Dr. Ishak B. Che Long,
  Director
60-3-294-7055 (Tel)
60-3-294-7033 (Fax)

Mexican Franchise Association
Insurgentes Sur 1783, #303, Col.
  Guadalupe Inn
Mexico, DF 01020, Mexico
Attn: Adolfo Crespo, Director
  General
52-5-661-0655 (Tel)
52-5-663-2178 (Fax)

Middle East Franchise &
  Distribution Association
P.O. Box 3093
Herzeliya 46590, Israel
Attn: Michael Emery, Chairman of
  the Board
972-9-576-631 (Tel)
972-9-576-631 (Fax)

Netherlands Franchise
  Association
Boomberglaan 12
Hilversum 1217 RR, Netherlands
Attn: Mr. A.W.M. Brouwer,
  General Secretary
31-35-243444 (Tel)
31-35-249194 (Fax)

Polish Franchise Association
Krolewska 27
00-670 Warsaw, Poland
Attn: Jolanta Kramarz, Chairman
48-22-27-78-22 (Tel)
48-22-27-78-22 (Fax)

Romanian Franchise Association
Calea Victorieri Nr. 95, Et. 4,
  Ap. 16, Sect. 1
Bucharest, Romania
Attn: Violeta Popovici, Chief
  Executive
401-3126889/6180186 (Tel)
401-3126890 (Fax)

Singapore International Franchise
  Association
71 Sophia Road
0922 Singapore
Attn: Mr. Tan Thuan Seng
65-334-8200 (Tel)
65-334-8211 (Fax)

Swedish Franchise Association
Box 5512-S., Grevgatan 34
Stockholm 11485, Sweden
Attn: Mr. Stig Sohlberg, Chief
  Executive Officer
46-8-6608610 (Tel)
46-8-6627457 (Fax)

Swiss Franchise Association
Lowenstrasse II, Postfach CH-8039
Zurich, Switzerland
Attn: Werner Kieser, President
41-41-225-4757 (Tel)
41-41-225-4777 (Fax)

**UFRAD - Turkish Franchising
  Association**
Istiklal Cad No: 65, Emgen Han,
  80600 Beyoglu
Istanbul, Turkey
Attn: Temel Sahingiray, Chairman
90-212-252-5561 (Tel)
90-212-252-5561 (Fax)

**Yugoslav Franchise Association -
  YUFA**
21000 Novi Sad
Mokranjceva 28, Yugoslavia
Attn: Dr. Zdravko Glusica,
  President
381-21-614-232 (Tel)
381-21-614-232 (Fax)

BUSINESS GROWTH RESOURCES
ON THE WEB

Over the past few years, hundreds of Web sites have been developed
to provide support to entrepreneurs and growing companies. Web sites
come and go quickly and change often, so it's probably best to use one
of the popular search engines and enter key words that will narrow the
scope of your search or particular resource need. Next time you are surf-
ing the Net, here are some Web sites worth visiting:

Name	Internet Address	Main Features
American Computer Resources, Inc.	www.the-acr.com	
The American Association of Individual Investors	www.aaii.org	Offers a basic guide to computerized investing and articles from the *AAII Journal* and *Computerized Investing*
American Society of Association Executives	www.asaecenter.org	Provides a newsroom, a bookstore, and links to various upcoming events and meetings
"Ask the Lawyer"	www.fairmeasures.com	A new Web site that offers practical advice for complying with employee law and preventing lawsuits

Name	Internet Address	Main Features
Business Journal	*www.bizjournals.com*	Features expert advice for small businesses on topics such as sales and marketing, technical, and business financing, and tips on shopping for business products and services
CareerBuilder	*www.careerbuilder.com*	Offers a database of national job offerings
CompanyValue.com	*www.companyvalue.com*	Site offering among the most thorough M&A advisory services on the Web
Dun & Bradstreet Information	*www.dnb.com/us*	A comprehensive source of financial and demographic information
EDGAR	*www.sec.gov/edgar.shtml*	A database that contains all corporate annual and quarterly reports (and exhibits) filed with the Securities and Exchange Commission
E-Span	*www.espan.net*	Used by human resource professionals to post jobs worldwide. Provides reference materials for human resource practitioners
GreatIdeasRadio.com	*www.greatideasradio.com*	Contains a searchable archive of radio interviews conducted with prominent people in business and technology